Theodore Roethke's Dynamic Vision

Published in Canada by Fitzhenry & Whiteside Limited,
Don Mills, Ontario
Manufactured in the United States of America

Library of Congress Cataloging in Publication Data

Blessing, Richard Allen.
    Theodore Roethke's dynamic vision.
    Bibliography: p. 226
    1. Roethke, Theodore, 1908–1963—Criticism and
interpretation. I. Title.
    PS3535.039Z58   811'.5'4   73-15282
    ISBN   0-253-35910-4

Theodore Roethke

THEODORE
ROETHKE'S
DYNAMIC
VISION

Richard Allen Blessing

INDIANA UNIVERSITY PRESS
Bloomington & London

Copyright © 1974 by Indiana University Press
Unpublished material from the Roethke papers may be reprinted
only by permission of Mrs. Beatrice Roethke Lushington

Published in Canada by Fitzhenry & Whiteside Limited,
Don Mills, Ontario
Manufactured in the United States of America

Library of Congress Cataloging in Publication Data

Blessing, Richard Allen.
   Theodore Roethke's dynamic vision.
   Bibliography: p. 226
   1. Roethke, Theodore, 1908–1963—Criticism and
interpretation. I. Title.
   PS3535.039Z58   811'.5'4   73-15282
   ISBN   0-253-35910-4

For Richard P. Adams and Richard Harter Fogle

relinquishing all claim to the produce of his fields, and sacrificing in his mind not only his first but his last fruits also.

THOREAU

Contents

Acknowledgments

Theodore Roethke's Dynamic Vision is distinguished, if in no other way, by the breadth and depth of its author's indebtedness. This book was begun with the aid of a grant from the American Philosophical Society, and most of the time spent on research and writing was created for me by the generosity of the John Simon Guggenheim Memorial Foundation. I am heartily thankful to both organizations.

Richard P. Adams and Richard Harter Fogle, the gentlemen to whom I have dedicated this work, have since my days as a graduate student at Tulane University served me well as models of what the life of the mind might ideally become. Both have supported me beyond professional obligation and beyond my deserving in this as well as in other of my academic pursuits. I would be extremely ungrateful if I were not to mention here Professor Robert Pack of Middlebury College and President Leslie H. Fishel, Jr. of Heidelberg College. I owe my original interest in Theodore Roethke to Professor Pack; he will, I hope, find in my approach to Roethke much that is derived from his own ways of reading Frost and Stevens. President Fishel assures me that my grants from societies and foundations can only mean that his letters of evaluation have been lost in the mail, but I thank him nonetheless for those letters and for other kindnesses too numerous to mention.

My study has benefited enormously from the willingness of Roethke's former colleagues, friends, and students to share with me their memories of the man. Especially worthy of thanks are Edward Bostetter, Dorothee Bowie, Robert B. Heilman, Richard Hugo, Jenijoy LaBelle, Arnold Stein, Joan Swift, and David Wagoner. I am doubly indebted to Professor Wagoner for letting me have a pre-publication copy of *Straw for the Fire.*

The photograph of Theodore Roethke which serves as frontispiece for this book was a gift to me from Professor Jenijoy LaBelle. It is reprinted with the kind permission of *The Seattle Times.* I am grateful to Viking Press for permission to quote from *The Complete Poems of D. H. Lawrence*, edited by Vivian de Sola Pinto and Warren Roberts (Copyright © 1964, 1971 by Angelo Ravagli & C. M. Weekley, Executors of the Estate of Frieda Lawrence Ravagli); to Macmillan Company for permission to quote four lines from *The Collected Poems of William Butler Yeats* (Copyright © 1933 by Macmillan Publishing Co., Inc., renewed 1961 by Bertha Georgie Yeats); to the University of Washington Press for permission to quote from *On the Poet and His Craft: Selected Prose of Theodore Roethke* (Copyright © 1965 by Beatrice Roethke as administratrix of the estate of Theodore Roethke), and from *Selected Letters of Theodore Roethke* (Copyright © 1968 by Beatrice Roethke as administratrix of the estate of Theodore Roethke), both edited by Ralph J. Mills, Jr.; to Alfred A. Knopf, Inc. for permission to quote six lines from *The Collected Poems of Wallace Stevens* (Copyright © 1954 by Wallace Stevens); to Doubleday and Company, Inc. for permission to quote from *Straw for the Fire: From the Notebooks of Theodore Roethke, 1943–63* (Copyright © 1971 by Beatrice Roethke as administratrix of the estate of Theodore Roethke); and to Doubleday and Company, Inc. and Faber and Faber Ltd. for permission to quote from *The Collected Poems of Theodore Roethke* (Copyright © 1966 by Beatrice Roethke as administratrix of the estate of Theodore Roethke). In the manuscript I have given page references to *On the Poet and His Craft, Selected Letters, Straw for the Fire,* and *The Collected Poems* parenthetically. I have used "SP" to stand for *On the Poet and His Craft,* "SF" to stand for *Straw for the Fire,* and "CP" to stand for *The Collected Poems.* "Letters" has been written out. Full bibliographical information can be found in the selected bibliography at the end of this volume.

I am grateful, too, to Beatrice Roethke Lushington for her permission to use the previously unpublished material contained in this book. In quoting from the Roethke Collection of the University of Washington's Suzzallo Library, I have given the number of the box within the collection first and the number of the folder within the box second. I have used the symbol # before notebook numbers to differentiate between notebooks and the loose-leaf pages in the folders. Please notice that the material so marked can be reprinted only with the special permission of Mrs. Lushington.

Theodore Roethke's Dynamic Vision

THEODORE ROETHKE'S DYNAMIC VISION

Introduction

I wish to present a way of looking at the poetry of Theodore
Roethke—not the only way surely, and perhaps not even the best
way—but the way that concentrates most closely upon what
seems to me to be the essential, vital quality of his craft. That
quality, as one might expect when one is dealing with a complex
man and artist, has been difficult to isolate and still more difficult
to limit and define. Nonetheless, I have had much help in my
efforts, help that leads me to hope that I am close to the heart of
what it was that Roethke tried to do and, at his best, was able to
do in his poetry. I have tried to build upon, rather than rely upon,
the best of the pioneering studies of Roethke, most notably Karl
Malkoff's book-length work, Arnold Stein's edition of critical
essays, and the impressive articles of such perceptive readers as
Stanley Kunitz and Kenneth Burke. Needless to say, I have made
use of Ralph J. Mills, Jr.'s selected edition of Roethke's letters and
of Allan Seager's biographical study, *The Glass House*. *Straw for
the Fire*, David Wagoner's beautiful arrangement of the chaos of
some of Roethke's notebooks, has also been helpful, but whenever
possible I have tried to quote from previously unpublished pas-

sages and from other of the notebooks so that Roethke scholars might have a piece or two more of the poet with which to do their own work.

Many of my colleagues at the University of Washington were among Roethke's closest friends, and I have been able to talk with them and with many of Roethke's former students. All of these people have been very generous with time and information, and I have plundered their experiences shamelessly, if informally, to learn as much as I could about what Roethke had to say about the creative process, about the writing of poems. Most helpful, of course, has been Roethke himself. The Roethke Collection of the University of Washington's Suzzallo Library is a treasure-house of rough drafts, letters, books, notebooks, undergraduate and graduate school papers, shopping lists, bluebooks, class lists, and the notes from which he taught. The collection is rich enough to support many scholars, and I claim only to have made a dent here and there in penetrating its secrets. Nonetheless, because Roethke was a teaching poet who labored lovingly to help his students discover the mysteries of his craft, and because he was a working poet who frequently pondered his poetic strategies in his notebooks, I believe I have been able to come to a clear idea of what he thought poetry ought to do, and to an idea, somewhat less clear, of how he went about making poems that did it.

Roethke had, by the time he was an undergraduate at the University of Michigan, begun to develop a dynamic view of the world. That is, he experienced life in terms of speed, energy, whirl —as unceasing and often violent motion. The papers he wrote in those years hint at such a vision and, years later, when he found himself teaching others, the jottings and notes which formed the skeleton of the classroom performance were often full of the vocabulary of dynamism. The key words, repeated in varying forms and combinations, are *energy, intensity, speed, movement, flow*. There are lists of devices for heightening intensity in a poem, for speeding the imagery, for creating energy in rhythm. There are aphorisms. "What is the most important element: energy." "Style: What is style but matter in motion?" "A poem means an

extra, a surplus of energy." "The enemy of intensity: grandiloquence." "When you're working on quality, you're also working on
action" (65, *passim*). There are questions, apparently from students, and hastily scribbled answers:

> Q. What do you want in the way of a rhythm, Mr. R?
> A. It's the nervousness, the tension, I think I value most.
> Blake's bounding line and old Willie's high imperial honk-
> ing. (28, 21)
>
> Q. You speak of energy in rhythm. What are the factors that
> seem to enter into, or contribute to, this force?
> A. They are so multiple that they constitute the whole art of
> writing; but I feel what comes to the aid are alliteration of
> initial sounds and a manipulation and a variation of interior sounds, (repetition of words) particularly vowels.
> The line—but the verbal forms particularly, particularly
> the "ing" participial form, impart, as would be expected,
> movement. *This may be because I see the world in motion*, but I don't think so. (67, 2) [Italics added]

The notebooks themselves are a hodgepodge of Roethke's
snatches of poems, invective and admiration for contemporaries,
complaints to his purse, remarks on his health, and comments on
poetry. It would be misleading to claim that all or even most of
those comments have to do with the need for dynamism in a
poem, for Roethke hardly had to remind himself of that require-
ment. There are, however, a number of remarks which, like the
teaching notes, suggest the need for increasing the energy that
constituted the poem: "Energy is the soul of poetry. Explosive
active language" (SF 259). Or "A poem is an extra—it announces
itself by its rhythmical energy: that energy proceeds from the
mind, the psyche of the person writing—or his unconsciousness"
(28, 21). Sometimes he teases the reader—and perhaps himself—
with a topic sentence followed by nothing at all: "There's a trick
in sustaining the energy of a poem" (23 #12). Sometimes
Roethke defines the thing he is: "Puts his thought in motion—the
poet." Or discusses the difficulties on the way to becoming that
thing:

> Movement: one of the hardest things a beginner (an honest one) has to learn is how to sustain the energy of a poem: in other words, the basic rhythm. He may have a variety of fresh subject matter, slick imagery, sharp epithets, but if he can't make the words move, he has nothing. (SF 172)

There is also the testimony of Roethke's former students, for he seems to have been unforgettable in the classroom. One of the best of them, David Wagoner, has told me that he remembers Roethke's saying, perhaps quoting someone else, that in poetry "motion is equal to emotion." Another, Oliver Everette, writes that Roethke used to snarl, "You've got to have rhythm. If you want to dance naked in an open barndoor with a chalk stuck in your navel, I don't care! You've got to have rhythm. I don't care how you get it." [1] He also remembers that Roethke stressed "motion in poetry," telling the class that "Motion or action should be found in every line. The poetic mind sees things in motion." [2] One of his students from the 1940s kept a notebook, which has been preserved in the Roethke Collection. She noted that Roethke told the class, "Please let me see evidences of an active mind. Don't be so guarded—let your mind buzz around. What you need is the energy to get it down" (73, 12). Once, in talking about the poetry of D. H. Lawrence, Roethke, himself a master of poetic technique, told the same group that "You don't need technique if the subject matter is big enough and you have sufficient energy" (73, 12). The catch, as Roethke well knew, is that such energy is not come by easily and that, once come by, enormous technical resources are required if it is to be transferred effectively to the printed page and beyond the page to generations of readers.

It seems to me that Roethke's problem as a classroom teacher was essentially the same problem with which he wrestled as a poet. Given that the poetic eye sees things in motion, given that energy is all, *by what techniques* does one transfer that motion and that energy to the page or to another's ear? How does one "teach" energy? Not, I think, entirely by telling people to alliterate initial sounds and manipulate interior ones, though I do not wish to undervalue the importance of just such devices. A better clue, I believe, to Roethke's success as a teacher comes from the coed who once told him, "I've learned a lot in this course. I don't understand a thing you say, but I just watch your hands" (SF 261). Or from Richard Hugo, now a fine poet in his own right, who says that he learned at least as much from Roethke's actions —from the boundless energy, what Hugo calls the "overstance," of the teaching performance—as he did from Roethke's words. In Roethke's classroom, apparently, the medium was, to an unusual degree, the message. How do you teach a beat? You don't. But many a student seems to have been surprised to find his foot tapping in time to Roethke's bear-like professorial dance.

But if the hands of the poet are not present to dance for us, he must rely on words and the arrangement of words alone to present the motion that is life. "Talent talks," Roethke wrote in one of his notebooks. "Genius does" (SF 171). And Roethke was more than talented. Therefore, the critic who concerns himself primarily with what one of Roethke's poems "talks about," with a paraphrase of "the thinky-think," as Roethke called it, has only a part—and not the best part—of the poem. In his great poems Roethke's "meaning"—never mind the ostensible subject—is always a celebration of the dance of being, the energy of life. To meet his own standards for genius he had to create a revelation of that dance for his audience, and he had to use every resource of the language to bring it off. To satisfy himself, he had to make the experience, not talk about it.

The purpose of my study is to discover, if I can, *by what techniques* Theodore Roethke was able to present dynamism successfully in a work of art. That his continuing subject was evolution, his own long journey—as man and as artist—out of the self, has been quite clearly established by critics who have gone before me. His almost defiant use of his various influences, his fascination with mysticism, his employment of Jungian archetypal patterns and Freudian symbolism—these matters, while of undeniable interest, are of concern to me only insofar as Roethke made them means to the end of producing "the most important element: energy." My intention here is to demonstrate that a sense of the terrible and beautiful dynamism of life is with Roethke from his earliest preserved writings and, beyond that, to trace his artistic evolution of strategies adequate to translate that sense into language, into poetry. Mine is a study of style: of rhythm, rhyme, diction, imagery, verb forms, the use of pun, paradox, compression, repetition, and yes, even alliteration of initial sounds and manipulation and variation of interior sounds. It is also a study of the uses of the past, of Roethke's treatment of time and space; of his search for structural devices which might be appropriate to a world view in which structure was, after all, an illusion; and of his search for subject matter which was appropriately energetic. In short, I wish to shake Roethke's bag of tricks for getting energy into a poem, turn it upside down, and dump as many of those tricks as I can onto the table for examination and appreciation.

I hope that my shaking and dumping produce so violent a disorder that it becomes, Wallace Stevens fashion, an order despite itself. I start before Roethke is Roethke; that is, I begin before the poetry, begin with his prose pieces written for undergraduate courses and with literary criticism that he wrote as an adolescent English major and later as a half-mature graduate student. I spend more time than some will think proper on the very early poetry, pieces Roethke himself judged unworthy of inclusion in that showpiece of his apprenticeship called *Open House*. But I have few real doubts about the value of studying the poet's earliest steps. Roethke's apprenticeship is fascinating, and fascinating not merely because much of it has received little critical attention while most of it has received none at all. Those earliest writings are important because, at least in retrospect, some of them show what may have been the Saginaw sources for his dynamic world view; because others of them point clearly to literary influences which doubtless strengthened that vision; and because all of them show the first fumbling strategies with which Roethke tries to render in language his sense of the motion that is life.

The larger portion of my study, of course, is concerned with the mature poetry, much of it anyway, upon which Roethke's literary reputation must finally rest. Because I have not been inclined to write "A Reader's Guide to Theodore Roethke," I have left many pieces of *The Collected Poems* untouched. Instead, my intention has been to work with Roethke at his best, by which I mean Roethke during those creative periods when his vision and technique come into wedlock and the issue is poetry of extraordinary intensity, extraordinary energy. During such periods, it seems to me, Roethke most often thinks and writes in units, not of single poems, but of sequences of poems. Therefore the Roethkean sequence has also become my unit of thought, my unit of writing. "The Edge of Many Things," that section of this book that follows the study of the apprenticeship, examines four of the large sequences written entirely or almost entirely in free verse. "The Formal Father," my final section, turns to a consideration of three major sequences of poems done for the most part in rhyme and meter. I have treated the texture of Roethke's poetry as if it could be unwoven and the individual strands—the particular stylistic techniques—examined separately. To put it another way, I have, in order to avoid repeating myself, shifted my approach slightly from sequence to sequence, each time trying to come at the poetry, at Roethke's dynamic vision, by emphasizing a different "trick" or device of his. I would prefer not to be misunderstood here. I am not so foolish as to think that Roethke himself, once he had mastered any device for generating intensity, ever gave it up again. He used every trick he knew, though some tricks fit some passages, some poems, and some sequences a little better than others. I have tried to respond to that "fitness" of things whenever possible, but my choice of which particular strand, which technique, to trace through any given sequence is admittedly a technical device of my own, an attempt to bring some order to this study of Roethke's vision and technique.

In my approach I have tried to emulate that coed who learned from watching Roethke's hands. And Richard Hugo, who stopped taking notes long enough to find meaning in the "overstance" of his professor's performance. By concentrating on the medium rather than the message, on how the poetry moves rather than on what it says, I think that I, too, have learned a lot from Roethke's course. As poet, as teacher, Roethke is a kind of magician, one charged with creating before our very eyes the illusion of life itself. To keep one eye on his performance, on his mastery of the tricks of his trade, not only increases one's appreciation of the illusionist's skill, it often gives new meaning and value to the illusion as well.

In a notebook entry dated early in 1946, Roethke wrote, "The mod. error in criticism: Someone uses a trick, therefore he is a trick" (36 #89). The ultimate "trick" in conveying dynamism is, of course, to have "A sense of intense life behind the verses" (36 #89), which is no trick at all, but life in earnest. Finally, one cannot fake that intensity of life which makes the poem. In his rough drafts for the prose piece called "On Identity," Roethke may have commented on one of the prices he paid for the energy found in his poems:

> Granted it may take spiritual guts to deliberately shake up, to disarrange the senses—and it can be done: by noise, by repeated music, by refusing to sleep and so on. . . . There's a terrific sense of exhilaration and terror on going down— But the unconscious is not neutral . . . therein dwelleth the devil, and what is called Original Sin, all the seamy sides of man. Ask these forces to take over and they may. You may be possessed of a terrible and terrifying energy: your adrenalin may leap like a shot. Your acceleration down may get entirely out of control. . . . The profound desire to live to the fullest may change into an even more powerful will to die. (28, 26)

The remarks were not included in the final form of the presentation, perhaps because Roethke felt a responsibility not to tempt would-be poets toward a break-up of the senses. As he claims to have told a younger poet once, "It's not nice work and you wouldn't like it" (28, 26).

I believe, as did Roethke, that the energy of the poem proceeds from the psyche of the poet; that, in a very real sense, the great man makes the great thing. But how Roethke came to be a great man is beyond the scope of this book. Indeed, it may be beyond the scope of any book. Certainly Allan Seager's biography gives few clues, and they are confusing and sometimes contradictory. "Yes," Roethke writes, "I was dancing-mad, and how / That came to be the bears and Yeats would know" (CP 105). I have, with much reluctance, left the "how" to Yeats and the bears and concentrated on the outward and visible signs of that dancing-madness—the style and the changes in style, which are always a kind of change in subject and which may well be a change in mind and spirit as well. I shall, it is true, concentrate on Roethke's "tricks," but I am not now, nor, I hope, ever shall be, guilty of thinking the man himself "a trick." It is only that the style is less elusive than the man, that one may get hold of poetic techniques with one's critical tools, while the process by which the artist's spirit evolves remains his secret to the end.

Roethke as Student

At the end of an undergraduate paper titled "Some Self-Analysis," Theodore Roethke wrote, "I'm either going to be a good writer or a poor fool" (SP 6). To which his instructor, a logical man bent on doing his duty, replied, "There are alternatives. Writing isn't the only thing worthwhile" (60, 1). One can sympathize with the instructor, who ought to have been right, as well as with Roethke, who, it turns out, was telling the truth. "If I can't write," he decided early, "what can I do?" and, in something like desperation, he pursued his vocation with remarkable single-mindedness. For Roethke there were no alternatives; writing *was* the only thing worthwhile.

He began, as every writer begins, with tools inadequate for the thing he wanted to say. His self-analysis is probably accurate but not *too* accurate.

> I have long wondered just what my strength was as a writer. I am often filled with tremendous enthusiasm for a subject, yet my writing about it will seem a sorry attempt. Above all, I possess a driving sincerity,—that prime virtue of any creative worker. I write only what I believe to be the absolute truth,—even if I must ruin the theme in so doing.

In this respect I feel far superior to those glib people in my classes who often garner better grades than I do. They are so often pitiful frauds,—artificial—insincere. They have a line that works. They do not write from the depths of their hearts. Nothing of theirs was ever born of pain. Many an incoherent yet sincere piece of writing has outlived the polished product. (sp 3–4)

That last sentence must have often come back to haunt him during his years as a teacher of writing, but as an undergraduate it represents an idea which is almost obsessive to Roethke. Over and over again he begins papers with pretended apologies, "To pour out one's heart in a rhetoric theme is not a customary practice perhaps" (60, 3), or with defiance masquerading as despair:

Soon the alert pupil realizes that it is a wise policy to keep his own silly thoughts out of most subjects and stick to thread-bare platitudes regarding things academic. . . . A pseudo-scholarship is preferable to honest conviction. . . . (60, 3)

Another Roethkean beginning, this one to a paper on *Dame Care*, a paper offered without footnotes and, one suspects, without research, remarks archly that

One can be quite learned and scholarly, read up on the subject, show the influence of so-and-so the novelist, and so-and-so the psychologist. This is all very fine and usually brings down an "A"; but the student usually realizes that what he says is pretty dull, second-hand stuff. On the other hand, one can endeavor to show what a delicately attuned, sensitive person he is. Such an honest fellow usually is crushed, for he finds that his own reactions are valueless, that he is judged flippant and superficial. (60, 3)

Perhaps it is worth noting that Roethke's own honest reactions to *Dame Care* earned him a B+ and, no doubt, confirmed his suspicions. It is also worth noting that Roethke played the academic game well enough to make Phi Beta Kappa and that he once asked a friend's opinion of his student themes with the written comment, "Please criticize the themes severely. I know they're quite school-boyish. Remember that they were written to fill assignments and to please an instructor" (60, 2).

Nonetheless, I think Roethke's "Some Self-Analysis" tells the truth mainly, though surely with a few "stretchers." A driving sincerity *was* his real strength as a writer, and many of his student themes, whether pleasing to instructors or not, do seem to have been written from the depth of his heart. Surely those qualities are the main strengths of those undergraduate papers, some of them biographical fiction and others of them fictional biography, in which Roethke created, and not for the last time, a kind of mythological Saginaw, a mythological past.

"Have I only been reciting a drab and sordid family history?" he asks at the conclusion of a piece called "Plot Material." "I think not. It is intense and bitter human drama. . . . A great story could be written about my father, for in many ways he was a truly great man" (60, 1). Roethke knew perfectly well that his student pieces were not great stories, that he had not created intense drama; but he knew, too, that his own history was charged with an energy of which something of value might be made, that a great story *could* emerge from the materials of his childhood and adolescence. It was knowledge that he spent almost twenty years in relearning, for it was not until some years after the building of *Open House* that he turned again for subject matter to the intense drama of Saginaw and his father and the great glass house.

To a reader with the lifetime of poems spread out before him, Roethke's student papers—his Saginaw Sagas—are of more than biographical interest. It is not merely that one occasionally finds the germs of poems scattered among the themes, for example, that one paper is called "Moss Picking" and demonstrates some of the same details and attitudes that appear in "Moss-Gathering," the *Lost Son* poem; or that in an essay called "Papa" the narrator dreams that "it seemed papa came in and danced around with him. . . . John put his feet on top of papa's and they'd waltz" (60, 1). The real significance of these themes, a significance clearly visible only in the light cast by the poems to come, lies in the value they place upon the dynamic values of change, growth, and development as opposed to the static virtues of order and stability. What makes these papers more unified than is usual in a batch of student writings is that the dramatic tensions in Roethke's mythological Saginaw are always the same. All that is creative, energetic, primitive, and (of course) honest is at war with that which is successful, restrictive, civilized, and merely slick. Roethke himself is frequently the hero poised between these force fields, much as Everyman is poised between the forces of Heaven and Hell.

The hero of the myth, the King who is quite literally identified with Nature and the energy of growing things, is Roethke's father, Otto the greenhouse keeper. It is he who grows flowers in order to create the beautiful out of nothing, who preserves and loves the wilderness, who is sexually and creatively potent. Roethke makes of him a kind of German Indian, a white primitive, a figure who shares in and adds to the energy that is life itself. Opposing Otto Roethke, most clearly in the piece called "Plot Material," is Uncle Charlie. Uncle Charlie is a partner in the greenhouse, but he grows flowers solely for their commercial value. Charlie is portrayed as being fickle, deceitful, and ineffectual; he is a social climber, concerned with status in a way that Otto is not. And, in a piece called "My Estrangement from Nature," Roethke contrasts his father's woodsmanship with Uncle Charlie's:

> Lean and hardy as a hickory sapling, he had the tirelessness of an Indian. His taciturnity and stoicness, too, were Indian-like characteristics. He never rhapsodized over anything as did Uncle Charlie (who, moreover, was too fat to be a good woodsman). (60, 2)

Roethke himself, sometimes thinly disguised as a boy named John, is the figure who, in most of the stories, must grow and change. The effort is usually to prove himself worthy of being Otto's son, to remove himself as far as possible from the horror of being—however symbolically—the illegitimate son of Charlie.

It is not always easy, for Roethke often depicts himself as being uncomfortably more like his uncle than like his father. He, too, is fat and inefficient in the woods. In "Fish Tale" he has been so incompetent—getting up late, forgetting his tackle, rowing poorly, accidentally knocking off Otto's hat—that the father refuses to let him go fishing with the men of his party. Left by himself, Roethke catches an enormous fish, accidentally loses his father's pole over the side, then rows after the pole until the fish is exhausted enough to be boated. When he gets credit for using "an old trick,—throwing your pole in the water," he is pleased because "I had been judged clever of mind and hand for the first time in my life. And I hadn't deserved it." Both the incompetence and the pleasure taken in deception are qualities more closely associated with Charlie than with Otto Roethke.

Moreover, Roethke often depicts himself contemptuously as the adolescent who sides with law and order, with civilization and its various restraints, against the primitive energy of love or sexuality, of the primitive. In "The Home Coming," calling himself "John," but apologizing to the teacher for writing what is almost biography, Roethke returns from college and displays a shallowness and a concern for petty rules most unworthy of Otto's son. His mother, a long-suffering figure bent over the dishes while her children go their ways, thinks with pride of her son John, who is "the best of the lot. So kind and sensible." But when John, symbolically a sophomore, comes breezing in from college, he carries a packet of her letters in his coat pocket. The mother is surprised and pleased: "Why you dear boy. . . . You've been keeping all my letters in your pocket. Did you like them?" And John's reply ends the story: "Well—of course, Mom. . . . But good Lord, here's what I wanted to show you,—you're [sic] grammar's become simply horrible and you spelled three words wrong." Clumsy as it is, the story illustrates the conflict between the energetic love of the mother and the affectation ("simply horrible") of obsessive concern with slickness, with the technical business of grammar and spelling.

In a story called "The Egg," Roethke visits Old Stevens, an

Indian who is critically ill. The boy is repulsed by the conditions in which he finds the Indian dying—especially when he finds that hens have the run of the house. He is sickened when one of the hens lays an egg, but he is then instructed by the wise primitive: "Ah . . . being a white man, you are disgusted. But you are not a philosopher. An egg is a good sign,—a symbol even in Christianity. It means birth, new life,—perhaps health for me. I'm favoured by the gods" (60, 1). From Old Stevens the boy learns, though the narrator leaves the moral unstated, something of the energetic thrust of life; that it goes on in the face of decay and dirt and excrement; that it is the white man's obsession with perfection and sterility that is ultimately deadening. The boy begins the story as a conventional member of white society and ends it as the narrator who is capable of viewing his role in the tale with some perspective. He has, to some extent, put on some of the dignity and strength of the primitive, has also taken on new life and health.

In other stories, too, Roethke finds himself envying the life-giving energy of those who, like Antaeus, are in contact with the earth. The hero of "A Pointless Narrative," Old Joe, is quite literally in contact with the dirt, for he is a street cleaner who, though past seventy, handles his shovel "as if it were a plaything." Like Old Stevens, Joe is taciturn and, as successful primitive, his work is "rhythmically languid," an effortless flowing in which he is totally at peace. When the son of one of Saginaw's "most august and virtuous" persons chases a ball into the path of a car, Old Joe saves the boy at some risk to himself. For his reward he is spit upon by the boy, whose mother, "in her most grieved accents," calls for her son to "Come away from that man." Contrived as the story is, Roethke as narrator has asserted the strength, courage, and dignity of the primitive in contrast with the fastidious social rigidity of the "civilized" woman and her son.

In another, this one based on his experiences is a pickle factory, Roethke finds himself taken outside by one of the woman workers, who begins to make love to him. "He felt he was being dominated.

That he wasn't a man. She laughed, curling her lips. He felt very
silly" (60, 2). Despite his failure, the boy is elated on the way
home. "His little peasant girl. He felt himself another youthful
Tolstoi." The girl, like the other factory workers, has a vitality
which frightens the boy and which he does not share. He would
write about his experience—compares himself with Goethe as
well as with Tolstoi—but does not command enough energy even
to force the woman onto the page. Nonetheless, the sexual urge,
the dynamic force of the "peasants," fascinates him, and he does
recognize that such vitality is a theme worthy of a great writer.

Roethke is most his father's legitimate heir when he writes
about nature, perhaps his favorite subject in these undergraduate
papers. In "Some Self-Analysis" he wrote,

> I have a genuine love of nature. It is not the least bit
> affected, but an integral and powerful part of my life. I know
> that Cooper is a fraud—that he doesn't give a true sense of
> the sublimity of American scenery. I know that Muir and
> Thoreau and Burroughs speak the truth. (SP 4)

Once again Roethke is playing off the genuine, the true, and the
powerful against the affected and the fradulent, but at last he is
clearly on the side of the angels. In the woods with his father he
is, at least in some essays, no longer the novice. In "My Estrangement from Nature," one of the papers which does indeed seem to
be born of pain, Roethke praises his father's woodsmanship and
suggests a closeness shared by man and boy on their hikes through
the 160 wild acres which Otto Roethke had bought and preserved as a place "where small game and birds could flourish undisturbed, where the barking of hounds and the roar of the shot-
gun would never be heard" (60, 1). In that place, Roethke recalls,
"You will feel a close harmony between external nature and your
inner self. . . . However irate you may be, you'll be soothed and
beguiled into a wonderful sense of peace" (60, 1). But, as the title
of the paper suggests, the preserve fails to preserve: "Now men of
vision in the Rotary Club have converted it into 'Woodlawn

Vista, the Subdivision Beautiful.' " (60, 2). The ordering forces
of society have marshalled the sprawl of nature into neatly arranged streets. And Otto Roethke, who was in his son's mind "in-
separably intertwined" with Nature, had died. "I don't care to
hike anymore. I always find myself expecting to see his head appear over the edge of the next hill" (60, 2).

Roethke wrote, as the representative passages just quoted suggest, a reasonably good prose during the Ann Arbor years. It
would, to be sure, have taken a keen eye to detect the mature
poet beneath the layers of undergraduate baby fat. But the tension between the dynamic and the static is there from the beginning, embedded in the subject matter, implied even in the
vocabulary. That early "Self-Analysis" draws the battle lines. On
the one hand are "tremendous enthusiasm," "driving sincerity,"
work "born of pain," "fire," "love," "nature," instinct, visions
which "flood," and "undercurrents of emotion" which go "surg-
ing within." On the other hand are the "glib," the "insincere," the
"line that works," the "artificial," and the "polished product"
(surely Roethke intends the metaphor to conjure up the static,
mechanized drudgery of the assembly line). To side with the
polished product is to be "bound," "dwarfed," and "cramped," to
spend a lifetime not daring to do things honestly for fear that one
will display "bad form." Roethke sensed that life was motion,
but he had not yet found the means by which to represent that
motion in words. He needed time to discover what was, for him at
least, to be a great truth: "The things that concern you most
can't be put in prose. In prose the tendency is to avoid inner responsibility. Poetry is the discovery of the legend of one's youth"
(SF 171).

Looking back upon those undergraduate papers from the lofty
perspective of the Harvard graduate school, Roethke complained
that "there has been too much attention to certain set forms; and
too little to attempting to coax into being the emotions that lie
close to the subconscious, the ideas only half formulated" (60, 9).
And he went on, as if reciting a *credo*, to map out the way that he
intended to go:

I claim that once a man has the true urge to write, which implies ability . . . he doesn't need a lot of rules or principles. He reads and assimilates and gradually forms a style all his own. Or even say he reads and *imitates*. That's what Blake says we should do, you know. (60, 9)

One can hardly imagine a world view more dynamic, more at home with radical and continuous change than that of Lawrence. And the preface to *New Poems* is a beautiful and persuasive statement of the dynamism of life, "the ever-present [which] knows no finality, no finished crystallization . . . emerging and flowing off, and never in any sense at rest, static, finished."[1] It is also a list of the requirements for a poetry of the instant present:

There must be mutation, swifter than iridescence, haste, not rest, come-and-go, not fixity, inconclusiveness, immediacy, the quality of life itself, without denouement or close. There must be the rapid momentaneous association of things which meet and pass on the forever incalculable journey of creation: everything left in its own rapid, fluid relationship with the rest of things.[2]

In the rough notes for his long graduate paper on Lawrence, Roethke says, "Mr. Lawrence is a literary barbarian, a savage," but we have already seen that Roethke respected the energy and force of the savage. If there was a part of Roethke that wanted to play the swell, affecting a fur coat so that "those Harvards" wouldn't have it over him, there was also Roethke the white Indian, the most elemental thing in the room." The craftsman in Roethke, quite aware of the unfinished quality of Lawrence's poems, something greater in him responded to Lawrence's strengths stored them for future reference:

Like all great artists, he wrote because he had to, he tore his poems out of his consciousness. But Lawrence's genius required a form that permitted plenty of freedom and movement. . . . What is important in Lawrence? The answer is this: the moment is important, perhaps as a revelation of life. . . . (60, 9)

stions of influence are always tricky. I do not know whethe[r] learned something about dynamism and its literary poss om D. H. Lawrence or whether Roethke chose to wor

The Student Literary
Criticism

Like any other English major and graduate student, Roethke had to write a good deal of what passed for literary criticism. This he did with enthusiasm and insight, but not, it seems to me, with much thoroughness or scholarly care. He footnotes seldom, and is sometimes chided for carelessness when he does. One Roethkean footnote characterizes his approach rather well, I think. Toward the end of a long and intense study of the influence of Henry Vaughan on William Wordsworth, a paper which begins by remarking on the need for a detailed consideration of the problem, Roethke makes reference to an article in *Modern Language Notes* by L. R. Merrill. Merrill's article is called "Vaughan's Influence upon Wordsworth's Poetry," and Roethke apologizes, "I did not find this work until my paper was practically finished." Since Merrill's paper appeared in 1922 and Roethke was writing in 1930, there is some evidence that Roethke was a better poet than he was a student of bibliographical methods. Nonetheless, Roethke's critical studies of D. H. Lawrence and of Vaughan's influence on Wordsworth may be important for having clarified for him his dynamic world view and for having suggested to him possible poetic strategies for communicating that view to others.

Roethke had a continuing interest in Lawrence. In fact, he did two papers as an undergraduate on Lawrence, another long study of Lawrence at Harvard, and refers to him frequently—if not al-

ways favorably—in the notebooks and in the class notes he as a professor. The two undergraduate papers show Roethke both fascinated and repelled by Lawrence's poems. One of written for "Teaching of Poetry" and called "Upon M rence," remarks that "His poetry remains incomplete and . . . it is less poetry for being material which is not c under the artist's control. We find no sense of finality in of Lawrence. There is no sense of complete achiever 5). And the other paper, "An Analysis of a Typica Poem" ("Late at Night"), lodges the same compla good demonstration of how a creative mind of a hi be possessed of a real emotion, yet fall short of (60, 3). One would expect the poet of *Open Hous* of tiny forms and well-made lines, to deplore the rence's free verse. But at the same time, Roe what it was that Lawrence was about. "The p to please the ear or the eye; he wanted to enter of the reader abruptly and suddenly and at th the dominant mood of the poem" (60, 3). H mark with two quotations from Lawrence's pr a piece of writing which may have influen deal. In his preface, Lawrence applies to po same divisions that Roethke had sensed There is, Lawrence writes, that poetry of " which is characterized by "finality," "syn pletion, and, above all, by "perfection." of poetry," Lawrence says, and Roethk rence talks about what that poetry is:

the poetry of that which is at h
In the immediate present there
mation, nothing finished . . .
of the instant present cannot h
motion as the poetry of the
ished. There is no rhythm
There is no static perfectio
find so satisfying because v

Que
Roethke
bilities t

with Lawrence because he saw in that poet and novelist evidence of energy and motion that mirrored his own. Perhaps it is safest to say that Roethke might have gained from Lawrence an awareness of the dynamic nature of time, an awareness which Roethke was—much later—to incorporate into the best of his own work. For Lawrence all time consisted of "the moment, the quick of all change and haste and opposition: the moment, the immediate present, the Now." "It inhales the future," wrote Lawrence in that preface which Roethke quotes, "it exhales the past. It is the quick of both, and yet it is neither." [3] The difficulties of representing such a moment in poetry were not lost on Roethke. "What falls away is always," he wrote years later, "And is near"; and "The Waking," like many of the great later poems, is an attempt to present through energetic thrusts and turns of the language that "always" which is Now and which falls away before a man can touch it with hand or word. It is a time "near" only because there is no time nearer, yet it remains as inaccessible as God. When Roethke seems to turn to the past for his subject matter (as in the greenhouse poems or the *Lost Son Sequences*), he does so not because he is interested in what is past but because he is interested in what is continuous. Sometimes Roethke is content to capture the vitality of a remembered moment, usually a moment in which the energy and motion of life are conspicuously present. In such poems he tries to arrest that energy much as one might confine steam in order to make its power more fully realized. But more often he sets out to show that the past is still contained in the immediate present, that the historical event (defined as broadly as possible) is never "finished," but that it retains a vitality which extends infinitely, moving forever in the eternal now. In one of the notebooks, Roethke quotes Kierkegaard as saying that "Life can only be understood backwards; but it must be lived forwards" (35 #65). To do both at once—to experience the forward thrust of an event in life while reaching back with the memory to assign meaning and value to the same event—is a feat to be accomplished, with luck, by the artist. To relive the event in all its energetic motion and at the same time to realize its larger context in the past and in the future is to experience most fully the dynamism of life.

Perhaps the most significant line in Roethke's study of Lawrence is one which never found its way into a final draft: "I should have to grow a great deal to write like that" (60, 9).

Roethke's study of Vaughan's influence on Wordsworth is the most ambitious of the M.A. essays to be found in the University of Washington's collection. As I have just said, the question of influence is a tricky one, and as a graduate student Roethke handles it gingerly and very unevenly. He cites the obvious similarities: both men are "Nature" poets, both might loosely be termed "mystics"; there is a shared vocabulary, an echo here and there, some tenuous resemblances in rhythm. Roethke leaves nothing out. Each man suffered an encounter with political reality; each was a man of some prominence in the circle in which he moved. None of this, as Roethke uneasily admits, is news: "Among commentators familiar with Vaughan, his influence upon Wordsworth has become a commonplace" (60, 12). Nevertheless, he plunges ahead. "The linking of Vaughan's name with Wordsworth's in both casual remark and formal study warrants, it seems, a more detailed consideration of the study than has been made" (60, 12).

The real theme of the study emerges slowly and is stuccoed with irrelevancies and false starts. But it is a theme which seems to be useful to a reading of both Vaughan and Wordsworth, though Roethke might have done better to drop the "influence" business as unprovable. "One of Wordsworth's chief contributions as a nature poet," writes Roethke, "has been his recognition of the 'active principle.' . . . Wordsworth often saw the world in movement. To him, Nature was a kind of dynamic energizing force, a vast impersonal power" (60, 12). To prove his point, Roethke cites lines from "Tintern Abbey,"

> And I have felt
> A presence that disturbs me with the joy
> Of elevated thoughts. . . .

A motion and a spirit, that impels
All thinking things, all objects of all thought
And rolls through all things. . . .

He takes the phrase *active principle*, of course, from "The Excursion," which he also quotes:

To every Form of being is assigned,
Thus calmly spake the venerable Sage,
An active Principle:—howe'er removed
From sense and observation.

Roethke does little with the idea beyond quoting passages which illustrate it, usually limiting his comment to an editorial italicizing of active verbs or of lines which demonstrate his point. Then he moves on to Vaughan:

But this sense of activity in nature—especially a divine activity—occurs with far greater frequency in Vaughan. He has been called "The Poet of Light," but light to Vaughan was only one kind of activity. . . . Vaughan was literally overwhelmed by movement in the world, not merely as movement but as a manifestation of the divine. (60, 12)

And again, many quotations later:

I have said that Vaughan crowded his poems with phrases and single words which show his peculiar sensitivity and emphasis upon movement. Thus springs are "vocal," winds "active," winds "quick," streams "rapid," powers "quickening." . . . This emphasis on activity is characteristic of other metaphysical poets, it is true; but none have carried it as far as Henry Vaughan. (60, 12)

He may not have successfully demonstrated the influence of Vaughan on Wordsworth, but Roethke's letters make it clear that he was himself much influenced by Vaughan. In a letter to Dorothy Gordon, for example, Roethke apologizes for the religious nature of the poem he then called "The Various Light" by saying that it was written "after reading Vaughan one time" (*Letters* 11). He also thought enough of Vaughan (as he did of Lawrence) to include him in the list of "minor or special writers for whom I have a real enthusiasm" (*Letters* 104), and, as is by now well known, to take a title, "Unfold! Unfold!" from Vaughan's "The Revival." It was, I am all but certain, Vaughan's sense of "movement in the world," his belief that God manifests Himself as pure motion and energy, which most attracted Roethke to him. Roethke's analysis of the techniques by which Vaughan presents that motion in poetry is rudimentary, not really going beyond a listing of those "phrases and single words" which indicate activity in nature, but his paper makes it clear that Roethke recognizes the dynamic element in Vaughan's poetry and that he admires it greatly—and this at a time when influences are especially important to Roethke.

At the bottom of a page from the rough drafts of the paper on Vaughan and Wordsworth, scrawled at a jaunty upward tilt, are two lines of poetry: "Dispell the shape of doom / From each wall of your room" (60, 15). The accents are carefully and heavily marked above the lines, as if to make sure of the meter. The couplet, somewhat altered, becomes a stanza of "The Conqueror," one of those poems which Roethke took to Robert Hillyer and of which Hillyer is supposed to have said, "Any editor who wouldn't buy these is a fool!" (SP 16). The ending—really the beginning—is happy. George Shuster of *Commonweal* proved himself no fool by printing "The Conqueror," one of Roethke's first significant publications, in 1931.

Uncollected Poems

The first fifteen years or so of Theodore Roethke's writing life —the years beginning about 1929 and ending about 1943 or 1944—constitute a lengthy and painful apprenticeship. In 1959, safely on the far side of a Pulitzer Prize, two Guggenheim Fellowships, a National Book Award, and a Bollingen Prize, he still remembers what it is to be a beginner:

> He isn't sure whether he is a thief or a fake. He may, critically, be far ahead of himself emotionally. He may be able to discuss, with real intelligence, Marvell or Pound or Stevens, but when he takes pen in hand the great models of the past may seem far away and even absurd, and the big names of his own time awesome, overwhelming. (SP 62–3)

Indeed, at the beginning of his apprenticeship, Roethke is far ahead critically of where he is emotionally. Like most beginners, he needs to learn to shake loose, to substitute associational powers for analytical ones, creative energy for critical precision. Richard Hugo puts it well, I think:

> Yeats's "What comes easily for the bad poet comes with great difficulty for the good" seems to apply to Roethke. He was a terrified man and writing was not easy . . . his urge to write was so strong that he often resorted to trivial versification both to learn how to write and to free his imagination. When writing is that hard, no effort is wasted no matter how weak the immediate result.[1]

27

The early notebooks are fascinating, for they are the battleground in which Roethke fought to catch up emotionally, to free his imagination, to shake something loose. Unlike his later notebooks, which often contain a good deal of confident prose—comments on poetry and other poets, strategies for teaching, remarks on the professorial life, evaluations of his mental and physical well- or ill-being—those from the very early 1930s are filled almost exclusively with lines of poetry. One exception, taken from the first notebook (apparently begun at Harvard in the autumn of 1930), is an aphorism which floats like a banner over the poems which surround and follow it: "Eloquence the enemy of precision" (32 #1). Years later Roethke echoes the phrase in his teaching notes, but changes it to read "The enemy of intensity: grandiloquence" (65, 14). The enemy is the same, though the mature Roethke defines "eloquence" more clearly and deals with it more effectively; but the vital organ of the poem, that essential quality which must be protected, is significantly different. One of the things Roethke's apprenticeship teaches him is that precision is not enough—that it is simply a tool, sometimes useful, for adding to the intensity, to the energy and motion, without which a poem fails to come to life.

Even with the notebooks in front of one, the process by which Roethke makes the poems of his apprenticeship remains quite mysterious. He seems to have worked on as many as four or five poems at one time, juggling them from page to page, abandoning one to work on another which, in turn, would be abandoned either for the first poem or for yet another. Sometimes he seems to fit lines or short stanzas from one poem into another, usually with surprisingly little modification. He gets away with it, clearly, because of the remarkable sameness in tone, vocabulary, meter, and rhyme of those early pieces. They are poems assembled from parts which are often all but interchangeable, and the notebooks are crammed with isolated lines or couplets—almost always in iambic tetrameter or trimeter, almost always with perfect rhymes or ending with words which will be easy to rhyme on—lines which seem to be waiting for a poem that they can be squeezed into or tacked onto.

In his effort to break loose, to stimulate the imagination, Roethke often begins by doodling with unusual, or what he hopes are unusual, combinations of adjectives and nouns. Typical examples —a small sampling culled from that first notebook—are *prurient rose, superb dead, valorous moon, angel days, vague virginity, supple virtue, accurate ecstacy, sombre untranquillity, terrible immediacy, fluid form, tragic taint, faultless clarity, cosmic innocence,* and *arrowed grace* (32 #1). These phrases are then set into poems which are already begun or else become the seeds from which new poems begin. *Arrowed grace,* for instance, seems to have been the phrase which triggered "Someday I'll Step," a poem which begins "Someday I'll step with arrowed grace / Into a brighter realm of space." [2] All of these phrases are, it should be noted, relatively easy to rhyme on and all have that regular alternation of stresses which enables them to be set easily into Roethke's early verse. Moreover, of the examples given above, only *rose, moon,* and—to a lesser extent—*dead* might be thought of as concrete nouns. The rest—*untranquillity, ecstacy, virtue, innocence, immediacy*—are about as abstract as nouns get. That quality of abstraction characterizes—and weakens—the early poems. The adjectives seem an attempt to solidify the unsubstantial, to give to ideas a hint of substance that will give them a connection, however tenuous, with the physical world.

Sometimes Roethke begins with even smaller units, with words alone. Like most beginners, he leaves margins full of rhyming words: "main, sane, vein, rain, brain, pain, grim, attain" (32 #1). Only *grim* offers relief from predictability in the list cited, but the early poems rely heavily on such exact rhymes. At times Roethke lists words that seem to have attracted him by their sounds, by being unusual, or by the meanings hidden in their roots: *incarnadine, concupiscent, centripetal, augury, infrangible, terrain* (32 #1). From such lists he creates phrases by adding adjectives or nouns ("concupiscent sun") and then sets the phrases into lines which eventually become poems or try to become poems. For this sort of word play he prefers the Latinate, the ornamental, and, despite his disclaimer, the eloquent.

Roethke may have been able to discuss, as he puts it, "with real intelligence," the dynamism of Lawrence or the active principle in Wordsworth, but the poems of the apprenticeship—particularly those poems which he did not include in *Open House*—are, for the most part, unsuccessful gropings toward such models. "The Conqueror," that early publication in *Commonweal*, might serve as a fitting representative of a group of poems including "Exhortation," "Essay," and "Statement."

> Be proud to live alone.
> Be murdered and undone,
>
> But do not seek escape,
> In visionary shape.
>
> Be brave, and do not keep
> A guardian for your sleep.
>
> Preserve your promised word
> Brighter than a sword,
>
> Your lively mirrors chaste,
> Uncheckered to the last.
>
> Erase the shape of doom
> From the walls of your room;
>
> Constrain the willing blood
> To virtue's platitude.
>
> Beneath a sturdy roof
> Live unconfused, aloof,
>
> The dreaming heart, the sense
> Remote from all pretense.
>
> O fear no little death,
> But live by truer faith
>
> And find through pure control
> The measure of your soul! [3]

Dynamism in this collage of hortatory advice on how to live, what to do, is confined to the exclamation mark at the end, a way of achieving a smash finale of which Roethke seems rather over-fond in his apprentice work. These "Exhortations" and "Statements" offer their wisdom, apparently, without the relief of irony, though it is hard to believe that a stanza such as "Constrain the willing blood / To virtue's platitude" is meant to be taken straight. Yet, since there is little or nothing in the rest of the poem to suggest that the poet's face is a mask, that his voice is cleverly disguised, there seems no choice but to take his advice at face value, to take the voice to be Roethke's, heightened slightly in the manner of a lecturer's when facing an audience he wishes to impress. It is hard to imagine a more static format for poetry, one less likely to result in "intensity."

Scanning rough drafts of "The Conqueror," one does not feel the handprint of necessity on the content. One draft, for example, opens "Be murdered and undone / But do not live alone" (32 #1). As he added, deleted, altered, and rearranged stanzas, Roethke seems to have decided that, in the interests of consistency (and perhaps of chastity), the conqueror ought to live by himself after all. And, finally, the character does take shape. He is one who preserves, controls, constrains, and measures. He lives "unconfused," without pretense and without evasion "In visionary shape." He is a model of constancy, and yesterday's promise is preserved today. The tight little couplets, fit together with perfect and near-perfect rhymes, all have the effect of being closed. Even when the stanzas run on, one has the sense that they might easily be complete in themselves, that they have been composed in two line units and later spliced together by coordinating conjunctions or by commas to make items in a series. Generally it is a form illustrating the virtues it extolls: constraint, control, and measure.

I suspect Roethke hugs the small forms so hard because they serve as rudimentary devices for freeing his imagination. The need to rhyme, the need to maintain a rhythm and to keep regular stanzas, are ways of distracting the conscious mind long enough to allow something from the subconscious mind to slip past. Like many beginners, Roethke seems to find a tight form to be a way of saying the thing he did not know he knew. And, as he grows more skillful, his powerful sense of the dynamism of life begins, quite naturally, to find its way into his themes and images.

In 1932, after several rejections, Roethke managed to persuade Harriet Monroe of *Poetry* to accept two poems, "Bound" and "Fugitive" (see *Letters* 3–5). Some of the rough drafts of "Bound" are headed "Variations on Mr. Kilmer's Theme," but Roethke— or Miss Monroe—wisely dropped that title. As it is, the four beat couplets and the unrelieved (save for the final stanza) perfect rhymes are enough to invite comparison with "Trees," whereas Roethke, I presume, wished to invite contrast. "Bound" is a poem about a tree, "A variously compounded fact / Denied the favor of swift act." It is that denial which fascinates Roethke:

> You are a bird, securely bound,
> That sings the song of voiceless ground,
>
> And builds a nest in sterile stone,
> Yet breeds no kin of flesh and bone.
>
> You are a bird denied, the blood
> Of earth in flying attitude.[4]

For Roethke, bondage, the prevention of motion, results in sterility and silence, conditions amounting to death for any poet. Nonetheless, the comparison of tree to bird, the fixed to the flying, gives a powerful sense of arrested energy. The denial "of swift act" is a terrific denial, one which makes the reader feel keenly the potential sweep and movement of the "bound" tree. Roethke practices the sculptor's trick of capturing his subject as if in mid-action—a trick which affirms and even accentuates for his audience the very motion that is being denied.

In "Fugitive," on the other hand, Roethke tries to present movement directly and is less successful.

> The supple virtue of her mind
> Is innocent and wild,

I claim that once a man has the true urge to write, which implies ability . . . he doesn't need a lot of rules or principles. He reads and assimilates and gradually forms a style all his own. Or even say he reads and *imitates*. That's what Blake says we should do, you know.   (60, 9)

The Student Literary
Criticism

Like any other English major and graduate student, Roethke had to write a good deal of what passed for literary criticism. This he did with enthusiasm and insight, but not, it seems to me, with much thoroughness or scholarly care. He footnotes seldom, and is sometimes chided for carelessness when he does. One Roethkean footnote characterizes his approach rather well, I think. Toward the end of a long and intense study of the influence of Henry Vaughan on William Wordsworth, a paper which begins by remarking on the need for a detailed consideration of the problem, Roethke makes reference to an article in *Modern Language Notes* by L. R. Merrill. Merrill's article is called "Vaughan's Influence upon Wordsworth's Poetry," and Roethke apologizes, "I did not find this work until my paper was practically finished." Since Merrill's paper appeared in 1922 and Roethke was writing in 1930, there is some evidence that Roethke was a better poet than he was a student of bibliographical methods. Nonetheless, Roethke's critical studies of D. H. Lawrence and of Vaughan's influence on Wordsworth may be important for having clarified for him his dynamic world view and for having suggested to him possible poetic strategies for communicating that view to others.

Roethke had a continuing interest in Lawrence. In fact, he did two papers as an undergraduate on Lawrence, another long study of Lawrence at Harvard, and refers to him frequently—if not always favorably—in the notebooks and in the class notes he kept as a professor. The two undergraduate papers show Roethke to be both fascinated and repelled by Lawrence's poems. One of them, written for "Teaching of Poetry" and called "Upon Mr. Lawrence," remarks that "His poetry remains incomplete and warped . . . it is less poetry for being material which is not completely under the artist's control. We find no sense of finality in the work of Lawrence. There is no sense of complete achievement" (59, 5). And the other paper, "An Analysis of a Typical Lawrence Poem" ("Late at Night"), lodges the same complaint: "It is a good demonstration of how a creative mind of a high order may be possessed of a real emotion, yet fall short of achievement" (60, 3). One would expect the poet of *Open House*, that volume of tiny forms and well-made lines, to deplore the sprawl of Lawrence's free verse. But at the same time, Roethke understood what it was that Lawrence was about. "The poet did not want to please the ear or the eye; he wanted to enter the consciousness of the reader abruptly and suddenly and at the same time strike the dominant mood of the poem" (60, 3). He backs up this remark with two quotations from Lawrence's preface to *New Poems,* a piece of writing which may have influenced Roethke a good deal. In his preface, Lawrence applies to poetry something of the same divisions that Roethke had sensed in his life in Saginaw. There is, Lawrence writes, that poetry of "the beginning and end" which is characterized by "finality," "symmetry," a sense of completion, and, above all, by "perfection." "But there is another kind of poetry," Lawrence says, and Roethke quotes carefully as Lawrence talks about what that poetry is:

> the poetry of that which is at hand: the immediate present. In the immediate present there is no perfection, no consummation, nothing finished . . . it is obvious that the poetry of the instant present cannot have the same body or the same motion as the poetry of the before or after. It is never finished. There is no rhythm which returns upon itself. . . . There is no static perfection, none of that finality which we find so satisfying because we are so frightened. (60, 3)

One can hardly imagine a world view more dynamic, more at home with radical and continuous change than that of Lawrence. And the preface to *New Poems* is a beautiful and persuasive statement of the dynamism of life, "the ever-present [which] knows no finality, no finished crystallization . . . emerging and flowing off, and never in any sense at rest, static, finished." [1] It is also a list of the requirements for a poetry of the instant present:

> There must be mutation, swifter than iridescence, haste, not rest, come-and-go, not fixity, inconclusiveness, immediacy, the quality of life itself, without denouement or close. There must be the rapid momentaneous association of things which meet and pass on the forever incalculable journey of creation: everything left in its own rapid, fluid relationship with the rest of things. [2]

In the rough notes for his long graduate paper on Lawrence, Roethke says, "Mr. Lawrence is a literary barbarian, a savage," but we have already seen that Roethke respected the energy and force of the savage. If there was a part of Roethke that wanted to play the swell, affecting a fur coat so that "those Harvards" wouldn't have it over him, there was also Roethke the white Indian, the "most elemental thing in the room." The craftsman in Roethke was quite aware of the unfinished quality of Lawrence's poems, but something greater in him responded to Lawrence's strengths and stored them for future reference:

> Like all great artists, he wrote because he had to, he tore his poems out of his consciousness. But Lawrence's genius required a form that permitted plenty of freedom and movement. . . . What is important in Lawrence? The answer is this: the moment is important, perhaps as a revelation of life. . . . (60, 9)

Questions of influence are always tricky. I do not know whether Roethke learned something about dynamism and its literary possibilities from D. H. Lawrence or whether Roethke chose to work

I've always thought it one of the best I've ever done, but
few people seem to understand. What I'm trying to say is
that light—so various and strange in its nature—is, after all,
the supreme gift of God—(Imagine my being religious!).
(*Letters* 11)

Roethke may have liked the poem because it is more interesting
metrically than are most of his apprentice pieces. The increase in
anapests, the movement toward prose rhythms, the longer line
(both in terms of accents and syllables) are all ways of counteract-
ing that "effect of dryness" that he once acknowledged to be one
of the "defects of my present technique" (*Letters* 5).

Light, as Roethke presents it, is a force which activates the
landscape that it illuminates: "Its pure effulgence may unbind the
form / Of a blossoming tree; it may quicken fallow mould." God's
"supreme gift" is not only "various and strange"; it is enormously
dynamic, is, as it was for Vaughan himself, "another kind of
motion."

> This light is various and strange; its luminous hue
> May transmute the bleakest dust to silver snow;
> Its radiance may be caught within a pool, a bead of dew;
> It may contract to the sheerest point; it may arch to a bow.

That protean quality of light, its ability to expand or contract, to
be a sliver of reflection or an immense rainbow, may illuminate
more than the landscape it alters. It also, as God's gift, casts light
on the nature of the giver, suggests that God Himself may be "various and strange." The ever-changing light "will never cease," its
constancy lying essentially in constant change. By following light
through its continuous transmutations one may, paradoxically, be
led "to eventual peace."

"Someday I'll Step" reverts to Roethke's four-beat couplets and
perfect rhymes, though there is more enjambment than in most of
the poems of the 1930s. The piece is clearly a celebration of motion, a longing for the day when the poet will "step with arrowed
grace / Into a brighter realm of space." Roethke makes, I believe

for the first time, an equation between motion in a poem and physical motion:

> With grave felicity of motion
> I'll tread an incidental ocean
>
> Lightly; wander minutely where
> Confederate clouds divide in air;
>
> Place accurate feet upon the brink
> Of nothingness; obliquely sink
>
> In crystal wind; more pure than flight
> Of curving bird, I'll walk the night.
>
> Death shall not drift my limbs apart
> When ancient silence storms my heart:
>
> Before my patterned dance is done,
> I'll pace on shadows to the sun. . . .

Surely the "accurate feet" and the "patterned dance" are puns which warn us that the poem is essentially about poetry, not space travel. "The patterned dance" is a kind of ritual for warding off the twin evils of death and ancient silence; it is as if the "felicity of motion" that is poetry has the power to serve as an immortal substitute for the felicitous motion of the body. At this stage Roethke thinks of the motion of successful poetry as light, minute, accurate, pure, patterned, and delicate. Later he will be less delicate, more intense and violent.

The rest of the *American Poetry Journal* sequence of poems is less interesting, and it would be repetitious to go through the poems individually. In "Prepare Thyself for Change" and "Now We the Two," Roethke implies that death, like life, is motion. The first of the two has the soul escaping from the "Corrupting machine of lust . . . In unbewildered flight," and the second, an elegy to a dead lover, has the girl escaping from the "vice-like . . . grip of lips" into continuous motion, a hiding in "caves of mind," a wandering in dreams. In each poem it is as if one moves beyond mortal motion, that gradual entropic slowing, into a ceaseless and never-slowing motion. "Exhortation" demands that the poet be freed from "Infertile quietude" and "The barrenness of pause," which have trapped him in "sodden ease." He longs for the "sudden miracle," which presumably will lead him back to the fertility which he associates with motion. In one way or another, the subject matter of seven of the eight poems touches upon change, motion, and energy, though few of them handle those qualities in very effective ways. Roethke is still talking about experience, not creating it.

There are two other peoms, never collected, from Roethke's apprenticeship that seem to me worthy of attention. "In the Time of Change," published in *The Atlantic* in 1937, begins with the poet's implied desire for "some imperishable bliss," as Wallace Stevens puts it in "Sunday Morning."

> All things must change: the vision pass,
> The shadow lengthen on the grass,
> The ship go down behind the sun,
> The passion of the heart be done.
> The flower droops: we cannot stay
> The lovely miracle of May.[7]

But that rather conventional plaint and equally conventional apology for the limitations of the poetic power to preserve is followed by a stanza in praise of the holiness of "the time of change." .

> But in the time of change, a rare
> Illumination fills the air.
> There is a shift, a holy pause
> Between what is and what once was.
> The senses quicken with delight;
> The scene grows pure upon the sight.
> Our fixity is lost; the eyes
> Look out with passionless surprise,
> And in that instant we may see
> The shape of an eternity.

History, as Roethke presents it here, is experienced as a series of rather jerky shifts from state to state, an experience something like watching a series of slides being projected on a screen. Instead of conceiving of change as a smooth flowing in which each instant present contains all past and present instants, "In the Time of Change" concentrates on an imagined "pause," a space between *is* and *was* in which the emptiness somehow contains "The shape of an eternity." Such a conception is, I suppose, one way to reconcile one's sense of change and motion with one's desire for permanence, for the purity of eternity is found in the hypothetical interstices between moment and moment. Confusingly, perhaps confusedly, change *is* pause in this poem; and the eternity which one glimpses in the instant of change has a shape, whereas physical things—the shadow on the grass, the drooping flower—are so protean as to be considered shapeless. The poem is not clear, but it is one of Roethke's early attempts to grapple with pure process, to give to energy itself, if not a local habitation, at least a shape.

The following year *Poetry* published seven more of Roethke's poems. By 1938 he had polished his techniques a good deal, and of the seven poems, four were to be included in *Open House*. One of those not included is called "The Pause," and it is interesting because it is another attempt to present—this time more dramatically—that "holy pause / Between what is and what once was." The central metaphor of the poem—one which Roethke will use again—is that of the journey:

> I have walked past my widest range,
> But still the landscape does not change.
>
> The branch that scrapes across my face
> I once saw from a distant place,
>
> But never closer than a mile.
> I lean against the bark a while. . . .[8]

The exploration promises to be endless, an infinite journey motivated by a desire for change that never seems to come. Yet, there is some hope that the country beyond is untravelled, that it, at least, has not yet been tamed by any human presence:

The last worn wheel-ruts disappear.
Rain-beaten rocks lie sharp and clear.

.   .   .   .

Two wind-blown hemlocks make a door
To country I shall soon explore.

For a poet who is to dream of journeys repeatedly, it is a good start. As a symbol of spiritual and poetic growth—perhaps, for Roethke, the same thing—his exploration indicates an urge to fare forward, to widen forever one's "widest range." Strangely enough, however, it is the pause which implies the need to go on. During Roethke's apprenticeship motion is most keenly felt through its absence. He is better at creating the feeling of potential energy than he is at presenting kinetic energy, the motion that is life.

Open House

The title of Roethke's first volume buzzes with various promises, most of them misleading. An open house is, one imagines, an invitation to all readers, and surely Roethke did wish for the widest possible reading audience. But the title (and the title poem) also suggests an openness, that now at last the raw, brutal, naked truth will be told. We have only to compare *Open House* with, say, *The Lost Son* to realize how truly cautious a volume, how tightly closed a house, that first book is. An open house suggests informality, a kind of unstructured, free-floating gathering in which guests come and go pretty much as they please. But Roethke's *Open House* is so traditional in its strategies and so formal in its techniques that his party takes on an ambience of butlers and engraved invitations and dinners served promptly at eight. Finally, an open house is highly dynamic; it is marked by a continuous changing of guests, a coming and going which alters the nature of the affair with each arrival and departure. But the poems seldom convey that sort of dynamism, nor do they often generate the energy that the change and motion of a truly open house might deliver.

The poetry of *Open House* differs little, if any, in kind from the uncollected poetry of the 1930s. Karl Malkoff tries to argue that Roethke excluded "the more obviously derivative poems" from his first volume, but he is not very convincing. He suggests, for example, that "The Pause" is too obviously derived from Auden because the poem's "dominant imagery" includes "Auden's landscape equivalents of the human mind,"[1] but such equivalents are, as Malkoff himself later points out, the stuff of which many of the poems of *Open House* are woven. Moreover, if Roethke leaves out "In the Time of Change" because it is derived from other poets and "there is no room for second-hand emotion," [2] why does he include "No Bird," a poem which Jenijoy LaBelle has convincingly demonstrated to be an imitation of Emily Dickinson? [3] The answer is that the process of selection is not a matter of whether or not a poem is derivative, for by that standard Roethke would have had to exclude most of *Open House*. As he says quite plainly, "Imitation, conscious imitation, is one of the great methods, perhaps *the* method of learning to write" (SP 69). And *Open House* is a collection of learner's pieces, as Roethke eventually realizes better than anyone else. I believe that the principle of selection is much simpler. Roethke just takes the best he has, using his own critical judgment and that of Stanley Kunitz and a few other friends whose experience he respects. If *best* need be defined, I would suggest that even in his first volume Roethke equates his best work with his most intense, not with his least derivative.

I think Malkoff also errs in his extensive concentration, however ingenious, on the structure of *Open House*. He begins by quoting John Holmes, Roethke's colleague at Lafayette, on the "wholeness" of the book. According to Holmes,

> Mr. Roethke has built it with infinite patience in five sections. The first is personal pronoun; the second the out-of-doors; the third is the premonition of darker things—death among them; the fourth is the purest of metaphysical wit, something very rare in our time; and the fifth contains still another side of the poet's nature, the human awareness of which he has become capable in his recent development.[4]

"This," Malkoff says, "is good as far as it goes." [5] But it has already gone too far. The first section is no more "personal pronoun" than the others, if by that one means that the poetry of the section is written in the first person. And the fifth section seems no more—nor less—humanly aware than the other four sections. The concept is so vague as to be meaningless. Malkoff does no harm, I suppose, in trying to demonstrate a unity beyond Holmes's, an organization based on Roethke's attempts to define the self. However, it ought to be remembered that almost any volume of lyric poetry is likely to be in some sense "an epic of the I's," and occasionally Malkoff allows his thesis to force him into readings which Roethke's text does not justify. There is no reason, for example, to assume that satiric poems like "Academic" or "Poetaster" are Roethke's views of himself, and it seems rather heavy-handed to read "For an Amorous Lady" as a way of coming to grips with the question "What Is Man?" The sections do maintain a kind of loose unity within themselves, but it is a unity of tone as much as anything else. The second, third, and fourth sections respectively are, as Holmes suggests, poems dealing with nature, the darkest poems of *Open House,* and the lightest. The first and fifth sections seem to me to resist any sort of rigid categorizing, though I think the last section of the book is somewhat darker, more ominous in its implications, than is the first section.

The structure of *Open House* is not, as Malkoff would have it, "more complicated" and "subtler" than the structures of Roethke's later books. It is, rather, a loose arrangement of poems which had been composed to stand as independent works, an arrangement tacked together for the most part by the limitations of Roethke's early poetic techniques and by the shape of his personality. When Roethke later begins to think—and write—in organic sequences of poems rather than in units of one poem at a time, it is a sign that his apprenticeship is over and it marks one of his significant technical advances toward an adequate presentation of the dynamism of life. At any rate, the way Roethke builds his *Open House* is not so much complex and subtle as it is artificial and tenuous.

Although *Open House* is often, as Roethke himself describes it in one of the notebooks, "over-neat, mere Jacobean doo-dads," it seems to me—given the advantage of hindsight—that Roethke's first volume does foreshadow in some faint ways the terrific energy of the later poems (28, 34). Most obviously he tries to compress the great emotions—rage, anguish, love—into the tightest forms imaginable. By forcing enormous psychic energies into tiny containers, Roethke sometimes manages to give impressions of real force and power. At his best, he achieves an effect something like that rigidly controlled hysteria that one often feels in Emily Dickinson. The obtrusiveness of the mechanics—one is almost always aware of the orderly pattern of rhyme and meter— and the sense of compression caused by short lines and small forms are played off against the energy of rage or terror or love in such a way, Roethke hopes, as to make those emotions "feel" more emphatic as we experience the poem.

This technique is the common property of most of the poetry of *Open House* and is, for that matter, common to the formal lyric as it is presented by most skillful poets. However, in such poems as "Open House" and "Silence," Roethke seems to achieve an effect beyond the usual tension that exists between form and passion. Both poems use language to assert that language is incapable of building "a complement to rage," an adequate symbol of the nameless "What" that "shakes [the poet's] skull to disrepair" (CP 22). In other words, the poem before us on the page conveys the turmoil of Roethke's inner world by saying, as if through clenched teeth, "I can't talk about it." In "Open House" the *love* of the first stanza, the *anguish* of the second, and the *anger* and *Rage* of the third all reveal themselves in action, in the poet's every deed and gesture and—apparently—in the very look of him. It is as if the energy of the inner life translates itself clearly into pure act. The energy is too powerful for speech and all attempted statements about it turn false even as they are uttered:

> The anger will endure,
> The deed will speak the truth
> In language strict and pure.
> I stop the lying mouth:
> Rage warps my clearest cry
> To witless agony. (CP 3)

Like "I Sought a Measure," "Open House" tries to back into success by claiming failure. Something is achieved by talking around the emotional life, by articulating one's sense of the inarticulateness of rage, but it is a limited something, the trick of a man of talent with a gift for "talking about," not the trick of a genius who creates for us the agony and the rage. In "Silence," Roethke comes closer to presenting the inner rage:

> There is a noise within the brow
> That pulses undiminished now
> In accents measured by the blood.
> It breaks upon my solitude—
> A hammer on the crystal walls
> Of sense at rapid intervals.
> It is the unmelodic ring
> Before the breaking of a string. . . .   (CP 22)

The rage, grief, confusion—whatever—is expressed as rhythmic sound, a kind of pulsing vibration that threatens to shake to pieces the structure which confines it. The pulses, the accents at rapid intervals which build to a steady and ominous ring, become intolerable, become almost as terrifying as the "Funeral" Emily Dickinson feels in her brain. And yet the energy, expressed as vibration, cannot be transmitted or released:

> If I should ever seek relief
> From that monotony of grief,
> The tight nerves leading to the throat
> Would not release one riven note:
> What shakes my skull to disrepair
> Shall never touch another ear.   (CP 22)

To sing would be to release the forces within, but again Roethke insists upon the failure of the singing apparatus. The idea that emotional energy is like physical energy is carried out by the image of "touching" another ear, the denied possibility of finding a voice which might create vibrations in the air, vibrations which might, in turn, transmit to another those "accents measured by the blood" which grind so terribly in the poet's skull. In "Silence"

the confinement of such energy between one man's ears is parallel
to the confinement of powerful—if unspeakable—feelings within
the rhymed couplets of the poem itself.

For the most part, however, the celebration of motion is, in
Open House, a matter of making direct statements or a matter of
the manipulation of images. In "The Signals" nameless "objects"
flash, wheel, dart, flicker, and slip past before the poet can put
his "glance upon them tight" (CP 8). There is a sense of almost
pure motion, for the "objects" remain unidentified and unidenti-
fiable, felt along the pulse rather than caught by the eye or hand:

> Sometimes the blood is privileged to guess
> The things the eye or hand cannot possess. (CP 8)

The blood, itself in motion, perceives the rhythms of things and
their motion by its own answering leap and surge. "Genesis" is a
hymn to energy, to the "elemental force" which pervades the
cosmos and which is narrowly channeled, "locked in narrow
bone." And again, power and force are felt along the blood stream.

> This wisdom floods the mind,
> Invades quiescent blood;
> A seed that swells the rind
> To burst the fruit of good. (CP 18)

The force that floods, swells, and finally bursts—the concept of a
terrible energy straining to be free—is, I think, the real strength
of *Open House*. It is that sense of "elemental force" locked in the
narrow bones of Roethke's tiny forms which warns us of the
poetry he is later to write.

One of the finest of Roethke's early poems celebrating motion
is "Night Journey," the final poem in *Open House*. The poet is on
a train riding west, a direction which may be symbolic, though I
think little is added to the poem by having it so.

> Now as the train bears west,
> Its rhythm rocks the earth,
> And from my Pullman berth

I stare into the night
While others take their rest.　(CP 34)

The rocking of the train, the rhythm it imposes upon the earth
itself, is an expression of pure speed and power. Significantly,
while others are at rest, the poet remains awake to share in that
rhythm and to try to re-create it in his poem. The landscape is
experienced as a series of rapid images, one to each three-beat line,
and impressions of speed are heightened by the clever use of the
adjective turned noun in a phrase like "A suddenness of trees."
Although critics have enjoyed ferreting out the sexual symbolism
of Roethke's later poems, to my knowledge none has yet noted
the feminine imagery associated with the earth which must bear
the rocking motion of the train. Bridges, for example, are seen as
"iron lace," and the poet finds himself plunging into "A lap of
mountain mist." Gradually he comes to identify with the train,
takes on its straining rhythm:

Full on my neck I feel
The straining at a curve;
My muscles move with steel,
I wake in every nerve.　(CP 34)

The appeal to the kinesthetic sense is highly successful here, and
the body of the poet and the body of the train are experienced as
one body. To signify this shift, Roethke moves to the first person
plural, so that now it is "We" who "thunder through ravines / And
gullies washed with light," and "We" who "rush into a rain / That
rattles double glass" (CP 34). The poem concludes with the
rush and rattle and shake and jerk and shove of verbs that thrust
the lines onward much as the pistons drive the train onward. The
sexual motif is, I suppose, consummated by the concluding rhyme
of "shove"/"love," and the motion that is life is made one with
the motion that creates life. The rhythms of journeying are both
celebrated and felt, and the poem becomes more than an experience that is "talked about." The night journey is lived, is absorbed into blood, muscles, and nerves.

Like most of us, Roethke is sometimes afraid of the dizzying pace of life in the twentieth century. "Highway: Michigan" evokes that pace, but this time Roethke is outside of the sweep and movement, is, quite literally, a bystander as the auto workers race from the factories to their homes at the end of the day.

> Acceleration is their need:
> A mania keeps them on the move
> Until the toughest nerves are frayed.
> They are the prisoners of speed
> Who flee in what their hands have made. (CP 33)

There is, as in other poems of *Open House*, a sense of a speed which increases and increases until disaster is inevitable. The body, the machine, cannot withstand the terrible energy within. Roethke may not have intended it, but the workers with their mania for motion and who "flee in what their hands have made" are, in some ways, like the poet. For the poet, too, energy, speed, and acceleration are the great need; a poem must move, as Roethke knew, and the formal arrangement of words which is the poet's "machine" is never quite up to the pace. The poet is also a kind of prisoner of speed, one who "gets away" in what his hands have made, though the "getting away" and the prison are one and the same. "Highway: Michigan" ends in violence, and the motion of life is "escaped" through death.

> The pavement smokes when two cars meet
> And steel rips through conflicting steel.
> We shiver at the siren's blast.
> One driver, pinned beneath the seat,
> Escapes from the machine at last. (CP 33)

It is change and energy which most fascinate Roethke in his early poems of "the out-of-doors," as John Holmes calls them. "The Light Comes Brighter," "Slow Season," and "The Coming of the Cold" are all pieces which view nature in process, in "the time of change." "The Light Comes Brighter" and "Slow Season" seem to be companion pieces, the first dealing with that "season" between winter and spring and the second with the interval, the pause, between late autumn and winter. In each poem, change is first noticed as a change in light, itself a kind of motion. "The Light Comes Brighter" is a poem in which the pace of things and their motion quickens, a celebration of the time in which ice shifts and thaws, rivers overflow, water escapes, roots stir, and in which one anticipates the unfurling of leaves and the swelling of fruit. "Slow Season" reverses the process, and all things hang, thicken, and gather toward sleep. In each poem the rhythm of the seasons is absorbed by the observer. In "The Light Comes Brighter," Roethke imagines the energetic stirring of nature to set up vibrations in his "inner world."

> And soon a branch, part of a hidden scene,
> The leafy mind, that long was tightly furled,
> Will turn its private substance into green,
> And young shoots spread upon our inner world.   (CP 11)

In "Slow Season" the rhythm of the dying year is "known" along the pulse, for "The blood slows trance-like in the altered vein; / Our vernal wisdom moves through ripe to sere" (CP 12). "The Coming of the Cold" is, I think, a much less successful poem, partly because it evokes the rhythms and moods of the "slow season" without any sense that those rhythms set up vibrations in the inner world, partly because the language is about as phony as any Roethke ever uses. Nonetheless, it is significant that the seasons which Roethke chooses as subjects are those seasons in which change makes itself felt in the rhythms and motions of both our outer and inner worlds.

Another way of demonstrating the energy of the "out-of-doors" is to capture the violence of a storm in a poem. This Roethke tries to do twice in *Open House*. In "Interlude" the rage of the storm builds and builds but, like the inner rage of "Silence," never finds release. The air itself turns violent, uncontrollable:

> The element of air was out of hand.
> The rush of wind ripped off the tender leaves

And flung them in confusion on the land.
We waited for the first rain in the eaves.   (CP 6)

But it is not chaos which terrifies. Finally it is the absence of
motion, the stasis of the interlude which creates a fear felt—once
again—in the rhythms of the poet's blood stream:

> The rain stayed in its cloud; full dark came near;
> The wind lay motionless in the long grass.
> The veins within our hands betrayed our fear.
> What we had hoped for had not come to pass.   (CP 6)

The speed and energy of the elements build and build to a dizzying
"What," but the "What" remains unexperienced and unnamed.
There is no release from the tension that has been established,
and the blood races to the tempo of fear. In "Mid-Country Blow"
the storm rages all day and all night, "Until I could think there
were waves rolling high as my bedroom floor" (CP 12). The entire first stanza creates a frenzy of roaring, rolling, sweeping, and
lashing—a frenzy which creates belief, which continues until it
becomes possible "to think" of the violence of a storm at sea.
The second stanza shows the contrast of the dawn of the second
day, a morning "I would not have believed."

> The oak stood with each leaf stiff as a bell.
> When I looked at the altered scene, my eye was undeceived,
> But my ear still kept the sound of the sea like a shell.   (CP 12)

The poem is, in part, a poem about what can be believed, what
can be thought. What the eye sees and what the ear hears now
belong to separate scenes, to different "realities." The ear has re-
tained the violence, the energy of that metaphorical sea which
had been believed in—or nearly believed in—during the blow;
but the eye sees the oak and the "stiffness" of the altered scene
and, since seeing is believing, the "I" is undeceived. The poet and
the reader, of course, have it both ways at once. The remembered
storm and the present calm, the violence and the stasis, are both

to be "kept" as partial truths about our planet and its wide weather.

When Roethke writes about what Malkoff terms "the self . . . in its social context," [6] he almost always does so after the fashion of classical comedy. That is, he sets the energy of the life force against the rigid codes of the social order and lets nature take its course. The "Ballad of the Clairvoyant Widow" sets up the order of the quotidian in the widow's first vision:

> "I see ten million windows, I see ten thousand streets,
> I see the traffic doing miraculous feats.
>
> The lawyers all are cunning, the business men are fat,
> Their wives go out on Sunday beneath the latest hat.
>
> The kids play cops and robbers, the kids play mumbley-peg,
> Some learn the art of thieving, and some grow up to beg. . . .
>
> I see a banker's mansion with twenty wood-grate fires,
> Alone, his wife is grieving for what her heart desires." (CP 27)

The world that the widow sees is very much like the world of Saginaw that Roethke portrayed with scorn in his undergraduate papers. The lawyers and business men have no individuality; religious experience is reduced to fashionable experience; and there is no passion anywhere. But when asked if she sees "any sign or semblance of that thing called 'Hope,'" the widow lady has an answer:

> "I see the river harbor, alive with men and ships,
> A surgeon guides a scalpel with thumb and finger-tips.
>
> I see grandpa surviving a series of seven strokes,
> The unemployed are telling stale unemployment jokes.
>
> The gulls ride on the water, the gulls have come and gone,
> The men on rail and roadway keep moving on and on.
>
> The salmon climb the rivers, the rivers nudge the sea,
> The green comes up forever in the fields of our country."
> (CP 28)

Hope is motion. Grandpa goes on living, pointlessly, except that life is good in itself. Humor survives, even among the unemployed, and, like grandpa's survival, it is a sign of enduring human courage, of dogged willingness to keep going. The men, the salmon, the rivers, the green stuff of life all go on forever and in their incessant coming and going there is joy. The real hero of the poem is the earth itself with its eternal cycles, those turnings darkly praised by Ecclesiastes. In a letter to Earl Robinson, a composer who apparently wished to set "Ballad of the Clairvoyant Widow" to music, Roethke wrote that "by the last couplet I mean to imply that there is a deep and abiding energy in all living things which can aid our human strength and contribute to our destiny. I don't think this is just mystical bunk; even the anthropologists seem to believe this" (*Letters* 97).

In "Idyll" and "Sale" and "The Reminder" one is made to feel the inadequacies of the barriers that men raise to protect themselves against the darker implications of that deep and abiding energy. "Idyll" sets up the complacency of suburban life by stressing that the lawns have been "well-groomed" and "fresh-cut" as a temporary stay against the green that comes up forever in the form of dandelion and crabgrass. The suburbanites sit "in the porch swing, content and half asleep" (CP 33). But the last stanza of the poem reminds us of the darkness surrounding the peaceful lawns:

> The world recedes in the black revolving shadow;
> A far-off train blows its echoing whistle once;
> We go to our beds in a house at the edge of a meadow,
> Unmindful of terror and headlines, of speeches and guns.
> (CP 33)

Instead of the white at the edges of the poem, we have blackness. Outside of the order of lawns, the order of rhymes and five-beat lines, chaos and old night have their reign. And to be "Unmindful" is not the same as to be safe. "Sale" offers material possessions as an ineffectual wall between oneself and the terrifying

energies of time and process. The list of articles for sale, together
with the sense of the ordered lives which had helped maintain
those articles, is set off against change and decay:

> The dining room carpet dyed brighter than blood,
> The table where everyone ate as he should,
> The sideboard beside which a tall footman stood
> —And a fume of decay that clings fast to the wood.   (CP 32)

The ordered structure, the house with rooms that the children
had never been in, stands against the running of the blood,
"tainted" and "too thin." And the blood, emblem of time and its
turning, has the final word. "The Reminder" is a poem of remembrance, remembrance occasioned by the orderly ticking of a
cheap clock in a disordered room. The remembered person, perhaps a former lover, more likely Roethke's mother, is associated
with all tidy arrangements, with "the crossing-tender's geranium
border" and with "The bronze wheat arranged in strict and formal
order" (CP 29). For the absent woman, if it is a woman, precision
"was ultimate law."

> The handkerchief tucked in the left hand pocket
> Of a man-tailored blouse; the list of shopping done;
> You wound the watch in an old-fashioned locket
> And pulled the green shade against morning sun.   (CP 29)

All of the ordered gestures, the tucking and listing and winding,
the pulling of the shade against the sun and the cosmic energy
it represents, fail to ward off chaos:

> Now in the misery of bed-sitting room confusion,
> With no hint of your presence in a jungle of masculine toys,
> In the dirt and disorder I cherish one scrap of illusion:
> A cheap clock ticking in ghostly cicada voice.   (CP 29)

The ordered time measured by clocks is "illusion," a fictive pattern of precise measurement imposed upon the sprawl of experience, a rhythm that has nothing to do with the ever-changing
rhythms by which we live our lives.

Death is, of course, the ultimate stillness, the final order, and Roethke contrasts it with the movement of life in "No Bird" and in "Death Piece." "No Bird" becomes, it seems to me, a better poem if it is written in memory of, as well as in the manner of, Emily Dickinson.[7] Not only are such phrases as "one who knew / The secret heart of sound" and "The ear so delicate and true" quickened by application to a specific poet, but there is also a giving and taking of cadence and manner, a use of tradition which keeps the voice of the poet alive and which subtly suggests the triumph of the creative life while seeming to acknowledge the victory of death. Less important, perhaps, is the fact that life goes on, that breezes swing and grasses stir, while the dead woman lies motionless in a sleep that will not be broken. "Death Piece" works that contrast harder, setting the speed of the living mind off against the rock-like immobility of the empty skull.

> Invention sleeps within a skull
> No longer quick with light.
> The hive that hummed in every cell
> Is now sealed honey-tight. (CP 4)

The image of swarming bees representing the activity of the mind suggests enormous vitality. Roethke shifts the image in the next stanza, likening the curve of the skull to the curving prow of a ship, as if the curve and sweep of the forehead all but demanded motion. The prow is, after death, "moored to rock," and the thrust of time, the explosive minutes, "burst upon a brow / Insentient to shock" (CP 4).

However, promising as it may seem in retrospect, the incipient dynamism of *Open House* cannot conceal that "chilly fastidiousness" and "austerity of vision" which, as David Wagoner has remarked, are the curse of Theodore Roethke's apprentice work.[8] Roethke needs to see that, while he is himself his proper subject, it is a subject which must be treated dynamically; his "self" is not so much to be his material as are the energetic transformations of that self. And for such a subject he will need new forms, new structures. In "An American Poet Introduces Himself," a piece

written in 1953 to be broadcast over the BBC in late July, Roethke
says, "In those first poems I had begun, like the child, with small
things and had tried to make plain words do the trick" (SP 10).
An earlier version of that sentence, one found in the notebooks,
is, I think, more honest: "I began, like the child, with some
things, the little, narrow forms. I thought in these I might learn
to write verse and perhaps poetry would happen" (37 #110). I
believe that Roethke often did, in more ways than one, "begin"
with the forms of his poems. Though he was fond of telling his
classes that a form was a sieve for catching certain kinds of material and not a mold into which material might be poured
(*Letters* 106), there is some evidence that, when the writing
got tough, Roethke the apprentice was not above pulling out a
stanzaic "mold" and filling in the blanks. The early notebooks
contain several such "molds," some of them with lines scratched
in here and there as if the pouring had begun and stopped. For
example, one finds this sort of pattern in one of the notebooks of
the mid-thirties:

4 a
4 a
3 b
4 c
3 c
4 a
4 d
3 e
4 f
4 f   (32 #11)

Even if such diagramming is the skeleton of someone else's poem,
which I doubt, it nonetheless suggests the attitude that form
exists prior to and outside of the experience that it "contains."
It is an attitude very different from that found later in the teaching notes: "A poem becomes independent of you. The experience
dictates the form it insists on: an exasperating answer" (65, 5).
At any rate, if the human experience is highly dynamic, then one
must find the technique, discover the "form" which that experi-

ence "dictates" and "insists upon." It is the evolution of forms as protean as the experiences out of which they grow that constitutes Roethke's continuing triumph during the seven years between *Open House* and *The Lost Son*.

The Notebooks:
1938-1948

To my mind, the transformation of Theodore Roethke from a poet of "lyric resourcefulness, technical proficiency, and ordered sensibility" to a poet of "indomitable creativeness and audacity . . . difficult, heroic, moving and profoundly disquieting" [1] is one of the most remarkable in American literary history. Only Walt Whitman's growth from a maker of newspaper verse to the *Leaves of Grass* poet would seem comparable, either in magnitude of transformation or in poetic significance. With all of the poetic returns in, the critic may speak easily of Roethke's growth as if it had all been inevitable enough:

> Current criticism has been eager to seize upon the notion of a sudden change, but there is no need to depend upon so mysterious an explanation. What seems to be a drastic revision of method is actually a perfectly logical, and rather gradual, shifting of emphasis. . . .[2]

It is true that the change was hardly sudden. It had been paid for during the years of apprenticeship, those years of hard-won skills and self-loathing, of tiny poems and enormous rages. But such growth could hardly have seemed inevitable to the man struggling to attain it, nor does it seem "perfectly logical," save through those distortions by which hindsight always makes the wonderful occurrence seem to have been in the works all along. The slow growth which Roethke endured seems to me both wonderful and mysterious, and I am willing to leave it so, to admit that the real secrets of creative energy are never revealed. However, unlike Walt Whitman between, say, 1845 and 1855, Roethke has left us the notebooks, half diary and half work sheets, which may offer some hints about the changes in the man and his working methods between *Open House* and *The Lost Son*. There are in the Roethke Collection approximately ninety-five notebooks written between 1938 and 1948, and they demonstrate some significant shifts both in methods of working and in the concerns and obsessions which made up the furniture of the poet's mind.

As Allan Seager's biography makes clear, the gestation period of *The Lost Son* was a time of enormous personal turmoil for Roethke. He had had his first mental breakdown in 1936, and he had lost a job at Michigan State because of it. He spent seven years at Pennsylvania State College and, out of a kind of academic snobbery and other, more legitimate grievances, was never very happy there. In 1942 he had an almost fatal attack of pneumonia, a close call which, the notebooks indicate, both terrified and stimulated him. In 1943 he began teaching at Bennington, a curious experience which might be best described by remarking that although his students called him "the best teacher we ever had,"[3] and although he had earned a Guggenheim Fellowship while teaching there, he was about to be fired by 1946. The same energies and enthusiasms which drove him as poet and teacher seem to have troubled him at what Arnold Stein calls "a more ordinary level of living."[4] In 1946 Roethke suffered a second mental attack, this one perhaps more terrifying than the first because he was given electric shock treatments—"they'll turn my brain to jelly," Seager quotes him as saying.[5] It was a decade of triumphs and terrors; of having his teaching praised effusively and fearing that he would have no job, of quickening mental powers and the worry that his brain might be turned to jelly. It was the period in which, Seager tells us, Roethke used to dress and undress four or five times a day, a "ritual of starting clean like a baby, casting one's skin like a snake and then donning the skin again. It was not exhibitionism. No one saw. It was all a kind of magic."[6]

David Wagoner, who surely knows the notebooks as well as anyone, remarks in his introduction to *Straw for the Fire* that "If the notebooks show nothing else, their extensiveness and their intensity show the most wholehearted, energetic, even uncanny devotion to poetry I have ever known of, an apparently almost total commitment of time and attention" (SF 14). But I have also heard him remark that perhaps the strongest impression that one brings away from the notebooks is that of how desperately Roethke sought to find God. That search is one of the marked differences between the notebooks of the forties and those of the thirties. It is a search which begins with intimations of Roethke's desire to *be* more, to go beyond the man he has been. A notebook entry for July 1942 puts it about as baldly as one could wish: "I want to live on a higher, a nobler level" (33 #28). In the same notebook, he writes,

> I only know that I am moving toward, or I should be moving toward a richer experience, the best I have done should be but hints. I believe in faith: and that faith I shall not define. I believe in the dignity of man, all men.

And then he adds, "Oh, if it were true that some great impulse for good were driving one's life" (33 #28). Over and over, Roethke refers to the struggle to "go beyond," to be more than he has been. "It's the poet's business," he writes, "to be more, not less, than a man" (36 #77). And the necessary capital in that business seems to have been faith, at first simply a faith in faith itself. "I don't think there is a God," he says at one point, "but to try to believe one is one of the noblest human efforts" (34 #53). At another place, he writes, "For belief is noble. We say I believe and we do" (34 #33). The effort to believe that "some great impulse for good" might be the energy which drove his life shows in Roethke's comments after his bout with pneumonia. Even illness, he believed, or tried to believe, was a source of power:

> I suppose it's a dangerous feeling of power that you get after a successful duel with death. . . . For some reason

this illness seems to have shaken loose powers. I am alive
with ideas, some bad no doubt, but there is more vehemence,
more energy, more contempt, more love. (34 #52)

One of the quotations which he copied into his notebooks, in this
case without naming the author, combines the search for God
with his own drive to move forward as a man and artist: " 'For he
who mounts and enters and goes above and beyond himself, he
truly mounts to God' " (36 #93).

After his first mental breakdown, Roethke had told Peter De
Vries that he had had "a mystical experience with a tree and he
learned there the 'secret of Nijinsky.' " [7] And later he told Allan
Seager that "For no reason I started to feel very good. Suddenly
I knew how to enter into the life of everything around me. I
knew how it felt to be a tree, a blade of grass, even a rabbit.
. . ." [8] Still later he told his wife that his trouble had been self-
induced " 'to reach a new level of reality.' " [9] Whatever happened
to Roethke, and he had so many versions of the episode that it is
impossible to know, the notebooks do reveal an incessant effort to
break out of the self, an effort to know more and to love more,
the twin goals of the mystics, for whom love and knowledge
finally merge into a perfect whole. At times the notebooks suggest
that, like Nijinsky, Roethke felt that God had, in fact, entered his
mind or his body. "Not I," he quotes, "but God in me," or "As
soon as you are ready, God will pour Himself into you" (36 #93).
More often God was felt as a terrible absence:

> Wait. Watch. Listen. Meditate. He'll come. When? No,
> I know He won't come. He doesn't care about me any more.
> No, I mean Him, the Big He, that great big three-cornered
> Papa. (SF 168)

The notebooks also confirm what many astute critics have already surmised. Roethke read widely in and around the literature
of mysticism; for example, he knew *Love in the Western World*
thoroughly by 1943, and he apparently read Evelyn Underhill's
Mysticism more than once. In a note tentatively dated in April of

1946, he reminds himself to "go back" to that book and follows his reminder with a brief outline of the mystical experience:

1 Awakening—to a sense of divine reality.
2 Purgation of self, when it realizes its own imperfections.
3 An enhanced return to a sense of the divine order, after the self has achieved detachment from the world. (36 #84)

Roethke was not much of a mystic if, indeed, he was one at all. Less than a year before his death, he wrote in one of his notebook entries,

> Have I experienced the Beatific Vision: Not that I know of. I have in certain states of consciousness experienced a shimmer of iridescence that lasted for a considerable time. This was not a blurring thing that faded away. (43 #208)

But mystic or none, Roethke was a considerable poet and a poet who believed that the search for God and the search for poems reflecting a greater intensity of life were closely related. He seems at times to have been troubled by the conflict which he thought might exist between the life of the pure seeker after God and the life of the creative (and competitive) artist. In 1948 he notes uncomfortably that "Creativeness requires that a man forget about his own moral progress and sacrifice his personality—If a man feels nothing but humility and a perpetual sense of sin, he can do no creative work" (37 #267). However, if I read his notebooks correctly, Roethke seems to have come to hope that creativeness might serve as a way of forgetting the self, that it might, if a man could detach himself sufficiently from its fruits, take the place of the more conventional mystic's asceticism. In saying this, perhaps I am only restating what Arnold Stein has put better: "What contemplation was to some philosophers, composition was to Roethke." [10] Roethke may have put it most accurately of all—"A rich mystic: that's what I want to be" (SF 169). You didn't get rich by writing poems, but you did gain prestige and some measure of power. It was the fruit of the action, at once barrier and goal.

"We live by fictions and myths," Roethke noted in 1944 or 1945. "They seem as necessary as food. If there is no God, we invent one etc." (35 #61). Roethke seems to have invented a God according to his need, a God especially for poets; and, having created God, the poet began to live by Him and found Him, at least on occasion, to be there. By 1952 Roethke's faith in faith had yielded the experience of which he speaks in "On Identity":

> Suddenly, in the early evening, the poem "The Dance" started, and finished itself in a very short time—say thirty minutes, maybe in the greater part of an hour, it was all done. I felt, I *knew*, I had hit it. I walked around, and I wept; and I knelt down—I always do after I've written what I know is a good piece. But at the same time I had, as God is my witness, the actual sense of a Presence—as if Yeats himself were *in* that room. . . . That house, I repeat, was charged with a psychic presence: the very walls seemed to shimmer. I wept for joy. At last I was somebody again. He, they—the poets dead—were with me. (SP 24)

That "extra," that "surplus" of energy which Roethke believed was the poem, has taken on the aspect of God, and the great dead stand by like saints, capable of creative intercession on behalf of the living. Roethke's is indeed a religion for poets, a faith in which poems finish themselves and in which it is appropriate to offer prayers of thanks for a good piece after it has been "given." I do not know how literally one should take all of this. Sometime between 1942 and 1944 Roethke wrote in one of the notebooks that "I'll find a way or fake it" (34 #43). Perhaps he began by faking a way and found it true; perhaps the mystical experiences of which he wrote were never more than metaphorically "true." It is no matter. The enormous growth in the power of the poetry is there as evidence of his continued fath. And there is, of course, no way of faking the poems. Finally, as Roethke says, "The poem that moves is engendered spiritually" (35 #59).

It was probably the obsession with reaching a new level of reality and with making a poetry which might represent that reality which led Roethke to begin to fill the notebooks with accounts of his dreams. Sometimes the descriptions are long and detailed, sometimes brief:

> Dream: Was going to box; left arm was hurt: Dr. said why not lead with right. I said you can't fool a pro. (23 #12)

Frequently Roethke's father appears in these dreams, sometimes in his own form, sometimes thinly disguised. In most cases, the father acts as Roethke's antagonist:

> The Dream: I was trying to get home (Saginaw) through streets I did not know; I got involved in a deserted garden which had high hotbeds and a kind of greenhouse for walking around there, along the boards, pulling aside great strings of dead growth like dried brown smilax. I was apprehended by the owner. I had a feeling of guilt, but he said "I know you didn't want to steal anything. Do you know how I could tell? By your tone when you answered." At this point a woman with closely cropped hair came up and threw herself on her side, but almost face down, in the wet ground. She was brown and naked. (36 #92)

I do not know what a psychiatrist might make of Roethke's guilt here, nor of his appeasing the greenhouse owner by the quality of his voice. I suspect that Roethke himself was not so much interested in what the dreams might "mean" as he was interested in plundering them for poetic material and in using them to study the motion of the subconscious mind. What is the rhythm of a dream? How does that rhythm differ from the rhythms of the waking mind? How does the dream manage to compress narrative so effectively, to present such protean characters, and to absorb us so totally in actions which are not, on the face of things, particularly arresting? So far as I can tell, Roethke never actually made a poem of any of the notebook dreams, but he did, I believe, adopt in his poetry, particularly in the poetry of *The Lost Son* and of *Praise to the End*, something of the dynamic symbolism, something of the heightened speed of narrative movement, that all dreams possess.

The notebooks from 1938 to 1948 reveal a growing interest in mythology, an interest related to the increasing fascination with dream material. Roethke begins to jot down summaries of myths, and he cites a definition of *myth* as "a story—a symbolical figure —as simple as it is striking—which sums up an infinite number of more or less analogous situations" (33 #31). During this period there are quotations from Jung in the notebooks, though they need not have come from reading Jung himself. As a member of the academic community, Roethke could hardly have avoided hearing about the collective unconscious, and indeed, at one point he complains that perhaps we now know *too* much about such things, that we are in danger of intellectualizing it all to death (36 #92). I also suspect that the Roethke who subscribed to the *Dial* when he was in the seventh grade is not likely to have missed reading or rereading T. S. Eliot's 1923 article on the mythic method as James Joyce had used it in *Ulysses*. Like his use of dream techniques, Roethke's study of mythology seems to have been part of his effort to transcend himself, to stand beyond the limitations of the rational mind.

Roethke's desire to "break through" to a more intense and nobler life shows itself not only in prose entries of the sort I have been quoting but also in the changed methods by which he went about writing poetry. The changes grow out of an attempt to suggest in his new poems that quality of "over-aliveness" which characterizes the mystic, the madman, the lover, the primitive, the child. As Allan Seager points out in his chapter called "Working Methods," the notebooks of this period are "looser" than those of the *Open House* days. It is not so much, however, that "he begins to write funny, even scatological doggerel occasionally," though Roethke does begin to do so. It is more that the rough material which appears as poetry is less censored, less pressured by the need to fit any particular poem which he is working on at the time or, indeed, by the need to fit any poem which he might ever conceivably wish to publish. I suspect that Seager is quite accurate, perhaps even generous, when he judges that "Of all the lines of poetry [Roethke] wrote, a rough guess would estimate that only about 3 percent were ever printed." [11] No amount of reading and rereading of notebooks can help us know exactly how Roethke came up with his thousands and thousands of lines:

> Who has my hands? I'm cold; I'm cold all over. Rub me in father and mother. I'll take the old scow riding. I'm a real toad in imaginary shapes. Who says the worm has no shadow?   (36 #70)

Nonetheless, I cannot resist speculating. My best guess is that at least part of the time Roethke begins by free associating words denoting the most primitive elements in the human experience: air, earth, fire, and water. These terms, of course, have their variants —wind, light, rain, dirt, dust, stones, rivers, waves, and so on. And in the primitive world that he weaves of these elemental nouns, Roethke, like God Himself, places his beloved minimals, the toads and slugs and birds and fish. The word, the right word, was one way to plunge into the intensity of one's childhood, into "the imagination of the race." As Roethke said in "Some Remarks on Rhythm," "we know that some words, like *hill, plow, mother, window, bird, fish,* are so drenched with human association, they sometimes can make even bad poems evocative" (SP 80). One way, then, of creating in language that state of "over-aliveness" characteristic of a dog or a saint was to allow the mind to leap about freely, beginning and remaining loosely with those words which are "shot through with appeals to the unconscious" (SP 80). As a result, the notebooks are often repetitious, often silly, and often chaotic. But when it works, when the line takes on the psychic energy of the speaker, his nervousness and tension and quality of motion, Roethke seizes upon it and draws a circle about it. He will worry it into a context at some other time.

In addition to these lines and phrases which are spread all over pages, seeming to add up to nothing if one does not recognize the published lines as they fall and imagine them in their eventual places, Roethke makes a few comments on his craft which may help to explain the reasons for some of the changes he was making in his poetry. For one thing, even by 1938 he was tired of the "well-made poem." In that year he wrote, "Modern poetry has been cursed with too many 'well-written' poems: the tiny emotion expanded ludicrously beyond its own shape and size" (23 #15). The antithesis of such poems, presumably, was described in the same notebook: "Elemental poems—when we are outside ourselves" (23 #15). To achieve both the rhythm and the effect of being "outside" of the self, the "right mind" in which we ordinarily live, Roethke turned to nonsense cadences, the tunes of rants, mad songs, and children's games. At one point in the notebooks he quotes William Pitt, who says, "Don't tell me of a man's being able to talk sense; every man can talk sense. Can he talk nonsense?" And he follows the Pitt quotation with a snatch of his own nonsense:

> Mips & ma to mooly moo
> The likes of him is biting who
> A cow's a care and who's a coo,
> What footie does is final.   (32 #12)

It was the rhythm, the pace of nonsense which fascinated him. In July of 1949 an entry reads "Nonsense cadences escape so fast. The wonderful snatch always just beyond" (37 #104). To be "beyond" or "outside" was the key, and getting there required more speed, a quicker rhythm than the staid, "sensible" consciousness was able to manage. Speed is almost always "wonderful" for Roethke. "The energy of the nursery rhyme!" he exclaims (35 #54). "How wonderful the short line is!" (36 #87).

No amount of excerpting can give a fair sense of Roethke's notebooks. One is always forcing an order, a pattern, upon an outpouring of words which becomes nearly as formless as the subconscious mind itself. The lines tumble out, vertically, horizontally, diagonally on the page. Things are crossed out, circled, written over. The handwriting changes, the inks change, sometimes two or three times on one page. It is impossible to tell, in many cases, what was written originally and what was added later.

Dating is haphazard. But gradually tendencies do emerge. The search for God becomes more and more important. The characteristic feeling that emerges on the page is this one:

> The feeling that one is on the edge of many things: that there are many worlds from which we are separated by only a film; that a flick of the wrist, a turn of the body another way will bring us to a new world. It is more than a perpetual expectation. Yet sometimes the sense of richness is haunting: It is richness and yet denial. In living a half a step, as it were, from what one should be. . . . (36 #86)

And the mystical and the mythic are ways of trying to penetrate those worlds, ways of flicking the wrist or turning the body another way. The life of the dream has the same haunting sense of richness and denial. A little quicker rhythm, a slight shift in the speed with which the eye sees or the hand grasps, and one might find himself in another world, a new level of experience. The nonsense rhythm, the speedy short line, the rapid jumps of free association were techniques by which one might storm the Kingdom of Heaven. Composition, like contemplation, could be a finding of the way. The notebooks show only directions, never the place itself. But perhaps, as Robert Penn Warren has Jack Burden say in *All the King's Men*, "Direction is all."

The *Greenhouse Sequence*

Critics have had difficulty in Roethke's greenhouse. Though almost everyone agrees that the first section of *The Lost Son* contains some of the finest poems that Roethke ever wrote, no one seems quite comfortable in talking about them. Louis L. Martz, for example, calls the sequence "one of the permanent achievements of modern poetry," and goes on to say, "its poems deserve to cling to future anthologies like Marvell's 'Garden' or Wordsworth's poem about the daffodils." [1] John Wain is equally enthusiastic: "It is a wonderful sequence: I would say that it marked a point of Roethke's emergence, from a gifted minor poet among gifted minor poets, into a poet of the first importance with something absolutely individual to communicate." [2] But despite such praise, critics have tended to hurry past the greenhouse poems on their way to the more difficult poems of the *Lost Son Sequence* or of the sequence which begins with "Where Knock Is Open Wide!" Even Kenneth Burke, after more than two decades still the most perceptive reader of Roethke's poems of this period, uses the *Greenhouse Sequence* as "the best way-in" to a highly detailed study of the more complex sequences. He, too, skims them, going into only "Big Wind" at any length, remarking that some of the poems seem "Clearly the imagistic figuring of a human situation," [3] but not telling us how this is made clear; remarking that Roethke has endowed "his brief lyrics with intensity of *action*," [4] but suggesting only one of the many ways in which this endowment has been made.

Perhaps the difficulty in dealing with the greenhouse poems has been that, in many ways, they are too simple. Critical apparatus is not designed for a primitive, descriptive poetry, a poetry with few tropes, no allusions, a clear vocabulary and syntax, and almost no abstractions. Such poetry does not require an explanation of its "meaning" as, say, the poetry of Wallace Stevens or T. S. Eliot often does. Instead, most critics have been content to admire the greenhouse sketches, noting only that the plant life described does seem analogous to human life, that the sequence does bear symbolic weight. And of course, some have fastened upon the possibilities of Freudian analysis in Roethke's glass house, though, as Karl Malkoff rightly notes, the implications of these poems "are hardly dependent upon extra-literary references." [5]

Let us get the "meaning" of the sequence out of the way first. Morse Peckham has implied that symbolism is a device growing naturally out of a complex, organic, and dynamic world view, for a symbol is itself complex, organic, and dynamic. [6] That is, the relationships among the concrete figures of a poem may be analogous to the relationships among a potentially infinite number of abstract ideas, and that as the relationships in the literary work shift and develop, so, too, do the ideas they may represent shift and develop. Roethke, by using as few abstractions as possible and by insisting that, for the most part, both tenor and vehicle of his metaphors will be rooted in the physical world, has left the range of interpretation almost as wide as did the original greenhouse in which he grew up. If the reader is to make meanings of the urge and wrestle of plant life, he must do so at his own risk and with little help from Roethke. What does the growth of a plant mean in the physical world? That's what it means here, too, says Roethke; though by focussing our attention on the nubs and stalks, he has, of course, invited us to meditate on the energies displayed. This relationship between reader and poem is somewhat new in Roethke; he is no longer making statements or writing essays or giving advice. Whereas in *Open House* the reader's difficulty was most likely to be in following the abstractions that Roethke offered, in the greenhouse sequence the reader is asked to supply the abstractions himself—or to leave them out, if he prefers. This relationship between reader and poem is much more dynamic. He is asked to do more work, to join in the act of creation and complete the experiences of Roethke's childhood by meditating upon them as Roethke has done and will continue to do.

Nonetheless, Roethke has offered a clue or two as to some of the "meanings" which he himself finds in the greenhouse experience. The second poem in the sequence, the one everyone always seems to quote in its entirety, is "Cuttings (*later*)." In it, Roethke makes the analogy between the plants and himself very plain, but directs the analogy to two specific resemblances that he wishes the reader to see:

> This urge, wrestle, resurrection of dry sticks,
> Cut stems struggling to put down feet,
> What saint strained so much,
> Rose on such lopped limbs to a new life?   (cp 37)

The struggle "to put down feet" suggests, for Roethke is never careless with words, the poet's struggle to put metrical feet down on paper, and the saint's straining toward "new life" is that effort to be "more than a man" which the notebooks show to have been Roethke's preoccupation throughout much of his life. David Wagoner is very astute in his observation that Roethke must have seen an aspect of himself in the vine, the growing climber and clinger that goes where it must. "This was," Wagoner says, "his illumination, the shape of his thought." [7] At any rate, the "meaning," the "lesson" of the greenhouse, grows out of the terrible energy of tropism, the mysterious forces by which plants grow down to their food and reach upward toward the light simultaneously. That energy, Roethke sees, is the perfect figure for all creative energy, for the energy of life itself. It is an analogy which fits Roethke's creative struggle, but it fits other struggles as well, and it is unfair to the poems to apply the comparison too narrowly.

If the real *meaning* of these poems is the energy they convey, that "intensity of action" of which Kenneth Burke speaks, then the most worthwhile question about the greenhouse sequence is that of how that intensity is achieved, by what devices Roethke manages to make the energy of tropism a felt experience. Roethke himself is of some help in finding an answer. For one thing, a notebook entry for 1946 offers "My design in short poems: to create the situation and the mood as quickly as possible = etch it in and have done; but is that enough? No. There must be symbolical force, weight, or a gravity of tone" (36 #84). We have already seen that "symbolical force" is attained in these poems, partly because poetic focus on any part of nature invites symbolic attention, partly because Roethke chooses his words and his tropes carefully to nudge us toward such a reading. But it is hard to imagine poems getting under way more quickly than do the greenhouse poems. In 1934 Roethke the apprentice had written Dorothy Gordon that "I'm poor at titles. Do they really matter?" (*Letters* 15). But the Roethke of the greenhouse poems is a master at titles, making sure that they matter. For example, the title "Weed Puller" establishes the protagonist and the rough setting immediately and allows the poem to begin with specific place and with *activity*:

> Under the concrete benches,
> Hacking at black hairy roots,—
> Those lewd monkey-tails hanging from drainholes,—
> Digging into the soft rubble underneath,
> Webs and weeds,
> Grubs and snails and sharp sticks,
> Or yanking tough fern-shapes,
> Coiled green and thick, like dripping smilax,
> Tugging all day at perverse life. . . . (CP 39)

The hacking and digging and yanking and tugging goes on as pure action, without pause to identify the actor, for ten lines before we come to Roethke himself, "Crawling on all fours, / Alive in a slippery grave" (CP 39). Like Emily Dickinson's hummingbird, the subject of the poem emerges gradually from behind a flurry of movement, a buzz of activity. In "Child on Top of a Greenhouse" the entire setting is contained in the title, and such efficiency enables Roethke to concentrate his poem entirely on action. Though grammatically "Child on Top of a Greenhouse" is composed entirely of subjects without verbs, the use of the participial forms gives an effect which is just reversed. It is as if the poem has no subject except pure action, a *billowing* and *crackling* and *flashing* and *rushing* and *plunging* and *tossing*. The title provides the information, the frame of reference, which enables Roethke to make a poem without ordinary subject-predicate constructions, a poem in which the actor and the act, the child and the energy sweeping around him, become one. There is no separation between the rushing and tossing of man and nature and the rush and toss of the boy's blood flow. His exhilaration and terror is mirrored in the motion of the plunging air. Most of Roethke's titles in the *Greenhouse Sequence* establish either subject or predicate, a situation which enables the poet to begin *in media res*, without explanation or background, at the heart of the action where the poem lives or dies.

Roethke has another comment which is of some value in discussing the energy of the greenhouse poems, this time a note I have already cited in my "Introduction." In the teaching notes Roethke answers the question of what factors contribute to "energy in rhythm."

> I feel what comes to the aid are alliteration of initial sounds and a manipulation and a variation of interior sounds, (repetition of words) particularly vowels. The line—but the verbal forms particularly, particularly the "ing" participial form, impart, as would be expected, movement. (67, 2)

Listen to several lines at random from this sequence:

This urge, wrestle, resurrection of dry sticks. . . (CP 37)

Where were the greenhouses going,
Lunging into the lashing
wind driving water. . . (CP 41)

Cannas shiny as slag,
Slug-soft stems,
Whose beds of bloom pitched on a pile. . . (CP 43)

Nothing would sleep in that cellar, dank as a ditch,
Bulbs broke out of boxes. . . (CP 38)

Vines tougher than wrists
And rubbery shoots,
Scums, mildews, smuts along stems,
Great cannas or delicate cyclamen tips. . . (CP 38)

It is hard to imagine harder-working sound effects, tighter manipulation and variation of vowel and consonant. To concentrate, even momentarily, on Roethke's use of alliteration and assonance is to realize that for him free verse had to be even harder working than did formal pieces. The absence of a regular pattern of accents frees him—but frees him to pile accents together as closely as possible and to call attention to that energetic rush and thrust by accenting syllables which alliterate, which clack and clatter against each other like train wheels over a track. The ideal line in the greenhouse sequence, the line Roethke reaches toward but never quite achieves, is the line of pure spondee, the line totally free of unaccented syllables. At any rate, if Roethke is right—and I think he is—in asserting that alliteration of initial sounds and manipulation and variation of interior sounds have much to do with the "energy" of a poem's rhythm, the energy of the *Greenhouse Sequence* must owe much to just those devices.

Roethke's use of "the 'ing' participial form" to impart movement to his poems is equally apparent. "Transplanting" and "Child on Top of a Greenhouse" have almost no other verb forms, though "Transplanting" does have the verb "goes" mid-way through the poem. Other poems are not far behind in the use of participles. Frequently Roethke uses them in catalogs of action, as

in "Weed Puller" or as in "Big Wind," in which the violence of
the storm is portrayed as *lashing, driving, flailing, flinging, veering,* and finally *whistling,* while the greenhouse and its keepers
answer by *lunging, pumping, watching, stuffing, ploughing,
bucking,* and at last "Carrying her full cargo of roses" into the
calm of morning.

The use of participial verb forms is appropriate to the *Greenhouse Sequence* in another, somewhat related, way. It seems to
me that the dynamism of Roethke's greenhouse poems is very
much dependent upon the way that the experiences they represent are presented as existing in time. Roethke's interest in these
events is not to create a sense of the past, but rather a sense of
the continuous. To represent successfully the flow of the continuous in time is difficult; to do it without merely talking about
it is doubly difficult. The use of the present participle to suggest
ongoing activity, to suggest the thing being done rather than the
thing done, is one of Roethke's tools for presenting time and
process in a dynamic way. On the one hand, by writing out his
personal history, by depicting himself as a child in (or on top of)
a greenhouse, Roethke begins every poem with an implied past
tense. On the other hand, only five of the fourteen poems—"Root
Cellar," "Moss Gathering," "Big Wind," "Old Florist," and
"Frau Bauman, Frau Schmidt, and Frau Schwartze"—are actually written in the past tense, and the predominant verb forms
of the sequence are the simple present tense and the present
participle. The effect is that of a partially recaptured moment, a
past which breathes again and moves again and is again even
while we are aware that it is totally lost. It is as if the big wind,
the old florist, the fraus, the experience of weed pulling, reach
out, as the growing plants reach out, beyond themselves into the
future. It is as if the energy of the moment—or of some moments
—is so intense as to set up vibrations in the mind and, more than
the mind, in the pulse and nerve endings, and thereby refuses
to give up life, keeps on breathing its small breath. Roethke aug-
ments this effect by clever use of pronouns, speaking of *"This"*
urge of dry sticks, *"These"* nurses of nobody else, but of *"That"*

old rose-house and of *"that"* cellar, dank as a ditch. Parts of the sequence treat the greenhouse as not present, as removed by distance and time, while others treat the glass house and its inhabitants as if they were in the room with the poet, as if they existed in an eternal present in which the urge and wrestle of sticks was always "this" urge.

The poems of *Open House* are almost always written in the simple past or simple present tense; events (or lectures) are either completed or there is the pretense that they are taking place as the poet records them. But the glass house, a truly open structure, exists in the past and the present simultaneously. It is as if the imagination and memory are testing their powers to re-create the lost event and thereby demonstrate the continuity of the historical instant. Despite their ingenious after-the-fact arrangement, the poems of *Open House* were presented as spots of time with no real sense of connecting energies. Time is treated, I suspect unconsciously, as it is in "In the Time of Change," as a flickering rather than a flowing, as a series of stage settings, each of which requires a curtain and total darkness to be set up and another to be struck for the next setting. But to think and compose in sequences, to present a series of events, each of which insists upon its context, each of which quickens and is quickened by the events to which it is joined, allows the poet movement and complexity and continuity in his symbolic representation of the world. In the *Greenhouse Sequence*, context does matter. Poems do quicken one another. And there is movement, not only within the poems as Kenneth Burke has shown, but among the poems as well.

The simplest and most obvious kind of movement from poem to poem is seen in the white space between "Cuttings" and "Cuttings (*later*)." The sticks-in-a-drowse have awakened; the change which is going on in the first poem continues across the paper that separates it from its companion piece and is there, too, though more strained, more urgent. Even the energy and rhythm of the struggle to a new life changes, though that energy is change itself. The advantages of the sequence are immediately clear when one tries to imagine how "Cuttings" would impress him if he were to come across it, the unfortunate captive of some mad anthologist, stripped of its context as the poem of entry into the greenhouse world:

> Sticks-in-a-drowse droop over sugary loam,
> Their intricate stem fur dries;
> But still the delicate slips keep coaxing up water;
> The small cells bulge;
>
> One nub of growth
> Nudges a sand-crumb loose,
> Pokes through a musty sheath
> Its pale tendrilous horn.   (CP 37)

We have lost the full impact of the poem as perfect beginning place, the contrast between the drowsy coaxing and the later urge and wrestle; we have lost most of the awareness of the analogy between sticks and human beings and all of the direction to the specific human conditions of spiritual growth and creative effort; and, most important, we have lost all of the energetic tension between past and present, between the sense impressions of the greenhouse boy and the meditations and memories of the greenhouse poet. "Cuttings (*later*)," of course, fares better as anthology piece, but I would argue that it still loses the force that results from the contrast of its rhythm and energy with that of its companion piece and that it becomes a weaker poem when removed from its context, its place in the several patterns of movement which hold the sequence together.

Karl Malkoff has pointed to one such pattern of development. By concentrating on Roethke-the-protagonist, Malkoff shows that the sequence may be read as a struggle to grow to maturity, specifically sexual maturity. Thus, the first poems are part of the effort to be born; the middle poems "deal with the development of a more self-conscious sexuality"; and, gradually, having realized "a more adult kind of sexuality" in "Big Wind," the boy Roethke confronts in the final poems "the triumph and terror of emerging from the greenhouse world of childhood." [8] I have no quarrel with this particular description of the movement, the development, of Roethke's greenhouse poems; however, there are other movements in the sequence which interest me more and which, though too energetic to march nicely down patterned paths, seem no less realized than does the movement which Malkoff witnesses. There are many windows in a glass house and, one suspects, more than one kind of motion going on.

Roethke begins the sequence as one totally immersed in the vegetable life of the greenhouse. His personality, his subjecthood, barely intrudes, and when it does so, it is only to assert a oneness with the plants which surround him:

> I can hear, underground, that sucking and sobbing,
> In my veins, in my bones I feel it,—
> The small waters seeping upward,
> The tight grains parting at last.
> When sprouts break out,
> Slippery as fish,
> I quail, lean to beginnings, sheath-wet.   (CP 37)

Gradually he begins to separate himself from the greenhouse, first emotionally, when in "Weed Puller" he resents "the indignity" of tugging at perverse life and finds himself crawling in "a slippery grave" like some root or pulpy stem while all above him everything is blooming, "Whole fields lovely and inviolate (CP 39). Next comes physical withdrawal, the journey out and back which takes place in "Moss-Gathering." The sense of emotional disturbance with the greenhouse routine is reintroduced, for

> afterwards I always felt mean, jogging back over
>   the logging road,
> As if I had broken the natural order of things in
>   that swampland;
> Disturbed some rhythm, old and of vast importance,
> By pulling off flesh from the living planet;
> As if I had committed, against the whole scheme of
>   life, a desecration.   (CP 40)

The next excursion is straight up—the direction that calls attention to itself—to the top of the greenhouse. The boy has separated himself spatially from those below him, but he has also committed what must have been, to say the least, against the whole scheme of greenhouse life, a desecration. The guilty exhilaration at having defied Papa and the accusers below indicates that more than altitude and glass removes him from the world beneath him. Finally, in "Frau Bauman, Frau Schmidt, and Frau Schwartze," the greenhouse boy has withdrawn all the way into "Now," the word toward which the entire sequence moves, that state of furthest distancing from the glassed-in-world in which he was nurtured. The journey out of the greenhouse begins as a journey through space, shifts to the dimensions of the spirit, and at last combines these movements with the journey through time, the journey to the "Now," when we find the poet "alone and cold in [his] bed."

The sequence also drifts from the poetry of concrete physical sensation to the more complex poetry of meditation. Like Faulkner's *The Sound and the Fury*, the greenhouse poems begin with the life of the eyes, the ears, the nose, and the fingertips. We see the bulge of cells, hear the sucking and sobbing of small waters, smell the congress of stinks, feel "rubbery shoots" and "Vines tougher than wrists." When the orchids

> lean over the path,
> Adder-mouthed,
> Swaying close to the face,
> Coming out, soft and deceptive,
> Limp and damp, delicate as a young bird's tongue . . . ,

we feel and see them simultaneously. Later we take in "their musky smell" and feel the coming of the cool night, the touch of the orchids' "Soft luminescent fingers." But "Moss-Gathering," a poem beginning in pure sensory experience, turns reflective when all the moss is in. In the swamp the moss is part of the flesh of the "living planet," but in the cemetery basket, uprooted and dying, it speaks only of death. The boy senses the meanness of it, a meanness that the poet calls "a desecration," though he softens the term by saying that it is "*As if*" he had committed, "against the whole scheme of life, a desecration" (CP 40). It is life that is celebrated in the poem, the "rhythm, old and of vast importance," which drives the sequence line by line and which lifts the carnations toward the light. The poet has the advantage of the florist, for he may handle living material—indeed, he must handle it—but he keeps it alive, preserves the rhythm of life undisturbed. Malkoff points to the onanistic nature of the action, a reading clearly reinforced by such phrases as "something always went out of me" and "pulling off flesh." [9] It would be very wrong, however, to read the poem as a thinly veiled treatise on masturbation. Roethke is, as always, too much the craftsman for the word choices to be accidental, but the poem *is* about moss-gathering and the verbal traces of onanistic imagery operate as almost subliminal metaphors, as aids in establishing the sense of guilty meanness which is the central feeling of the poem. Onanism, Roethke seems to suggest, is comparable to moss-gathering in that it is another kind of break with the natural order, another enemy of "the whole scheme of life." "Moss-Gathering," then, is not a poem "about" masturbation; it is a poem celebrating the energy that greens the earth.

Like the early poems in the sequence, "Big Wind" begins with a flurry of sense impressions. But unlike the earlier pieces, Roethke's account of the storm is set in the past tense, a strategy which allows him to give order and meaning to the events of the night. The violence of the storm has, thanks to the shaping powers of memory and the imagination, a beginning, a middle, and an end. The energy of the "big wind" is made meaningful by the reflection that only the passage of time allows. Essentially, the poem is one in which inner and outer violence collide; the fury of the storm is held off by the furious activity of the men in the glass house. In order to preserve the beautiful order of the greenhouse against the vicious flowing of wind and water, one must, paradoxically, meet force with force, counter change with change. So the men drain the manure machine for the steam plant, stuff burlap into spaces where glass ought to be, and break the pattern of their lives by staying in the rose-house all night. The formula for endurance in a world of motion is one of continuous adaptation. For Roethke the poet, looking back across time to the night of big wind, the uncontrolled violence of the storm has come to represent the "ugly," while the inner violence, the controlled energy "under glass," preserves and nurtures that which is beautiful. In a sense, "Big Wind" is a figure for the poet's life, that continuous activity of the mind pressing out to preserve itself from the violence of time and change. If the memory and imagination were not to press outward against the storm on the other side of the glass, Roethke's entire past, the Edenic greenhouse world, would surely cave in. It is entirely appropriate that the poem ends with a single extended figure of speech, the only such figure in the *Greenhouse Sequence:*

> But she rode it out,
> That old rose-house,
> She hove into the teeth of it,
> The core and pith of that ugly storm,
> Ploughing with her stiff prow,
> Bucking into the wind-waves
> That broke over the whole of her,
> Flailing her sides with spray,
> Flinging long strings of wet across the roof-top,
> Finally veering, wearing themselves out, merely
> Whistling thinly under the wind-vents;
> She sailed until the calm morning,
> Carrying her cargo of roses.   (CP 41)

Thus the poem which begins with a question—"Where were the greenhouses going . . . ?"—suggesting that the outer violence has the upper hand, ends with a metaphor, evidence that the mind of the poet has the power to transform the chaos of his world and make of it what he chooses. The greenhouses are going to sea, to become ships, to sail at last into the harbor of morning. The violence turns to calm; the questions turn to answers; the chaos of sense impressions turns to the order created by the imagination. The beautiful, artificial figure of the ship is very like the beautiful, artificial life inside the greenhouse. Like his father before him, the poet creates a world and preserves it by energetic motion. The energy of the poem is the rhythms by which it moves, and that movement rides out the flux which breaks over it. Only by "sailing" does the glass house stand still; only by movement do words reach the stillness.

The final poem in the sequence as it is printed in *The Collected Poems* is "Frau Bauman, Frau Schmidt, and Frau Schwartze," a piece first published in 1952 and first inserted into the greenhouse poems in *The Waking*. Both there and in *Words for the Wind* the Fraus are sandwiched between "Old Florist" and "Transplanting." Louis L. Martz has complained of the intrusion, arguing that the poem belongs to Roethke's period of "Yeatsian imitation" and that "it breaks the natural, intimate presence of those earlier poems, and it ought to be printed elsewhere in future editions of Roethke's poetry." [10] I believe very strongly that the poem does belong in the *Greenhouse Sequence*, and I feel it is especially appropriate as the final piece in the group. Although its subject matter, style, and tone relate it closely to the other poems in section one of *The Lost Son*, "Frau Bauman, Frau Schmidt, and Frau Schwartze" is, in its treatment of time, the most complex and the most interesting of the sequence.

The poem conveys an impression of an elusive, darting "reality," for the three Fraus move so swiftly as to manage to be in two places at once, to be "Gone" and "still hover[ing]" simultaneously. The ladies, like the Old Florist, have the power to transfer their energy creatively into the life around them, and it is that power which commends them to the memory and to the apotheosizing power of the imagination. The Fraus are glimpsed through a blur of active verbal forms—*creaking, reaching, winding, straightening, tying, tucking, dipping up, sifting, sprinkling, shaking, standing, billowing, twinkling, flying, keeping, sewing, trellising, pinching, poking,* and *plotting.* Even nouns such as *Coils, loops, whorls, nurses, seed, pipes,* and others are potential verbs, reminding us that the names of greenhouse things are squirming with metaphorical action. The ladies are never still, for even when they stand astride the greenhouse pipes, their skirts billow and their hands twinkle "with wet." Their movement is always that of "picking up," and the movement of the poem, like the movement of the climbing roses, is upward from the earth toward the sun. So swiftly do the ladies scurry that the memory blurs fact into fiction, the historical ladies into the mythic. Flying "like witches," they become more and more enormous in their activity until at last they trellis the sun itself, giving support to that strange flower which is the life of our planet.

As the remembered ladies become apotheosized into mythic figures, Roethke imagines them to take on the fecund powers of earth mothers. They straddle the phallic pipes of the greenhouse, pipes belonging to Roethke's father, until their skirts billow "out wide like tents"—as if someone might live there. They have, we are told, the power to "tease out" the seed, to undo the lifeless "keeping" of the cold. And finally, they give the poet himself a symbolic birth. Acting as midwives to themselves, they pick him up, pinch and poke him into shape, "Till I lay in their laps,/ Laughing,/ Weak as a whiffet" (CP 44). The ladies, trellisers of the sun, also trellis "the son," the boy fathered by the greenhouse owner.

Though the old women are, as the first word of the poem indicates, "Gone," they "still hover" in the air of the present. All of the verbs in the first stanza are, as one would expect in a remembrance, in the past tense. Nevertheless, Roethke refers to the Fraus as "*These* nurses of nobody else" as if they were present, as if the memory had established them in the poet's room. And, of course, he says that "Now, when I'm alone and cold in my bed,/ They still hover over me,/ These ancient leathery crones. . . ." The relationship between poet and crones is a highly dynamic one. On the one hand, the hovering mothers "still" have the power to give him life. He lies like a seed, cold and in his bed, and they breathe over him the breath of life, a snuff-laden blowing that lifts him from the keeping of the cold into a life that manifests itself in poetic blossoms. On the other hand, it is the poet who "keeps" the Fraus alive, whose breath gives to the dead the power to move and be again. Their energy is entirely dependent upon his ability to intensify the language until their movement becomes tangible in the empty air, becomes an event in the viscera of the reader. The poem itself takes its cadence not from a màn named Yeats, but from the German Fraus—takes it and gives it back again. As for the poet, he has, by the end of the poem which is the end of the *Greenhouse Sequence*, lost himself in two places at once. He is in his bed and the time is now, yet the crones who hover above him breathe "lightly over [him] in [his] first sleep," presumably that sleep from which one wakes at birth. They are the remembered gateway to the house of glass, these witches capable of collapsing time so that the cold sleep of the adult is as one with the first sleep from which he wakened into life. They are the means by which Roethke demonstrates the dynamic reach of the "Now" in which we always live; for, through the Fraus who were, through the Fraus mythologized, and through the Fraus who remain as a felt presence, he has made a poetic representation of the living extension of the past into the ever-moving present.

Thus, the fourteen greenhouse poems move from simplicity to complexity, from pure sensation to meditation and memory, from Paradise to Paradise Lost and part-way back. The shifting pattern laid down by Roethke's personal history is, as he knew well, the pattern of all human experience. The sensual world of the greenhouse is the first garden from which we have all emerged, and the attempt to make meanings of it, to recall the energies of that place, occupies us all in the lonely chill of our adult beds. The message spelt from Roethke's leaves reads that life is dynamic, not static; that the energy of the moment from the past preserves it, in part, in the present; that experience is a continuum, not a collection of dead instants preserved and pinned on walls we have left behind.

The Opening Knock
and the Lost Son

It is wisest to begin with Roethke's letter to us all, for in it he tells us not only what the fourteen poems which open *Praise to the End* "mean," what they "are," but also how we must read them:

> you will have no trouble if you approach these poems as a child would, naively, with your whole being awake, your faculties loose and alert. (A large order, I daresay!) *Listen* to them, for they are written to be heard, with the themes often coming alternately, as in music, and usually a partial resolution at the end. Each poem . . . is complete in itself; yet each in a sense is a stage in a kind of struggle out of the slime; part of a slow spiritual progress; an effort to be born, and later, to become something more. (sp 37)

Despite such help, few have been the critics who have been able to become as little children, for naivete is not what is ordinarily required of us. Perhaps the trouble has been, in part, that Roethke, having told us that the poems are *about* a "slow spiritual progress," and, moreover, having given us (in the same "Open Letter") a quick sketch of his methods, has stolen our usual occupations from us. Nonetheless, after leading us through "The Lost Son" section by section, the poet insists that "This crude account tells very little about what actually happens in the poem" (SP 39). The attempt to tell the rest of "what actually happens" and how it happens has occupied various Roethke scholars since the "Open Letter" appeared in 1950.

83

Those who have fared worst, it seems to me, have tried to do line-by-line "close readings" of these poems; that is, they have tried to illuminate the obscurities of the *non sequitur*, the nonsense, the oracular pronouncement, and the cryptic command or question as each occurs, a step at a time. In letters not so open as the one I have been quoting, Roethke offers an indirect warning against this sort of approach. Writing Kenneth Burke and, later, Babette Deutsch, he quotes with obvious pleasure from a review by John Theobald.

> "It is Hopkins, we remember, who distinguishes two sorts of illumination of obscurity: first that which yields step by step with the construing of the sentences (e.g. Browning's *Sordello*), and second, that which shines from every sentence, withholds itself from the poem as a whole on repeated readings, but when it does yield 'explodes.' Brinnin's poem exposes itself to the first, Theodore Roethke's *The Long Alley* (*Poetry*, July '47) . . . does to the second."
> (*Letters* 138, 140)

Roethke's twice quoting Theobald's remark is indication enough that the poet approved of that judgment; to Burke he added, "In my childish way, I was pleased," and to Ms. Deutsch, "Is it childish to cherish this remark, and hope that this will often, eventually, be the case with those whose opinions I value?"

It was not childish, I think, and other poets—whose opinions Roethke surely valued more highly than those of "text creepers" —have offered ways of looking at these difficult poems which seem to indicate that, for them at least, the desired "explosion," the "illumination," has taken place. Such an illumination usually takes shape as a metaphor, an overriding comparison which cuts through the difficulties of constructing sentence by sentence paraphrases and comes at once to what actually happens in the poem, to what is happening to Roethke as he grunts, bellows, and sings his way from "Where Knock Is Open Wide" to "O, Thou Opening, O." For Stephen Spender,

> Mr. Roethke has really made a Noh drama of himself: a monologue in which, wearing a mask painted with a fixed

smile of pain, he visits a pond in a wood which is haunted
by a nymph-like ghost, and performs a very slow and solemn
pirouetting dance, whilst pronouncing some very strange
serious-mock words. . . .[1]

For Stanley Kunitz the poems are a quest for spiritual identity in
which the hero, in order to find himself,

> must lose himself by reexperiencing all the stages of his
> growth, by reenacting all the transmutations of his being
> from seed to maturity. We must remember that it is the
> poet himself who plays all the parts. He is Proteus and all
> the forms of Proteus—flower, fish, reptile, amphibian, bird,
> dog, etc.—and he is the adversary who hides among the
> rocks to pounce on Proteus, never letting go his hold, while
> the old man of the sea writhes through his many shapes
> until, exhausted by the struggle, he consents to prophesy in
> the *claritas* of his found identity.[2]

And I have heard David Wagoner offer yet another figure to represent the struggles of the lost son who moves through the two
sequences.[3] Wagoner likens Roethke's protagonist to the tribal
shaman, the man who gathers wisdom at the dangerous edge of
human experience, that edge at which man and beast become all
but indistinguishable. The shaman dresses in the skins of animals
—the deer, the fox, the panther—in order to take on their powers,
their instincts. By becoming less than human he can, paradoxically, take on powers which transcend the human and so can become almost god-like. In a sense, for the shaman the way back
is the way forward, a thought echoed by Roethke himself in his
by now well-known comment that "I believe that to go forward
as a spiritual man it is necessary first to go back" (SP 39).

These metaphorical illuminations have some things in common. All, for example, get at the "texture" of the lost son's experience. That is, they manage to convey something of Roethke's
down-the-rabbit-hole quality of dream, of ritual, of magical transformation. All three poets have, in their figures, pointed out the
ability of Roethke's hero to be more than one character at the

same time; as in dream and nightmare, all of the figures seem to be different aspects of the single self who speaks his words of love and terror. Moreover, Spender, Kunitz, and Wagoner all emphasize the masks, the disguises which the protagonist takes on, the deliberate playing of roles in order to confront—at last—the thing that he is. The prince in his toad suit is both cursed and blessed. If he is less than he is, less than a fully human being, he is at least temporarily protected from the burdens of human responsibility and guilt. A toad need not wish the Father-King dead in order to come to his inheritance. And if one wishes news of the well, one goes to the toad, just as one goes to the mole for news of the pit. By reenacting the journey out of the womb, by playing out the old drama of ontogeny, the hero takes on the wisdom of his phylogenic ancestors and does, indeed, speak at last with something like "the *claritas* of his found identity." At any rate, only a dynamic metaphor, the image of Proteus writhing with transformations or of the shaman living on the edge of many lives in the skins of many beasts, is able to give an adequate sense of Roethke's slippery hero.

The three poets also suggest in their metaphors a quality which others have also noted in these poems—that atmosphere of mythic power which plays over the entire sequence. Spender's Noh dancer is a ritualistic figure, a character in a psychodrama; Kunitz's Proteus is, of course, a character drawn from mythology, and one who acts out the process of psychic and physiological growth by which we live; Wagoner's shaman is also a ritualistic figure, one who represents the beast-man of nightmare and fantasy who, by descending into the darker regions of the ancestral mind, comes at last to unusual illumination. Kunitz was among the first to point to Roethke's use of mythic patterns in the lost son sequence. Noting that Roethke knew, if not Jung, at least "Jung's disciple Maud Bodkin," Kunitz summarizes Jung's discussion of progression and regression in *Contributions to Analytical Psychology:*

> Before "a renewal of life" can come about, there must be
> an acceptance of the possibilities that lie in the uncon-

scious contents of the mind "activated through regression . . . and disfigured by the slime of the deep." [4]

Kunitz goes on to point out that the principle is embodied in the myths of the journey under the sea or the journey to the underground from which the hero returns to the light. "The monologues of Roethke," he concludes, "follow the pattern of progression and regression and belong unmistakably to the rebirth archetype." [5]

Little of this will be news to critics of the 1970s, those who have teethed on the work of Bodkin and Northrop Frye. What may be less apparent, however, is the effect, the impact, that the use of myth has on Roethke's poetry. It is not merely that, "by manipulating a continuous parallel" between the journey of his lost son and the archetypal journey of that mythic hero of the thousand faces, Roethke has found, in T. S. Eliot's words, "a way of controlling, of ordering, of giving a shape and significance" [6] to the chaotic experience of his—and everyman's—history. Nor is it merely that the myths themselves are charged with primal emotional power, though they may indeed reach the deep center of our consciousness. At times Roethke himself seems to have been skeptical of the powers sometimes attributed to myths, and he once complained to Kenneth Burke that "Most of the myths are a bore, to me" (*Letters* 147).

Roethke's boredom ought not to be taken too seriously, for he returns to the myths again and again in his writing. However, I believe he was never so much interested in the myths themselves as in their usefulness as a tool for directing the violent energies that he wished to set in motion. The advantage of a "mythic structure" is that, in a sense, it is no structure at all. A myth is itself pure action, the motion of a hero through time and space, usually toward more abundant life. What counts is not the sequence of particular events falling into a chronological order, but the urge, wrestle, and resurrection, the thrust toward the light, which drives the hero onward. The power of the myth is not a matter of plot, but of tropism, not a function of structure, but of energy and direction. The "structure" of the myth, like the "structure" of the atom, is a kind of artificial construct, a graspable metaphor created to stand for the unstructured flowing that is life itself. If, as Roethke believed, energy is the most important element in a poem, the discovery of a dynamic way of directing that energy is an important development in becoming the kind of poet he wanted to be.

One advantage of the "mythic method," as Eliot called it, is that it is always dynamic in its treatment of time. In the *Greenhouse Sequence*, Roethke had suggested by manipulation of point of view and of verb tenses something of the energetic thrusting on of the historical event as it moves through time and space. In the lost son sequences, the mythic parallels force upon us a sense of experiences "so powerful and so profound . . . that they repeat themselves, thrust themselves upon us, again and again, with variation and change, each time bringing us closer to our own particular (and thus most universal) reality . . ." (SP 39). "Everything has been twice," cries the child in "Where Knock Is Open Wide," but he knows only what his short life has taught him, and so his count is understandably low. The experience of death and rebirth repeats itself again and again—in the pattern of the seasons, in the evolutionary process, in the turning of human generations, in the psychic and spiritual journeys of everyman and of any man. What is emphasized, however, by Roethke's use of mythic parallels, is not the sense of repetition, but that of power, of thrust, of "variation and change." Though "everything" may, as the lost son has it, have been "twice," nothing is ever "twice" in exactly the same way. "Any history of the psyche (or allegorical journey) is bound to be a succession of experiences, similar yet dissimilar," Roethke says in "Open Letter." "There is a perpetual slipping-back, then a going-forward; but there is some 'progress'" (SP 39). The detail of the pattern—that rocking back and forth of regression and progression—may be movement, but the total "pattern," at least as Roethke envisions it, is motion as well. There is always some "progress" toward "reality," toward light within light.

Like William Faulkner, Roethke does not allow his reader to

pin his work to a single and particular myth, to read the *Lost Son Sequence* as, say, "Nothing but" the Oedipus myth or Christ's story or the dark way of mysticism or of Jungian psychodrama. Instead Roethke manipulates image and situation so adroitly that we associate his lost son, at various times, with a bewildering variety of shifting identities. He is Christ, Aeneas, Oedipus, Hamlet, Persephone, Narcissus, Adam, Cain, Adonis, Ulysses and Telemachus, the questing knight, the clever son of folklore, and rat and dog and fish and cat. And foetus and phallus. And Ted Roethke, the greenhouse keeper's boy. My list is by no means exhaustive. By confronting his reader with several different but compatible myths at as nearly the same time as possible, Roethke underscores the protean nature of the human experience, our dynamic ability to grow, change, and develop. In the fight to come out of the self, Roethke knew well, it is necessary to take on other selves, to undergo an almost continuous shape-shifting. I do not think that Roethke—or his lost son—ever come like Proteus to some final shape, to an identity which is, as Kunitz has it, "found." I think, rather, that it is Roethke's joy and terror to go on creating selves and, perhaps more important, to go on creating a language out of which each self may prophesy in the imperfect *claritas* of an identity which is always falling away.

One of the important changes that takes place in the protagonist as he evolves from the opening lines of "Where Knock Is Open Wide" toward the concluding passage of "O, Thou Opening, O" is that he becomes more and more aware of himself in his role as creator of a world made of language. It is not simply that the vocabulary becomes less primitive, that abstractions begin to appear and such fancy adjectives as *pelludious* or *vestigial*. It is more that we find the narrator beginning to call attention to himself as a performer, a shaper responsible for selecting the words and rhythms by which he moves and makes us move. The most obvious example occurs in "O, Thou Opening, O," when the hero calls time out to denounce himself in prose for inadequate "rage" and "indignation" and announces—like an eighteenth-century novelist—his intention to mend his ways:

> I'm tired of all that, Bag-Foot. I can hear small angels
> anytime. Who cares about the dance of dead underwear or
> the sad waltz of paper bags? Who ever said God sang in
> your fat shape? You're not the only keeper of hay. That's
> a spratling's prattle. And don't be thinking you're simplic-
> ity's sweet thing, either. A leaf could drag you.
>
> Where's the great rage of a mocking heart, the high rare
> true dangerous indignation? Let me persuade more slowly.
> (CP 98)

There are other such instances. In "The Long Alley" the poet
calls attention to himself by asking "Shall I call the flowers?" before he does so. In "Unfold! Unfold!" he self-consciously addresses himself to the voice he has been using, remarking, "What
a whelm of proverbs, Mr. Pinch!" And he offers his performing
self encouragement in "O, Thou Opening, O" when he cries,
"Dazzle me, dizzy aphorist./ Fling me a precept." It is as if he is
at once in the audience and on stage—performing, commenting
on his performance, and aware that the comment itself is but
another performance which might be judged. Occasionally he reminds us that—whatever the action he may seem to present—his
real performance is the tracing of words, the making of proclama-
tions. Thus, in "I Cry, Love! Love!" he remarks, "I've traced
these words in sand with a vestigial tail," and later, in the same
poem, he proclaims that "I proclaim once more a condition of
joy."

In one of the notebooks—this one variously dated from December of 1948 to August of 1949—Roethke talks about the
linguistic strategy of the lost son poems. "All you have to do," he
told himself,

> is take it cozy, play it loose—the aphorism, the adage and
> short hard shots with the language in, I hope, a charged
> language, with the motion of the mind when it's under
> stress, under pressure, from terror, from fear, from anxiety.
> . . . (37 #106)

One senses, reading through the complete sequence in the final arrangement that Roethke gave it in *The Waking*, how difficult it

must have been to maintain such "a charged language," how difficult to preserve through fourteen poems a verbal intensity that would be equal to "the motion of the mind when it's under stress." The poems, after all, like those "powerful and . . . profound" experiences of which Roethke speaks in "Open Letter," do "repeat themselves . . . again and again," and at times their similarities seem more apparent to the casual reader than do their differences. "It is a dark world in which to work," Roethke writes in that same letter, "and the demands, other than technical, made upon the writer are savage" (SP 42). But the purely technical demands are savage, too, and Roethke goes on to give some indication of what a poet must do with the language if he wishes to write "this kind of poem":

> His language must be compelling and immediate: he must create an actuality. He must be able to telescope image and symbol, if necessary, without relying on the obvious connectives: to speak in a kind of psychic shorthand when his protagonist is under great stress. He must be able to shift his rhythms rapidly, the "tension." He works intuitively, and the final form of his poem must be imaginatively right. If intensity has compressed the language so it seems, on early reading, obscure, this obscurity should break open suddenly for the serious reader who can hear the language: the "meaning" itself should come as a dramatic revelation, an excitement. The clues will be scattered richly—as life scatters them; the symbols will mean what they usually mean—and sometimes something more.   (SP 42)

The "actuality" which Roethke creates is, as he says, a "struggle out of the slime . . . an effort to be born, and later, to become something more" (SP 37). We experience Roethke's "actuality" on many levels simultaneously—the spiritual, the psychic, the mythic, the sexual, the evolutionary—and at each level the dynamic force of creative energy struggles against the repressive forces of doubt, of guilt and fear, of the monsters of the deep, of impotence and sterility, of death itself. But all of these struggles exist for us only in the language which Roethke has fought to shape from the slime of the blank page, which he has charged with the energy that is life and which he has battled to preserve from the deadening influences of the slack, the familiar, the easy, and the merely conventional. The real subject of the poem, it seems to me, is the emerging poem itself—the struggle to make an "actuality" out of the inadequate symbolism of language and to *create* an experience in the reader's blood and nerves when the temptation to *talk about* experience is always present. And the real hero of the lost son poems, beneath whatever disguises, is the poetic voice, the voice that sings itself awake, that creates out of nothing a world of terror and delight, then comforts us against the terror and celebrates for us the delight. I do not wish to say that these are poems "about" poetry in the usual incestuous sense of the phrase. If anything, they are poems "about" the energy that is life, but insofar as that energy is present in their rhythms, in their telescoped images and symbols, in the "psychic shorthand" which is part of their rhetorical strategy, they are, in fact, poems which have themselves as a subject.

Roethke's verbal strategy begins with his selection of a mask through which to speak, though in the course of the sequence both the mask and the voices coming from behind it alter a good deal. Roethke tells us that "The earliest piece of all (in terms of the age of the protagonist) is written entirely from the viewpoint of a very small child. . . . To keep the rhythms, the language 'right,' i.e. consistent with what a child would say or at least to create the 'as if' of the child's world, was very difficult technically" (SP 41). The rest of the sequence, he says elsewhere, includes the voice of "the young adolescent, half a child, then the randy young man boasting and caterwauling; and finally more difficult passages in which the mind . . . roves far back into the subconscious, later emerging into the 'light' of more serene or euphoric passages . . ." (SP 12). As apprentice, Roethke wrote "Statements," "Essays," "Exhortations," all in the voice, however self-conscious and "public," of Theodore-Roethke-the-poet. In the *Greenhouse Sequence*, though the perceptions were sometimes those of the child, the voice was always that of the adult, the language of the man cold and alone in his bed. But in the *Lost Son Sequence* Roethke's mask allows him to make important changes in rhythm and diction, changes which contribute much to his development as a poet. One of the notebooks, dated August 1949, contains the following "prayer": "Give me the madman's hidden insight and the child's spiritual dignity" (37 #105). The disguised voice which came through the mask became, I think, a partial answer to that request.

The voice of the entire *Lost Son Sequence*, though particularly the voice of the earliest poems in Roethke's arrangement, the voice of "Where Knock Is Open Wide" and of "I Need, I Need," takes its cadences from jump-rope songs, nonsense verse, Mother Goose rhymes, and, Roethke says, "Elizabethan and Jacobean drama, especially the songs and rants" (SP 41). "Rhythmically," he insists, "it's the spring and rush of the child I'm after . . ." (SP 41). For Roethke, a shift in the rhythm of composition is also a shift in the rhythm of thought itself, a change in the pulse rate of meditation. In Evelyn Underhill's *Mysticism*, that book which the notebooks prove that Roethke absorbed thoroughly, there is a passage which describes the process by which the intellect breaks up the world of our perceptions into units of "useful" size and feeds them to us at a pace which enables us to take them in and live by them. "Thus we treat," says Underhill,

> the storm of vibrations which we convert into "sound" and "light." Slacken or accelerate its clock-time, change its rhythmic activity, and at once you take a different picture of the world. . . . Let human consciousness change or transcend its rhythm, and any other aspect of any other world may be ours as a result. Hence the mystics' claim that in their ecstasies they change the conditions of consciousness . . . cannot be dismissed as unreasonable.[7]

To recapture the "spring and rush of the child" in the rhythms of one's thoughts and perceptions is, perhaps, to take on the child's "spiritual dignity," much as the shaman puts on the slyness of the fox when he clothes himself in its skin. And to become as a child, to make our consciousness take on the rhythms of childhood, is one way of entering the Kingdom of Heaven, one of the ways by which the jaded adult may find himself once again alert as a dog or a saint.

The lyrics often smack more of dog than saint:

> Even steven all is less;
> I haven't time for sugar,
> Put your finger in your face,
> And there will be a booger. (CP 75)

This passage is the beginning, Roethke's prose informs us, of a part of "I Need, I Need" in which "two children are jumping rope. The reader isn't *told* the children are jumping rope: he simply hears the two reciting, alternately, jingles to each other" (SP 10). I do not think that a reader could reasonably be expected to know that jumping rope is what is going on, but surely the nonsense cadences do take us back to our first, most primitive experiences with poetry, to those chants and songs by which a game is played or by which work is done. Such poems grow naturally out of the vigorous rhythms of the human body, and their success or failure as poems depends not upon what the words "mean" but upon how adroitly their rhythms are able to "measure time by how a body sways." The wisdom of the jump-rope song is the wisdom of the body, the special "knowing" of muscle and blood and nerve and bone. And the appeal of such rhythms is very directly to the kinesthetic sense, that sense most often ignored in art and most often employed in life.

As I have suggested, a change in rhythm, a shift to the pace of the child's heartbeat or to the motion of the mind when it's under stress, is more than a *tour de force*. A change in the rhythm of experience is a change in experience, one which well may lead to "a different picture of the world," to "a dramatic revelation, an excitement." Equally important is Roethke's adoption of the vocabulary, first of the child and later of the mind as it "roves far back into the subconscious." Our first words are likely to be terms for those things which most comfort and terrify us, those words which, to use Roethke's example, "like *hill, plow, mother, win-*

dow, bird, fish, are so drenched with human association, they sometimes can make even bad poems evocative" (SP 80). And the language of the subconscious is, of course, the language of our obsessions, essentially the same primitive language spoken by dreams, by myths, by primitive peoples, by ourselves as children. It is a restricted language, composed of a limited number of emotionally charged but simple nouns and a rather inadequate supply of active verbs which bear the burden of demonstrating relationships among the things of the world. The result is a great deal of repetition of word and phrase and idea, an effect Roethke once termed "the very essence of poetry" (SP 77) and an effect which very quickly comes to produce something like that telescoping of images, that psychic shorthand, that he was after in these poems.

Roethke has made a world of words in which nothing is its solid self, or, more accurately, nothing is its solid self alone. Instead, such common words as *cat* or *tree* or *fish* or *bite* or *have* become a whirl of associations, some growing out of literary tradition; some out of psychological convention; some evolving out of their previous uses in the sequence and, naturally, reaching ahead to their subsequent uses; some coming from Roethke's personal history; and some, I suppose, from the reader's. Always, of course, the force of the word is dependent upon its particular context, its setting in the sequence of a whole. Thus, the word *fish* is a symbol meaning "what it usually means," and, as Roethke put it, "sometimes something more" (SP 42). In "psychic shorthand" it joins together Papa; the phallus; sperm; Christ; Roethke's phylogenic and ontogenic ancestors; that elusive treasure to be brought up from the depths; the poet's involuntary, neural life; and the self one might, with luck, catch behind the ears. *Fish* is also the word used to denote the fish, probably bullheads, which Roethke remembers catching on a jaunt with his father. Once one begins making associative lists, it is rather too easy to forget the literal denotation from which one must always begin. It is true, nonetheless, that a word, as Roethke uses words in the lost son poems, is a gathering of forces, a focussing of energies from many levels of spiritual and psychic life, and not a simple sign pointing to the dead end of a single denotation or, for that matter, of a single symbolic interpretation. Granted, any poet uses words this way to some extent, relying upon various traditional associations to flesh out his language. But I think Roethke forces us to feel the dynamism of his words by the verbal strategy he employs throughout the *Lost Son Sequence*. For one thing, the repetition of nouns—of *fish* and *pond*, *worm* and *rose*, *cloud* and *tree*—in unusual, even bizarre, contexts forces us to "think by association" if only because the literal puzzles us so thoroughly. When Roethke says, for example, "Once I was a pond" (CP 80) or "The holy root wags the tail of a hill" (CP 99), we are quickly aware that the words "mean" in a way quite different from that of everyday discourse. If these things are metaphorical, we wonder, where is the rest of the comparison? And, since the rest is not forthcoming—instead we are whirled off to another, equally puzzling sentence—we begin to assume that we are moving through a world that is totally metaphorical and in which all of the words hum with many meanings. The repetition itself gives us clues, for as figures appear again and again we find ourselves able to assign rough values to them. It is as if their "effects" (as opposed to their "meanings") grow by accretion until their forces, their energies, pull or prod us toward "a dramatic revelation, an excitement."

Thus Roethke's world of words becomes, as other readers have noted, though for different reasons, not nearly so "concrete" as a concordance might make it seem. The concrete nouns that swarm around us are less things in the physical world than they are a complex of stratified ideas, and they are less ideas than they are a whirl of psychic or spiritual or emotional energies. It is as if Roethke's words come to possess a kind of power of tropism and take on the ability to draw us either toward the depths or upward into the light.

One of the unfortunate practices in reading the *Lost Son Sequence* has been to interpret the poems by assigning a "meaning" to each of Roethke's figures and then to go through the poems as if Roethke had simply, for curious reasons of his own, chosen to

say "dog" when he clearly meant "repressed animal nature."
William Heyen is, it seems to me, guilty of this sort of oversimplification in his "Theodore Roethke's Minimals," an often
useful article which is marred by an insistence on flat equations:
"Weeds are a barrier to spiritual progress. . . ." or "In general,
fish in Roethke symbolize the Becoming of the spirit." [8] In more
skillful hands, such an approach can be enlightening. I have heard
David Wagoner assign values to the sub-human figures of the
lost son poems, but only after carefully insisting that his interpre-
tations were valid at one level of the sequence only, that level at
which the sequence is read as the poet's effort to grow, to become
"something more." It is a little like Wallace Stevens's glass of
water in which water and glass are seen to be—on both the physical and metaphysical level—merely "states" of many possible
states, existing between imaginary poles which are never to be
reached. But in this state, at the level of the poet's journey out of
himself, Wagoner suggests that many of the figures in the poems
may be read as aspects of the poet's self. The fish, for example,
corresponds to the poet's involuntary life, the life of the nerves.
The frog is that aspect of the self which lives in slime, yet remains clean. The toad is the prince's disguise, an ugly container
of the beautiful; Wagoner sees him as Roethke's figure for brooding and meditation. The spider and the moth are victim and
victor as well as representatives of two ways of searching—the
moth's frantic beating toward the light set off against the spider's
patient waiting. The fly is associated with that in the human
psyche which disgusts. The eel and otter are, in their slippery
playfulness, symbols of the unseen or half-seen aspects of the unconscious mind. Snail, slug, and worm are all identified with the
journeying human spirit, the snail by its lubricious movement,
the slug and worm as overtly visceral testing places for what
must be digested. Wagoner associates the dog, which is always
masculine for Roethke, with laziness, and the cat, always feminine, with aloofness. Finally the bird singing in its bush suggests
the spirit of the poet singing in his tangle of flesh and bones. [9]
All of this is excellent. But let the bird singing in its bush seem

for an instant to be the male organ throbbing in the nest of the vagina—an interpretation which is strongly suggested by the context in which the bird sometimes appears and the associations which grow about him—and we find ourselves in another "state," in which the landscape becomes as overtly sexual as any in American literature since Melville's "Tartarus of Maids." Biscuits that melt when eaten and the mouths that eat them, schools of fish and the ponds they swim in, bees and wasps and the blossoms they enter, the toad that turns into a prince and the lips that magically kiss him into transformation—it is a Freudian world to the end of it, and the protagonist's struggle is for potency rather than spiritual growth. Here, and in this state, the sequence has the libido as hero rather than the aspiring spirit. But the potential "states" are all but endless, and the thrust of Roethke's psychic shorthand is such that we are aware of the dazzling multiplicity of the lost son's world as we move through it beside him. Nonetheless, I think it is fair to say that in all states, on all levels of interpretation, the singing bird exerts a positive force; its energy as image is such that it draws us always toward the light.

In addition to the effects resulting from the repetition of these dynamic nouns, the limited verbs at the child's disposal have much to do with the nature of the world that Roethke builds of language. The first sentence of the sequence, for example, is "A kitten can/ Bite with his feet;/ Papa and Mamma/ Have more teeth" (CP 71). Clearly the kitten's feet do not "bite," but the childish mistake is one way of beginning to establish an entire pattern of biting and eating imagery, a pattern which comes to stand for the power to inflict pain, for the sexual "eating" done by the vagina, and, as the tongue is introduced into the pattern, for the power to take in experience and transform it into speech. The imagery of teeth and biting should not distract us from the child's greater fascination with "being able" (that potential power always expressed by *can* and *could*) and with "having." The child's real desire—established in the very first lines of "Where Knock Is Open Wide"—is to "have" power, to "be able," though he is quite confused as to what power might be and as to how it is to be "had." In his fine article called "The Vegetal Radicalism of Theodore Roethke," Kenneth Burke has noted that Roethke's verb choices are an effective rhetorical device:

> For instance, at the beginning of "The Shape of the Fire," there is a line "A cracked pod calls." As an image, the cracked pod belongs here. It is dead, yet there is possibility of a new life in it. Hence topically, the line might read simply "A cracked pod" . . . whenever there is no specific verb required, Roethke resorts to some word in the general category of *communication*. . . . There are possible objections to be raised against this sort of standard poetic personifying. . . . But it does help to suggest a world of natural objects in vigorous communication with one another. . . . To walk through his idealized Nature is to be surrounded by figures variously greeting, beckoning, calling, answering one another, or with little groups here and there in confidential huddles, or strangers by the wayside waiting to pose Sphinxlike questions or to propound obscure but truth-laden riddles. One thus lives as though ever on the edge of an Ultimate Revelation.[10]

Burke is very good here, and I would add only that the child's obsession with "saying," "crying," "singing," "whistling," and so forth is another way of emphasizing the power of language. His is a world alive in all of its parts, and the power of speech is one manifestation of the energy that is life.

The world of the child is a magical place, and the communication among natural objects is a part of that magic. Another example of the significance of Roethke's verbs in conveying a sense of such a world comes in a line from "I Need, I Need." After the child has seen "a beard in a cloud," after he has heard the ground cry his name, he asserts that "Love helps the sun./ But not enough" (CP 76). What does it mean to say that "Love helps the sun"? Perhaps that human love gives warmth, that love is one way of keeping off the dark and the cold; or that human love seems to make time (as measured by the moving sun) slow down, and so keeps the sun from going down to "death"; or perhaps it means that love brings life, as the sun brings life; perhaps there is a pun on Christ the Son, the suggestion that our love helps Him

with His work; or that Christ, who is Love, "helps" all of the
fallen sons of Adam; perhaps the line means, as Karl Malkoff suggests, that the love of the mother helps the son in the father's
absence.[11] My list is partial, of that much I am certain. Malkoff's
problem—and my own—is that the possible "meanings" of the
line roll past us so swiftly that formal analysis cannot hold them.
The real point, the real "meaning," lies in the dynamic complexity of the language itself. There is the wonderful suggestiveness
of the nouns, the abstraction *Love* lending itself readily to concrete readings (Love *is* God—or the sex act) and the concrete
noun *sun* possessing such a wealth of traditional associations that
it becomes almost immediately a symbol standing for time or for
the cosmic force or—as pun—for all those who are sons, for man-
kind. And, more to the point I have been making, there is also
the mysterious, magical vagueness of the verb which connects,
somehow, those two nouns. Love "helps" the sun only by the
logical illogic of dream and fairy tale. Yet the verb insists that
we make a connection—and an active connection—between the
world of the spirit (Love) and the physical world (the sun).
The verbs at the child's command are blessedly incapable of expressing an adult "intellectual" relationship—if such a relationship can exist—between Love and sun. But the squirming im-
precision of *helps* creates out of its own inadequacy a different
kind of relationship, one that is primitive, animistic, alive with
forces which are felt rather than understood. The ambiguity of
the relationship is part of its dynamism, and the child is content
to leave it so.

The lost son's universe is, for the most part, made up of strong,
active Anglo-Saxon verbs, verbs which connect the nouns in the
sequence by action rather than by expressing less vigorous relationships. There are few of the effete verbs of ordinary intellectual
discourse, of, say, literary criticism. Love "helps" the sun—it does
not "symbolize" the sun or "suggest" the sun or, worse still, "bear
an active relationship to" the sun. Because the verbs of Roethke's
created world are active, that world's relationships are active as
well. Ideas are as lively as fish; indeed, sometimes they are fish. In

his essay called "On Identity" Roethke once commented on the line "We think by feeling. What is there to know?" from his villanelle called "The Waking." "This," he said, "in its essence, is a description of the metaphysical poet who thinks with his body: an idea for him can be as real as the smell of a flower or a blow on the head. And those so lucky as to bring their whole sensory equipment to bear on the process of thought grow faster, jump more frequently from one plateau to another more often" (SP 27). Just as the jump-rope chants allow us to think once again with the body, so the lost son's primitive verb-hoard forces us to smell and feel ideas. Nothing is inactive for the narrator: "The plants wave me in . . . The minnows love me . . . The dark showed me a face . . . The light becomes me" (CP 88). Even "Eternity howls in the last crags" (CP 89). All things—even the most abstract ideas—draw upon our "whole sensory equipment."

The characteristic rhetorical devices of the sequence—the command, the question, the aphorism, the proverb or adage—serve to heighten intensity, to quicken the pulse rate of the poem and to achieve something like that "madman's hidden insight and . . . child's spiritual dignity" that Roethke was after. A comment in "Some Remarks on Rhythm," that hymn to poetic velocity, is useful here: "We say the command, the hortatory, often makes for the memorable. We're caught up, involved. It is implied we do something, at least vicariously" (SP 77). Questions, of course, make the same demand, albeit in gentler fashion. If one is looking for compelling, immediate language, the question compels us to find an answer, and preferably to find one immediately. There are sections in the lost son sequence which are built almost entirely around questions. For example, take that section from "The Lost Son" called *The Pit*:

> Where do the roots go?
>   Look down under the leaves.
> Who put the moss there?
>   These stones have been here too long.
> Who stunned the dirt into noise?
>   Ask the mole, he knows. . .   (CP 55)

Or take the opening stanza from "The Shape of the Fire":

> What's this? A dish for fat lips.
> Who says? A nameless stranger.
> Is he a bird or a tree? Not everyone can tell.   (CP 64)

Or one might turn to almost any part of "The Long Alley," a poem containing seventeen questions, these three among them:

> If we detach
> The head of a match
> What do we do
> · To the cat's wish?
> Do we rout the fish?
> Will the goat's mouth
> Have the last laugh?   (CP 60)

It is true that many of Roethke's questions have answers paired with them, but they are, for the most part, answers which answer nothing, which indeed are often more puzzling than the questions which occasioned them. *What* stones have been *where* "too long"? Who is the nameless stranger? What is the cat's wish? And what has the cat's wish to do with routing the fish? Finally the questions, both actual and implied, force us to confess our ignorance, to acknowledge the mysteriousness of things and the inadequacy of reason as a way of *knowing*. In his "Open Letter," Roethke makes certain that his readers will know the source of one of the many questions in "The Lost Son." "The line 'Hath the rain a father?' is from Job," he writes, adding that it is "the only quotation in the piece" (SP 38). The source is appropriate for many reasons, but one of them is surely that the question is among those which God—speaking from a whirlwind—uses to humble his already bothered and bewildered servant. "Where were you," God asks Job, "when I founded the world?" and He becomes angrier still, bombarding Job with questions, pausing occasionally for a sarcastic "Tell me, if you know all" or a "Tell me, if you have understanding. . . ." Finally Job must admit that he is of little account, that he has dealt with great things that he does not understand, things too wonderful for him to know. Roethke's questions, like God's, remain unanswerable—at least Roethke's are unanswerable at the conscious, rational level. They seem to work to tease us beyond thought and into the regions of wonder and awe, the regions in which madman and child presumably are more comfortable. It is as if the poems remind us, again and again, that we must rid ourselves of our pride in all that we *know* in order to confront the abyss, the immeasurable immensity of all that we do not know. Thus as readers we are drawn into the poem by being asked a question; frustrated and humbled by our inability to answer or to understand when answers are given; and, finally, left with something like the wisdom of Job for, like him, we have felt the energy of the whirlwind, though we have in no way comprehended it. In *Job* something of God's energy is suggested by the verbal whirlwind which buffets Job, the speed with which the questions come, the spring and rush of the language—the words which come from the Word which was in the beginning. Roethke, who also creates a world out of words, manages to convey a similar agitation and rush in his floods of questions, and the voice of these poems is, I believe, as close to the voice of whirlwind as one might find in recent poetry.

As confusing as Roethke's questions—perhaps more confusing —are his catalogs of proverbs and aphorisms, usually paced at one to the line and always offered without any connecting words to indicate in what way or ways, if any, each proverb is related to what comes before and after it. Consider, for example, section three of "The Shape of the Fire":

> The wasp waits.
> The edge cannot eat the center.
> The grape glistens.
> The path tells little to the serpent.
> An eye comes out of the wave.
> The journey from flesh is longest.
> A rose sways least.
> The redeemer comes a dark way. (CP 66)

Or this passage from "Unfold! Unfold!":

> This fat can't laugh.
> Only my salt has a chance.
> I'll seek my own meekness.
> What grace I have is enough.
> The lost have their own pace.
> The stalks ask something else.
> What the grave says,
> The nest denies.   (CP 91)

Or, to give proverbs equal time with questions, consider these, if they are proverbs, again from "Unfold! Unfold!":

> It's time you stood up and asked
>   —Or sat down and did.
> A tongue without song
>   —Can still whistle in a jug.
> You're blistered all over
>   —Who cares? The old owl?
> When you find the wind
>   —Look for the white fire.   (CP 89)

I think Roethke gives us a clue as to how these passages work in the line which follows the last section quoted above. The line is "What a whelm of proverbs, Mr. Pinch!" and the lines "Dazzle me, dizzy aphorist/ Fling me a precept" from "O, Thou Opening, O" help to confirm my suspicion. The "meaning" of these passages lies in their ability to overwhelm, bedazzle, bewilder, and balk the reason ("That dreary shed, that hutch for grubby schoolboys!") of which Roethke's audience is apt to be overproud. The speed with which these precepts are "flung" makes it impossible to catch many of them, and we find them bouncing off us in ways that are, indeed, almost physical. Our inability to grasp one proverb before we are hit by another, our sense of being overwhelmed by sheer speed—these sensations become a kind of revelation in themselves, a sudden excitement that crowds us toward —once again—the madman's insight and the child's dignity. The effect is something like the effect of those minute-long films which present all of American history as a bombardment of still shots flickering past so rapidly that the viewer must take in many of the pictures almost subliminally. In Roethke's "whelm of proverbs" and in such films the experience of the whole is quite different from the experience of the sum of the separate parts. In fact, the experience of the whole at one speed is very different from the same whole presented at another speed. A change of a single picture or a number of pictures, a change in the order of pictures, would, to be sure, alter the experience of viewing the film. But a change in the velocity with which the pictures zip past would, I submit, have a much greater impact upon the "created reality" which we take in. I believe the same thing to be true of Roethke's dizzying aphorisms. They are, indeed, "almost tail-flicks from another world, seen out of the corner of the eye" (SP 38).

This is not to say that these passages are created haphazardly. One can, to be sure, "interpret" them line by line; some of the lines do not even offer much difficulty. "What the grave says,/ The nest denies," for example, makes sense enough. Nest and grave, closely related images, suggest birth and death, and here the new life in the nest is a denial of the message of decay sent by the grave. Or, one might note that in the passage beginning "The wasp waits" the lines alternate between watchful repose and arduous and uncertain journeying. Or one might point to a familiar Roethkean pun in the line "—Who cares? The old owl?" since the association of the owl with the question that is his cry begins with "Where Knock Is Open Wide" and recurs throughout the sequence. But all of this is a little like explaining the impact of the American history film as if it had really been presented as a series of slides. It is to use a critical technique designed to illuminate that obscurity "which yields step by step with the construing of sentences" on poems whose meaning "shines from every sentence, withholds itself from the poem as a whole on repeated readings, but when it does yield 'explodes'" (*Letters* 138).

> The wasp waits.
> The edge cannot eat the center.

The grape glistens.
The path tells little to the serpent. . . .

As the reason fails to span the white space between lines or breaks
itself upon edge and center, we are thrown back upon the madman's insight. And in a world of language in which wasp and
grape and owl and wind are all holy mysteries, singing their own
songs, we may rediscover the child's spiritual dignity. And such
dignity and such insight are, I think, the illumination and excitement which finally "explode" from Roethke's whelm of
proverbs and questions and commands.

The dynamism of the *Lost Son Sequence* as a whole is implicit
in the quotation from Roethke with which I began this chapter.
"Each poem," he wrote, "is complete in itself; yet each in a sense
is a stage in a kind of struggle out of the slime . . ." (SP 37).
Each poem is complete in itself in that in each of them the lost
son grows, changes, or develops in some way. But the changing is
never completed, and each poem ends with an implied beginning,
with the sense that one is forever on the edge of something more.
And what is true of the individual poems is true of the entire sequence, for the effort "to become something more" is unending.
Even the final passage of "O, Thou Opening, O" insists that "going is knowing./ I see; I seek;/ I'm near" (CP 99). In one sense,
the sequence may be read as a search for "knowing," both the
sexual knowing that represents power—and love—and the mystical knowing that brings a man to some final illumination. But
what may finally be "known" is that we learn by going, that motion is all we know on earth, though not necessarily all we need to
know.

As I have already suggested, the opening of the sequence introduces the child's dream of potency, the dream of "having" something, of being able to "keep" it, of "being able" to do things, to
inflict pain with a bite or bring forth life as the cows do. "Where
Knock Is Open Wide" is a poem about the struggle to be born,
especially the struggle to create a self out of the language. The
child fights throughout the poem to assert an unqualified "I am."
He can say what he is not: "I'm not a mouse"; and he can say

what he was: "I was sad for a fish"; and he can say what he might
be: "Maybe I'm lost,/ Or asleep." But what he *is* seems quite
mysterious to him. At last he can say only that "I'm somebody
else now," a kind of partial knowledge, as if the "somebody" he
has become—better, to be sure, than being, or having, no body—
is still strange to him. But that uncertainty is appropriate, the
tentative questioning by which one journeys. "Have I come to always?" the child asks, and the answer is "Not yet" (CP 74). He
has come to nothing final, and the closing lines of the poem,
"Maybe God has a house./ But not here," suggest a setting out,
a dissatisfaction with "here" that serves as the motivation for
growth, for becoming as "high" as "have," high enough to have a
heaven like Papa, like God Himself.

The title of the second poem, "I Need, I Need" is appropriate,
for the lost son "needs" many things if he is to undertake so
perilous a journey. The boy finds himself trapped between fear of
his father ("Do the dead bite?") and disillusionment with his
mother ("Mamma, she's a sad fat"), and his weapons against these
emotions are knowing and wishing, the verbs on which the poem
turns. The jump-rope song of section two has one stanza made
entirely of wishes:

> I wish I was a pifflebob
> I wish I was a funny
> I wish I had ten thousand hats,
> And made a lot of money.   (CP 75)

The solution to "The Trouble" of the "No and Yes" of his
parents is to be something else, something more; to be, for example, a pifflebob, which, because it is nothing, might very well
be anything. To be a "funny" with "ten thousand hats" would
make the son ten thousand times more powerful than the mooly
man of "Where Knock Is Open Wide," a very potent figure indeed. And, of course, the wish to make a lot of money is a perfectly understandable symbol of adult power. Moreover, as the
old bromide has it, "knowledge is power." "A duck," the child
says, "knows something you and I don't," perhaps because the

duck is both diver and flier, capable of—in the boy's imagination
—visiting the bottom of the pond and soaring above the clouds.
In the final section of the poem, the boy makes ready to set out
again, presumably through the "gates" which are both sexual
and symbolic, gates to all adult experience. The "No and Yes"
which have been "The Trouble" have been replaced by affirmation—by "know" and "yes," a very different sort of thing:

> Her feet said yes.
> It was all hay.
> I said to the gate,
> Who else knows
> What water does?
> Dew ate the fire.
>
> I know another fire.
> Has roots.   (CP 76)

"Bring the Day!" is an appropriate title, for in this third poem
the son "rises" to encounter the darkness of that "cage" of skin
offered by a woman. The thinly disguised sexuality of bees and
lilies gives way to a clearer statement of sexual activity:

> The green grasses,—would they?
> The green grasses?—
> She asked her skin
> To let me in:
> The far leaves were for it.   (CP 77)

Section two of the poem concludes with a hymn to the boy's
awakening sexual prowess—as always a metaphor for development
of spiritual and creative power—which is a love song both to himself and to the quickening interaction of opposites by which the
world moves:

> When I stand, I'm almost a tree.
> Leaves, do you like me any?
> A swan needs a pond.
> The worm and the rose
> Both love
> Rain.   (CP 78)

"Bring the Day!" ends with a song in praise of wakenings. The past is given over: "Hardly any old angels are around any more. . . . The dust, the long dust, stays" (CP 78), and the boy who, in "Where Knock Is Open Wide," had asked "What's the time, papa-seed?" now has his answer. "It's time to begin!/ To begin!" (CP 78). The exclamation marks and repetition emphasize, of course, the beauty of beginnings, but the repetition forces us to hear the poem as ending "It's time to begin to begin" as well as to hear it as it is punctuated. In a world of continuous change, it is always time "to begin to begin," for—to reverse Eliot—the moment of birth is every moment. At any rate, the son's final emphatic declaration of independence commits him once again to life on the moving edge of the instant present.

The last three poems of part one of the sequence—"Give Way, Ye Gates," "Sensibility! O La!" and "O Lull Me, Lull Me"—all seem to me exercises in "knowing," specifically sexual knowing, but knowing in the broader sense as well. They have the rising and falling tensions of the sexual act, and one moves through repeated alternating passages of "over-aliveness" and torpor, urgency and release. So, Roethke might say, the spirit journeys. However, the imagery in which this journey is couched is decidedly of the flesh.

Roethke's "randy young man," no longer a child, now boasts of his capability. "I could love a duck," he says, "I could melt down a stone" (CP 79). Potency, the being able to be able, is his theme in the early going as the gates give way. Thus, the bird singing in "the bush of your bones" may—at some level—represent the spirit singing in the poet's flesh, but it also represents the phallus at creative play in the bush of the woman's pudendum. The (pussy) cat is after "great milk and vasty fishes" —a rather boastful description of masculine ejaculation—and the young man has let his nose out, his tail, his long bird, to poke about in the world of the "loved eye." The climax takes place at the end of section two:

> In the high-noon of thighs,
> In the springtime of stones,

We'll stretch with the great stems.
We'll be at the business of what might be
Looking toward what we are.   (CP 80)

As always when Roethke is at his best, the language stretches to
match his message. At the simplest level the "high-noon of thighs"
and "springtime of stones" suggest warmth and, perhaps, quickening life. But there is immense play in the idea of the thighs as a
kind of clock, with one phallic hand pointing straight (high) up;
and immense play in the pun on stones as testicles, coiling like a
spring to propel their contents. To "be at the business of what
might be" is a pretty fair description of creative work of any kind,
including the act of love-making, an act often consummated with
the partners facing one another—"Looking toward what [they]
are." But the "swinged instant" becomes the "aged instant" and
the long bird becomes a little owl. The transformation is both
frightening and humiliating:

Touch and arouse. Suck and sob. Curse and mourn.
It's a cold scrape in a low place.
The dead crow dries on a pole.
Shapes in the shade
Watch.   (CP 80)

There is the guilty sense of being watched, the unpleasantness of
"scraping" in a "low place." It is true that "Who stands in a hole/
Never spills" (CP 80), but it is equally true that "Who spills/
Never stands in a hole." What is most terrifying is that sense of
release, that yielding up of strength in the act that sixteenth
and seventeenth century poets termed "dying." The young man
must reconcile himself to dying in order to be reborn. He must remind himself that "What slides away/ Provides" (CP 80). We
create only by letting go; creation equals emission, and by such
"provision" does the world move.
    There is a temporary recovery in "Sensibility! O La!" when
the phallus—a truly protean hero—rises again:

A whisper of what,
You round dog?—
Is the wasp tender?
John-of-the-thumb's jumping;
Commodities, here we come!   (CP 81)

Once again the language, the rhythms, are "geared-up" to match the protagonist's excitement. Puns appear—is the wasp, for example, that great stinger, "tender" in the sense of being gentle or in the sense of being sore from over-work, a meaning quite plausible after his "cold scrape in a low place"? The jumping thumb takes us back to the father's rainbow thumb in "Where Knock Is Open Wide," joining wasp and rose and thumb and rose in an interaction of images which becomes more and more complex as the sequence goes on. And, of course, there is the delightful pun in which "Commodities" is heard as "come oddities," the sort of thing that one must hear if he is to get far in Roethke's world of words. The hero makes ready as "A shape comes to stay:/ The long flesh" (CP 81). But things go wrong; the final section of the poem turns into a nightmarish serial ordeal. There is an enveloping darkness peopled by figures that are never quite what they seem, beautiful shapes that turn into harpies and ghosts as the hero finds himself "alone with [his] ribs" (CP 82). The shape-shifting done by the phallus has been a cause of pride and delight, but the shifting now being done by the feminine principle creates uneasiness and anxiety. The "wrong wind" blows up, not the lovely "zephyr-hunted woodie," but the dark mother, Mamma in her "dark hood." Guilt and fear and loss of faith assail the lost son as he makes his way through the long grasses and the closing dark. "It's a long way to somewhere else," he realizes, and gathers his forces into a final, desperate affirmation:

My sleep deceives me.
Has the dark a door?
I'm somewhere else,—
I insist!
I am.   (CP 82)

The poem closes with the magic "I am" which, throughout the sequence, signifies strength and potency. The phrase is the *Shazam* by which the son takes on power; it is as if his words in this passage create a reality by insisting upon their own magical properties. The closing three lines may be read in many ways, but surely one reading might be that the hero, by insisting on being somewhere other than the terrible dark, finds that in fact he *is* "somewhere else." The tentative "I'm somebody else now" of "Where Knock Is Open Wide" has given way to an "I am," which, like "This is my body," has the power of creating, as Roethke puts it, "an actuality."

"O Lull Me, Lull Me" restores the lost son to grace as he passes through "the diocese of mice." "O lovely chink," he cries, "O white/ Way to another grace!" (CP 83). The way to grace in Roethke seems to be through the "O" of the "Opening O," a way that leads him to celebrate his own being and potency:

> For you, my pond,
> Rocking with small fish,
> I'm an otter with only one nose;
> I'm all ready to whistle;
> I'm more than when I was born;
> I could say hello to things;
> I could talk to a snail;
> I see what sings!
> What sings!   (CP 84)

It is a tribute to the power of love that the hero has arrived at his repeated "I am" by gazing at himself in the "pond," which he has stocked with "small fish." It is as if he learns what he is by seeing himself in the mirror of his loved one, his old nemesis. The phallic otter—a healthy specimen in a "diocese of mice"—is *all ready to* whistle, and *could* is the operative verb form of the passage. The lost son *could* say hello to things, *could* talk to a snail. The poem is open-ended, for one is left with a sense of enormous forces gathering, of energies about to be unleashed. The final lines echo in rhythm and construction the closing—which does not close— of "Bring the Day!" "It's time to begin!/ To begin!" (CP 78).

Part two of the sequence begins with "the dead cry" at Wood-lawn, with the "slamming of iron,/ A slow drip over stones." As the hero makes clear, "This is my hard time" (CP 53). What is needed is a Voice to come "out of the silence," one which will tell the lost son what he wants to know:

> Which is the way I take;
> Out of what door do I go,
> Where and to whom?   (CP 54)

The answers are various and confusing:

> Dark hollows said, lee to the wind,
> The moon said, back of an eel,
> The salt said, look by the sea,
> Your tears are not enough praise,
> You will find no comfort here,
> In the kingdom of bang and blab.   (CP 54)

But it must be the poet's own voice that comes out of the silence and creates the way by going where it has to go. The oddyssey takes shape only as the voice creates

> the pasture of flat stones,
> The three elms,
> The sheep strewn on a field, . . .
> the muddy pond-edge, . . . the bog-holes.   (CP 54)

The silence of tears is not praise enough, nor the banging of iron nor the blabbering condolence of cliché comfort enough. The words which must praise and comfort are to be created out of silence, and the artist is responsible for the making of the way and for the building of the door. In "The Lost Son" the way leads through the terror of *The Flight*, through the exhaustion of *The Pit*, through the frenetic activity, the rising agitation of *The Gibber*, and into the pure serene of memory in the beautiful sec-tion called *The Return*. Here at last the lost son finds a Voice—his own, or almost his own—capable of praise, and of comfort:

Once I stayed all night.
The light in the morning came slowly over the white
Snow.
There were many kinds of cool
Air.
Then came steam.

Pipe-knock.

Scurry of warm over small plants.
Ordnung! Ordnung!
Papa is coming!

A fine haze moved off the leaves;
Frost melted on far panes;
The rose, the chrysanthemum turned toward the light.
Even the hushed forms, the bent yellowy weeds
Moved in a slow up-sway.   (CP 57)

The moment in the greenhouse Eden when Papa brought light
and order, the moment in beginning winter when the light
stopped travelling over the field—these are Roethke's "white light
still and moving,/ *Erhebung* without motion," and, like comparable moments in Eliot, these experiences are the hints and
guesses upon which all faith resides. Because of such moments,
and because he may, in memorable speech, all but recapture them
though they are totally lost in the passages of time, he may wait,
and not without hope:

A lively understandable spirit
Once entertained you.
It will come again.
Be still.
Wait.   (CP 58)

Yet this passive state will not suffice. As Roethke puts it in his
long letter to Babette Deutsch, "the illumination is still only
partly apprehended; [the hero] is still 'waiting'" (*Letters* 141).
He must set out again, not to *find* an illumination but to *create*
one. The poet begins in darkness again and again, making the

light out of nothing but the magic of his voice. Poem after poem begins with the thought of death and with the language of death:

> A river glides out of the grass. A river or a serpent.
> A fish floats belly upward,
> Sliding through the white current,
> Slowly turning,
> Slowly.   (CP 59)

> Came to lakes, came to dead water,
> Ponds with moss and leaves floating,
> Planks sunk in the sand.   (CP 62)

> Eternity howls in the last crags,
> The field is no longer simple:
> It's a soul's crossing time.
> The dead speak noise.   (CP 89)

> Want weeping, little bones. But where?
> Wasps come when I ask for pigeons.
> The sister sands, they slipper soft away.
> What else can befall?   (CP 92)

The voice is anxious, the sentences terse and frequently truncated, without subjects. The imagery is oppressive, establishing a kind of wasteland as spiritual landscape. But out of such beginnings the poet sets about making a verbal gesture of cherishing, a gesture celebrating life and its motion. Some of Roethke's most fully orchestrated music grows out of the dead cry at Woodlawn, out of the noise the dead speak. Look, for example, at the closing passage of "A Field of Light" or "Praise to the End!" or "I Cry, Love! Love!" All "create a reality," a felt apprehension of sensory detail so lovely that it leads to an almost religious sense of unity. "The light becomes me" (CP 88), cries Roethke in the final line of "Praise to the End," a cry expressing the fullness of interpenetration between the self and the world. It is as if the long sought "illumination" is, at last, recognized to be as one with the self, with the voice that transforms silence into music, darkness into light. As in God's first "Let there be Light," *Light* and Light—word and event—"become" as one. The most perfect of all of Roethke's passages celebrating his world—lines which, to

my mind, are rivalled in American literature only by the closing
lines of Stevens's "Sunday Morning"—is the passage concluding
"The Shape of the Fire." In that poem the hero begins with an
imagistic portrayal of barrenness and sorrow, with the old scow
bumping over black rocks, the receding waters and the crying of
spiders. He goes on a terrible journey, going "Up over a viaduct
. . . to the snakes and sticks of another winter,/ A two-legged
dog hunting a new horizon of howls" (CP 65). He moves through
the dazzle of jump-rope chant and the whelm of proverb into—
once again—the serene of memory, "that minnowy world of
weeds and ditches,/ When the herons floated high over the white
houses . . ." (CP 66). And he comes for a moment to things
apprehended by, as he tells Babette Deutsch, "the mature man,"
the artist in full possession of his power:

> To have the whole air!—
> The light, the full sun
> Coming down on the flowerheads,
> The tendrils turning slowly,
> A slow snail-lifting, liquescent;
> To be by the rose
> Rising slowly out of its bed,
> Still as a child in its first loneliness;
> To see cyclamen veins become clearer in early sunlight,
> And mist lifting out of the brown cat-tails;
> To stare into the after-light, the glitter left on
>   the lake's surface,
> When the sun has fallen behind a wooded island;
> To follow the drops sliding from a lifted oar,
> Held up, while the rower breathes, and the small boat
>   drifts quietly shoreward;
> To know that light falls and fills, often without
>   our knowing,
> As an opaque vase fills to the brim from a quick pouring,
> Fills and trembles at the edge yet does not flow over,
> Still holding and feeding the stem of the contained
>   flower.   (CP 67)

To have; to be; to know. To extend in music the motion of light
until light becomes light within, the light that moves in us. "In

this kind of poem," says Roethke, "the poet should not 'comment' or use many judgment-words; instead he should render the experience. . . ." And then he adds, "You watch: What I say is true" (*Letters* 142).

The Old Woman's
Meditations and the
North American Sequence

In this chapter I intend to focus upon Roethke's dynamic imagery, imagery that comes to us through a mask and that evolves out of a need created by a dramatic situation. Roethke was never one to let go of a successful "trick" for creating energy in a poem, though he tried always to modify and improve such techniques as his career went along. It is not surprising then, that, having discovered in the *Lost Son Sequences* the advantages of speaking through a mask, Roethke should go on to develop more fully the possibilities inherent in the use of a dramatic persona. Of those *Lost Son Sequences* he had said, "To keep the rhythms, the language 'right,' i.e. consistent with what a child would say or at least to create the 'as if' of the child's world, was very difficult technically" (SP 41). In his new free verse sequences, *Meditations of an Old Woman* and *North American Sequence*, Roethke deliberately chooses to tackle the antithetical, and perhaps still more difficult, technical problem of how to keep his rhythms and language "right" for dramatic narrators who are as near death as the child narrator of "Where Knock Is Open Wide" is near birth. The new problem is, I think, more difficult because of the danger of falling into slack or "tired" rhythms which might, on the surface of things, seem justified by the slowing bodily rhythms of the old woman and the old man. In a letter to Ralph J. Mills, Jr., Roethke makes some comments that indicate that he was aware of that danger and that, indeed, he had written his "old lady poems," among other reasons, to demonstrate that meditative poetry need not be lacking in energy. Mills had written Roethke suggesting that parts of the *Meditations of an Old Woman* "seemed to contain parodies of Eliot," an observation which brought a rather strong rejoinder from the poet:

> Oh Christ, let's before the eye of God, try to wipe away the bullshit about both Willie & Tiresome Tom & say this:

> In both instances, I was animated in considerable part by arrogance: I thought: I can take this god damned high style of W. B. Y. or this Whitmanesque meditative thing of T. S. E. and use it for other ends, use it as well or better. Sure, a tough assignment. (*Letters* 231)

After a few remarks on his attempts to outdo Yeats's "god damned high style," Roethke returns to the matter of Eliot and his influence on the *Meditations of an Old Woman:*

> As for the old lady poems, I wanted (1) to create a character for whom such [Whitmanesque meditative] rhythms are indigenous; that she be a dramatic character, not just me. Christ, Eliot in the Quartets is tired, spiritually tired, old-man. Rhythm, Tiresome Tom. Is my old lady tired? The hell she is: she's tough, she's brave, she's aware of life and she would take a congeries of eels over a hassle of bishops any day. (*Letters* 231)

Though there are no letters to support my contention, I think the old man of *North American Sequence* is no more—and no less—"just" Roethke than is the old woman. He, too, is "tough" and "brave," an old codger with the spirit of a pioneer. When he says "Old men should be explorers?" the question mark reminds us that he is responding to (and challenging) Eliot. Roethke's old man will be "an Indian," the primitive in touch with the elemental energies of life, the daring redskin whose explorations take him ever deeper into the wilderness. His journey is to be no cook-out in the civilized campsite of religious ortho- doxy. Moreover, the dramatic tensions of exploration are height- ened, as they are for the old woman, by an awareness of impend- ing death that is present at every moment in every poem.

To be "aware of life," and both narrators have such an aware- ness, is to feel in one's muscles, joints, and pulse the thrust and surge of continuous change. Life is experienced as motion, and Roethke creates a kind of ethic out of how one responds to that motion. To be tough and brave is to refuse to give in to the fear of motion, or, better still, to exorcise one's fear by making musical gestures of cherishing and of celebration. Thus, old man and old woman become poets in their own defense, seekers after images by which they can represent the processes of time and change, seekers also after images by which they may make real their ap- prehension of the timeless and the changeless in the midst of flux. Perhaps those images by which they convey the dynamic energy which thrust them onward are not so much made as they are revealed, things torn from dreams, obsessions that will not let them go. To be "aware of life" is to be obsessed with journeying, with the dark drive into the swamp or out along a snowdrifted peninsula, with the blind plunge of black horses over a steep hill toward nothing the driver can see in time. "I dream of journeys repeatedly," says the old man; "Often I think of myself as riding," the old woman says. Confronted by such terrifying rhythms, such nightmarish imagery, it is difficult for them to find a language in which to be "brave" and "tough" to the end. The problem is, as the old woman puts it, "What Can I Tell My Bones?" for facile optimism, orthodox language, is not enough in the face of the gathering darkness, the rising waters. "It is difficult to say all things are well," the lady remarks, "When the worst is about to arrive" (CP 172).

At the most significant level, both sequences seem to me to be "about" an exploration in language, the search for rhythms and images which will give substance to those transcendent moments which both comfort and terrify. The old man and woman must discover or create—or half-discover and half-create—the experience of the eternal while being swirled about by the ever-flowing temporal. The narrators (and Roethke himself) must struggle to make an image of stillness which is intellectually and imaginatively as dynamic as the imagery of motion which runs through all of the poems. The paradox of "dynamic stillness," of how one may be still and still moving, is difficult to "talk about," still more difficult to "do" or present artistically. To outdo T. S. Eliot in writing about the same paradox is, for Roethke, part of the fun. To see the world in motion as Roethke did, and yet to have known moments in which his own motion matched the pace of that universal flowing so that it seemed as if he were not moving at all, as if he had attained a perfect stillness, made him rather intolerant of Eliot's more static world view and his—to Roethke's mind—facile mysticism. After all, Eliot had never risked his mind by intensifying the pace of life until "The profound desire to live to the fullest may change into an even more powerful will to die" (28, 26). "Not only is Eliot tired," Roethke writes to Ralph J. Mills, Jr., "he's a [. . .] fraud as a mystic—all his moments in the rose-garden and the wind up his ass in the draughty-smoke-fall-church yard" (*Letters* 231). The sequences, then, are journeys toward the stillness that grows out of motion, toward the image that combines the temporal with the eternal so effectively that the reader may experience the moment in and out of time and not simply be told about its existence. The energy of life is nowhere more felt in Roethke's poetry than in these strange images of moving stillness, of terrific repose.

I

In the bleak spiritual landscape of the butt-end of her life, Roethke's old lady begins by meditating on her condition. "[T]he sun," she knows, "brings joy to some," but for those to whom each day brings awareness of moving closer to death, the rising sun brings little joy. Indeed, "the rind, often, hates the life within," for the life within the fruit is that which surges and grows until the rind gives way, until ripeness becomes overripeness and finally decay. Moreover, though she is free from the geared-up over-aliveness of, say, the lost son, she is far from being at ease. There is a restlessness to her slowness, a paradoxical condition which she describes well:

> How can I rest in the days of my slowness?
> I've become a strange piece of flesh,
> Nervous and cold, bird-furtive, whiskery,
> With a cheek soft as a hound's ear.   (CP 157)

"Nervous" and "bird-furtive," the old, like the young, have their intolerable tensions, have the urge to do more and more with less and less time and with a body no longer always ready to cooperate.

The conditions of her life cause the old woman "Often" to think of herself "as riding," a thought which so captivates her that she turns it into an extended and extraordinarily concrete metaphor. She is alone, she thinks, riding on "a bus through western country."

> I sit above the back wheels, where the jolts are hardest,
> And we bounce and sway along toward the midnight,
> The lights tilting up, skyward, as we come over a little rise.
> Then down, as we roll like a boat from a wave-crest.
>
> All journeys, I think, are the same:
> The movement is forward, after a few wavers,
> And for a while we are all alone,
> Busy, obvious with ourselves,
> The drunken soldier, the old lady with her peppermints;
> And we ride, we ride, taking the curves
> Somewhat closer . . .   (CP 158)

This, the woman thinks, is her life—a bad trip through darkness and into the deeper darkness of midnight. Since there is nothing to see through the frosted bus windows, her impressions of motion are largely kinesthetic, the jolting over the back wheels, the bounce and sway, the rising and rolling as the bus takes the hills. Thus, the sense of forward motion is felt rather than perceived, and the woman is cut off by darkness from the pleasures of sight-seeing. Her loneliness is underscored by repetition. She tells us that she is riding alone and then—seven lines later—she remarks that "for a while we are all alone." She is not, of course, the only person on the bus, for the pronoun shifts from "I" to "we" and the journey is a collective journey, one containing a drunken soldier, a type-cast old lady. "All alone" becomes, I think, a pun, reminding us that all "journeys" through life are "the same" in that we are always strangers to one another, destined to get off as alone as we got on, finally busy, obvious, only with ourselves. The journey is already mildly unpleasant, for the jolting, bouncing, and swaying, the drunkenness of the soldier, the sense of overpowering loneliness, the outer darkness, perhaps even the scent of peppermints, all combine to produce a slight case of motion sickness. If life is a bus ride through the dark, it is, like most bus rides, a hard thing to endure.

Suddenly, however, as the passengers ride, they are passed by

> the trucks coming
> Down from behind the last ranges,
> Their black shapes breaking past;
> And the air claps between us,
> Blasting the frosted windows,
> And I seem to go backward,
> Backward in time. (CP 158)

It is difficult to tell from which direction the trucks pass the bus, but I prefer to think that they pass it "from behind," for such passing by a speedier vehicle would give an old woman on the bus the physical sensation of moving backward as the black shapes break past her window. Perhaps she has become so immersed in her thought, has allowed her metaphorical trip to become so real, that the illusion of moving backward on her purely imaginary bus "seems" able to take her "backward in time" to the greenhouse Eden of her childhood:

> Two song sparrows, one within a greenhouse,
> Shuttling its throat while perched on a wind-vent,

And another, outside, in the bright day,
With a wind from the west and the trees all in motion.
One sang, then the other,
The songs tumbling over and under the glass,
And the men beneath them wheeling in dirt to the cement
    benches,
The laden wheelbarrows creaking and swaying,
And the upspring of the plank when a foot left the runway.
(cp 158)

The memory is, as it were, preserved under glass—in this case
the glass walls of the greenhouse. And the return, the going backward in time, is the imagination's way of transforming the ugliness
of the present into the beautiful. The moment in the greenhouse
when the birds sang, like Eliot's moment in the rose-garden or
like Keats's moment in another garden when the nightingale sang,
seems one of those occasions set apart from the ordinary flow of
time, a "time" not in time when "reality comes closer." But
Roethke's old woman preserves her moment in motion. The bird
songs are heard melodies, not unheard ones; and the men and the
trees and the wheelbarrows and the planks of the runway are all
vibrating with energetic life. It is as if the instant and all of its
whirling forces are represented forever in the tumbling movement
of the music of the song sparrows. It is the shuttling throat, the
moving breath, the vibrations in the bright air that capture the
vitality of the moment and make it live again. "By singing we defend," says Roethke's old lady in her "Fourth Meditation"; by
singing one may create a moving pattern that reaches the still
point and is never wholly lost.

On the other hand, as Arnold Stein has correctly pointed out,
"Though the human witness of the scene can take it all in . . .
the interior scene of common human vitality leaves him out completely. Its motions are visible, audible, and near, but the activity
is also inaccessible—so fully engrossed in its own purposes, moving
by its own laws and interests, that the more exactly an outsider
sees and hears, the more he feels his remoteness." [1] In other
words, the memory cannot cheat so well as she is famed to do. As

the next section of the poem indicates, neither memory nor desire
—the mental journey into the past nor the mental journey into
the future—is wholly satisfactory:

> Journey within a journey:
> The ticket mislaid or lost, the gate
> Inaccessible, the boat always pulling out
> From the rickety wooden dock,
> The children waving;
> Or two horses plunging in snow, their lines tangled,
> A great wooden sleigh careening behind them,
> Swerving up a steep embankment.
> For a moment they stand above me,
> Their black skins shuddering:
> Then they lurch forward,
> Lunging down a hillside.   (CP 158–159)

The journey to the past is always blocked by the angel with the
sword. We have lost the ticket, lost the way through the last, remembered gate, have, as the saying goes, missed the boat. The
children who are waving are ourselves, and they are waving good-
bye to us, who can never rejoin them. And the journey into the
future is terrifying, marked by the terrific power of the horses and
the helplessness of the driver. The lines are tangled and the other
side of the summit can be known only by going where we have
to go. All that is certain is that we must follow the lurching
horses, careening out of control at a pace that—eventually—must
leave us breathless. Nonetheless, the song of the birds has provided
a basis for hope, though the bird song must be superseded by the
love song of the old lady herself, a chant of celebration that will
include both the stars and the stones.

Having established a metaphorical journey to represent the
motion of her flesh, and having established within that journey a
"seeming" movement backward through time—a movement of the
mind—the old lady turns her attention to the motion of the spirit
which, she has already told us, "moves, but not always upward"
(CP 157). "I believe," Roethke says in "Open Letter," "that to

go forward as a spiritual man it is necessary first to go back" (SP 39), and the third section of the "First Meditation" represents that slow progress. The woman offers two images for spiritual movement: the movement of a crab, tentative, hesitant, "sliding slowly backward"; and the movement of a salmon upstream, resting in back-eddy and inlet, and then swimming forward once again. The crab's retreat suggests escape from a spiritual blind alley, and this image of withdrawal combines with other imagery —such as the moon's paring itself to a thinness of nothing—to represent the "going back" that leads to "another life, / Another way and place in which to continue" (CP 159). The salmon's struggle against the current, "the rush of brownish-white water," leaves him "Still swimming forward" (CP 159). Roethke is very much aware of the pun on "Still" in that line, for it connotes more than the persistence of the fish. It also suggests that the spirit is "still and moving," that by vigorous effort against the motion carrying it toward death (and the sea) it manages to maintain itself in one place. The old woman seems to think of the spirit as journeying back toward its origin, and that it maintains its life by a thrusting back against time that is equal to or greater than the thrust of the current that would carry it down. The salmon's struggle is one way to maintain stillness in the midst of flux. There are others.

The final section of the opening meditation picks up the word *still* and connects it with happiness, happiness that prevails despite the absence of conventional faith in eternity. The old woman has searched the bleak landscape of "the waste lonely places / Behind the eye" and found only "the motes of dust in the immaculate hallways, / The darkness of falling hair, the warnings from lint and spiders" (CP 159). Amid these intimations of mortality there are no signs, "no riven tree, or lamb dropped by an eagle" (CP 159). There are, however, "still times," as the woman calls them, and again the pun is fully operative. They are not times of silence, for they are characterized by the songs of birds, but they are times that remain to her even among the warnings from lint

and spiders, times that seem—like the greenhouse moment—to
stand outside of the flowing of life.

> The cerulean, high in the elm,
> Thin and insistent as a cicada,
> And the far phoebe, singing,
> The long plaintive notes floating down,
> Drifting through leaves, oak and maple,
> Or the whippoorwill, along the smoky ridges,
> A single bird calling and calling;
> A fume reminds me, drifting across wet gravel;
> A cold wind comes over stones;
> A flame, intense, visible,
> Plays over the dry pods,
> Runs fitfully along the stubble,
> Moves over the field,
> Without burning.   (CP 159–60)

Once again, stillness emerges from the pure vibration, the motion,
that is song. The music of the birds takes on substance, becomes
"thin," is experienced as "floating" and "Drifting." Throughout
the sequence, bird song is the madeleine cake, the scent of tea,
that enables the old woman to be in two places at once, to be
still and still moving. Like the song of Keats's nightingale, the music takes us out of time and, however briefly, into eternity, for the
song is as it was and as it ever shall be. It is as if, at last, the song
bursts into flame, a moving energy that "Plays" and "Runs" over
the stubble but does not consume. The single bird "calling and
calling" creates a motion so intense that it becomes visible, like
flame, shapeless and dancing. Only in art, in song, does one create
the energy that feeds upon life and yet does not consume, the
fire that flares from pod and stubble, yet does not burn. "In such
times," the narrator concludes, "lacking a god, / I am still happy"
(CP 196).

As is so often the case in the Roethkean sequence, the narrator
has slipped back into spiritual despondency in the space between
poems. In "I'm Here," the old woman finds herself displaced by

"The prattle of the young," a kind of affront to her age. She cannot help a pang of jealousy when "young voices, mixed with
sleighbells" come toward her across snow. And though the sun
loosens the frost on her windows and sets the ice to glittering,
still there is a resistance involved, a part of her which declines,
which would shrink into a corner, sleep with her horse like a
witch.

As in the "First Meditation" when she wished to get off the
bus, the old woman seeks refuge by journeying backward in time.
The rhythms change, the questions disappear, the lines begin to
run on and the participles impart life and movement to her remembered girlhood:

> I was queen of the vale—
> For a short while,
> Living all my heart's summer alone,
> Ward of my spirit,
> Running through high grasses,
> My thighs brushing against flower-crowns;
> Leaning, out of all breath,
> Bracing my back against a sapling,
> Making it quiver with my body. . . .   (CP 161)

Even in repose, she is in motion, for her heaving energy sets up
vibrations in the sapling as she rests against it. And she recalls
another time, perhaps from her adolescence:

> I remember walking down a path,
> Down wooden steps toward a weedy garden;
> And my dress caught on a rose-brier.
> When I bent to untangle myself,
> The scent of the half-opened buds came up over me.
> I thought I was going to smother.   (CP 162)

These are the "ill-defined dyings" of growth, and the imagery of
smothering, of being "out of all breath," is a way of representing
the small deaths necessary to come to "another place and time, /
Another condition." In each memory the girl, and then the young

woman, is arrested in motion, and in each her stopping and her breathless condition coincide. At such moments

> The body, delighting in thresholds,
> Rocks in and out of itself.
> A bird, small as a leaf,
> Sings in the first
> Sunlight.   (CP 163)

The connection between the singing bird and the something that "rocks" in and out of itself is made here by juxtaposition and is made more explicit almost immediately in the closing stanza of section three:

> In my grandmother's inner eye,
> So she told me when I was little,
> A bird always kept singing.
> She was a serious woman.   (CP 163)

Surely Roethke intends us to feel the pun contained in this hearing "eye." The grandmother's inner "I" is, of course, her spirit, a sanctuary for the "happy melodist, unwearied," who may forever pipe songs forever new. Thus, for the first time, bird song and the inner "I," the "I" which sometimes stands outside one's self or runs before one "like a child," are joined.

Having devoted sections two and three of "I'm Here" to memories of moments of delight in thresholds, the old woman turns in section four to ways of keeping and holding in the present. She begins with the dying geranium, replanted again and again, but dying nonetheless, "Still leaning toward the last place the sun was" (CP 163). Like the geranium, the old woman is dying "for all I can do," but she, too, leans toward the light even when the light has gone. For example, she has learned the joys of "the fresh after-image," discovers she can "wear" roses by "looking away," as if, like Wordsworth, she discovers in the passing moment "life and food / For future years." Such "after-images" provide a "still" joy, exist "Without commotion." As if to offer an example, she says,

> Look at the far trees at the end of the garden.
> The flat branch of that hemlock holds the last of the sun,
> Rocking it, like a sun-struck pond,
> In a light wind.   (CP 163)

The image is, I think, one of Roethke's more successful presentations of a moving stillness, a dynamic "holding." Earth, air, fire, and water are combined in the figure of the garden and the fiery light that there metamorphizes into water and air. The hemlock branch "holds" the sun, that traditional symbol of time and flux, by rocking it; like the moments "held" by music, the light in the hemlock is preserved by motion, not by fixity. That last light becomes a pond, true, and not a river, but it is a pond vibrating at the touch of a light wind. Perhaps it is worth noting that it is the vigor of the mind in motion, the energy of the imagination, that turns light to water, air to light, and so preserves for us the moment with such music as poetry makes.

The poem concludes on a note of, as Roethke would have it, brave toughness. The old woman dismisses death, insofar as it is possible to do such a thing: "Even carp die in this river. . . . I've all the singing I would. . . . It's not my first dying" (CP 164). Finally she addresses the wind, that imageless image of energy without shape, the moving nothing which is one of her symbols for the flowing of all things:

> If the wind means me,
> I'm here!
> Here.   (CP 164)

In "Her Becoming," the old woman summarizes her education. She has learned to "sit quietly" while "In the back of my mind running with the rolling water, / My breast wild as the waves" (CP 165). The energy of the mind takes the place of the energy of the spirit; the soul must become more vigorous for every tatter in its mortal dress. Like her "serious" grandmother, the narrator thinks that her inner "eye" may contain a bird. "Am I a bird?" she asks, and goes on to say,

> A voice keeps rising in my early sleep,
> A muffled voice, a low sweet watery noise.
> Dare I embrace a ghost from my own breast?
> A spirit plays before me like a child,
> A child at play, a wind-excited bird.   (cp 165)

The image of bird and child, joined here for the first time, comes to stand for the "ghost from the soul's house," the eternal spirit which is here, as everywhere in Roethke, seen in motion, "rising," "playing," "wind-excited."

The poem then turns into one of Roethke's most extended figures for the mystical experience, for the time "when reality comes closer." The old woman remembers once again a sense of doubleness, of a self running ahead of herself—as if the greater velocity, greater energy, of the "inner I" might race into the elusive "Now" which we humans are never quite able to capture. Again there is the petit death of lessening breath, a momentary pause during which "All natural shapes became symbolical," and then "I shed my clothes to slow my daemon down. / And then I ran again" (CP 166). The shedding of clothes has, of course, the effect of renewal, and the rhythms of flight become more frantic, become faster and faster as they build to a climax in which breath grows out of breathlessness, song out of silence:

> Who can believe the moon?
> I have seen! I have seen!—
> The line! The holy line!
> A small place all in flame.
>
> Out, out, you secret beasts,
> You birds, you western birds.
> One follows fire. One does.
> My breath is more than yours.
>
> What lover keeps his song?
> I sigh before I sing.
> I love because I am
> A rapt thing with a name.   (cp 167)

As in the final lines of "First Meditation," fire and song merge, though here at last the breath of the poetic voice is "more" than the breath of the outer birds, those sparrows and vireos with their tiny cheepings. The spirit sings out of love—for the "loved fox, and the wren," and, presumably, for all the creatures which, in moments when "reality comes closer," become symbolical and reveal something of their creator. The closing section of "Her Becoming" is, to my mind, one of Roethke's most triumphant attempts to find images which manage to convey pure energy:

> Ask all the mice who caper in the straw—
> I am benign in my own company.
> A shape without a shade, or almost none,
> I hum in pure vibration, like a saw.
> The grandeur of a crazy one alone!—
> By swoops of bird, by leaps of fish, I live.
> My shadow steadies in a shifting stream;
> I live in air; the long light is my home;
> I dare caress the stones, the field my friend;
> A light wind rises: I become the wind.   (cp 167)

In the opening section of the poem, the woman has seen herself as "A mad hen in a far corner of the dark," and she returns to that image here by using the capering mice in the straw of the barn as references for the benign nature of "a crazy one alone." Again, there is the sense of doubleness, for the phrase "in my own company" is not merely a colloquialism as Roethke uses it, but suggests the presence of an "inner I" as well as an outer "I." To be outside one's self is, it seems to me, occupation for a madman or a saint, and Roethke's lady is choosing to be modest in claiming here to be the former. At any rate, the one who sings with a breath more than the breath of birds has become her music, "A shape without a shade," who hums "in pure vibration, like a saw." Becoming her voice, an almost pure motion, she lives by swoops and leaps, oscillating so rapidly as to be all but without a shadow. And paradoxically, her moving shadow "steadies in a shifting stream" because it shifts as the stream shifts and so comes to a kind of "steadiness" in constant motion. It is, as Roethke puts it in "The Waking," the shaking which keeps her steady. "I live in air," says the woman, both a pun on musical airs and on

the wind she is about to become, "the long light is my home."
Light, pure oscillation at the highest speed possible in the universe, is the perfect "home" for the "enlightened" one who
hums "in pure vibration." Once again light and wind merge as
co-images of shapeless energy when "A light wind rises," and
the old woman—she who "lives in air"—at last "becomes the
wind."

The "Fourth Meditation" begins with an ambiguous line: "I
was always one for being alone" (CP 168). Most obviously, it
tells us that the old woman was never a bridge-player, one of
those "Matchmakers, arrangers of picnics," whom she will casti-
gate later. She was, instead, one who sought—and sometimes
found—"eternal purpose," a search which is not, for Roethke, a
group undertaking. Less obviously, "I was always one for being
alone" suggests that the old woman was always one for seeking
pure "being" rather than the usual human experience of being
about to be or of having been. Her search has made her an edge-
walker, a searcher on the edge of fields, on beaches, along the
edges of "green embankments." From such perspectives she can
occasionally know both "the sinuousness" of the flowing waters
and the eternal calm of the "inner eye," that pool which moves
even as it is still:

> As a chip or shell, floating lazily with a slow current,
> A drop of the night rain still in me,
> A bit of water caught in a wrinkled crevice,
> A pool riding and shining with the river,
> Dipping up and down in the ripples,
> Tilting back the sunlight.   (CP 168)

The image of the riding pool made of night rain, still and yet
"Dipping up and down" and "Tilting back" the sunlight of day,
is another of those figures which manage to make a metaphorical
intersection of the timeless with time. In that eye-like "wrinkled
crevice," past and present, darkness and light, water and fire, pool
and river become a harmonious whole. There is an enormous
energy "caught" in the rocking stillness of that riding and shining
pool.

In section two, the old woman turns her meditation toward
self-definition. "What is it," she asks, "to be a woman?"

> To be contained, to be a vessel?
> To prefer a window to a door?
> A pool to a river?
> To become lost in a love,
> Yet remain only half aware of the intransient glory?
> To be a mouth, a meal of meat?
> To gaze at a face with the fixed eyes of a spaniel?   (CP 169)

Surely it is none of these things, for such static figures suggest a
kind of death-in-life which the old woman goes on to make more
specific as she thinks of the women about her, of "the self involved":

> The ritualists of the mirror, the lonely drinkers,
> The minions of benzedrine and paraldehyde,
> And those who submerge themselves deliberately in trivia,
> Women who become their possessions,
> Shapes stiffening into metal. . . .   (CP 169)

The "stiffening" shapes, the young "Frozen" into "baleful silence"
—such rigidity characterizes death, not life, and the old woman
is overwhelmed by pity which becomes prayer.

> How I wish them awake!
> May the high flower of the hay climb into their hearts;
> May they lean into light and live;
> May they sleep in robes of green, among the ancient ferns;
> May their eyes gleam with the first dawn;
> May the sun gild them a worm;
> May they be taken by the true burning;
> May they flame into being!—   (CP 169)

The passage reminds me of Roethke's attitude—as reported by
Allan Seager—toward his students at Bennington: " 'Ah, I know
it's lugging pork up Parnassus . . . but you get 'em up there
once, they see what it is. They're better then than they'll ever be
again.' " [2] Seager goes on to say:

He was out to create people anew, to implant or uproot, re-arrange, abrade if necessary, their sensibilities, to tear down and trample on all familial and social veils between themselves and the world as he saw it . . . and expose their little naked spirits, lift them up with love or drag them by sheer force of will up to the level where they could confront the most important thing in the world which was, of course, poetry, confront, comprehend, and sing it themselves.[3]

The desire is dynamic, an urge to stir things up, to "uproot," "re-arrange," "lift," "drag," and "lug" those minions of the mirror to the place where the soul makes its own authentic music, to the place in which they might, at last, "flame into being."

The prayer that the old woman utters becomes its own answer, for as she speaks the words of her wishing, the wish is transformed into a kind of musical vision. For an instant the women are seen as they might become, seen "as figures walking in a greeny garden, / Their gait formal and elaborate, their hair a glory, / The gentle and beautiful still-to-be-born . . ." (CP 170). The passage is a hymn to the evolutionary process, that motion by which the "descendants of the playful tree-shrew" grew thumbs, endured their slow changes, and became men, became women. The gentle and beautiful women are seen in motion which is the culmination of eons of motion, their stately and formal gait the beautiful, ordered culmination of the myriad "small beginnings" and the violent fury of the processes of time and change. The passage also celebrates the evolution of language from "the coarse short-hand of the subliminal depths" into a "grave philosophical language," and, in the celebration, combines the short-hand and the grave language into the fully realized language of poetry.

The "Fourth Meditation" concludes by affirming that "By singing we defend." "Is my body speaking?" asks the old woman.

> I breathe what I am:
> The first and last of all things.
> Near the graves of the great dead,
> Even the stones speak.   (CP 170)

If the breath that speaks becomes the body, becomes "what I am," then speech—the poem—becomes a kind of immortal equivalent for the tattered cloak of flesh. The poem is a moving pattern of sound which, by its motion and energy, reaches the still center of things and is not swept away. Thus, near "the graves of the great dead"—and for Roethke the great dead are always poets —"Even the stones speak." Hyperbole, to be sure. But is it possible to stand at the grave of, say, Robert Frost and not hear in one's "inner ear" the sounds of memorable speech? The energy that made his poems still vibrates in the receptive mind. And the landscape of New England through which he moved is colored forever by the sound of his voice, by the words with which he made the world he saw.

The final poem of the sequence, "What Can I Tell My Bones?" is a kind of summation of the whole. What to "tell" or "say" to the body "When the worst is about to arrive" is the question with which the old woman has been struggling all along. "Loved heart, what can I say?" she asks, for there are so many voices clamoring to be heard:

> The self says, I am;
> The heart says, I am less;
> The spirit says, you are nothing.   (CP 172)

The ego affirms itself; the clock in the body says it is diminished; the spirit, standing aside from the flesh, sees the bones as "nothing." Small wonder the woman lives in a whelm of questions: "The cause of God in me—has it gone? / Do these bones live? Can I live with these bones?" The need for answers prompts a desire to escape the rational, to be delivered "into the realm of pure song." The juxtaposition of stanzas suggests to me that "the realm of pure song" is that state of being in which one finally achieves that moving stillness which partakes of the eternal:

> To try to become like God
> Is far from becoming God.
> O, but I seek and care!   (CP 172)

I do not know exactly what Roethke means when he speaks of becoming "like God." Perhaps simply to be immortal, something which song can—in a limited way—achieve. Perhaps he was thinking of God as did Henry Vaughan, who, in Roethke's words, "was literally overwhelmed by movement in the world, not merely as movement but as a manifestation of the divine" (60, 12). If so, pure song and pure movement—movement without shape or shadow—are again being equated.

The final section of the poem and the sequence is a gradual altering from "The barest speech of light among the stones" into a fully orchestrated music introduced by the old woman's ecstatic assertion that she is "released from the dreary dance of opposites," that she lives "in light's extreme," stretches "in all directions" (CP 173).

> The sun! The sun! And all we can become!
> And the time ripe for running to the moon!
> In the long fields, I leave my father's eye;
> And shake the secrets from my deepest bones;
> My spirit rises with the rising wind;
> I'm thick with leaves and tender as a dove,
> I take the liberties a short life permits—
> I seek my own meekness;
> I recover my tenderness by long looking.
> By midnight I love everything alive.
> Who took the darkness from the air?
> I'm wet with another life.
> Yea, I have gone and stayed.   (CP 173)

The passage is a song of becoming. Some things are left behind—the secrets of the deepest bones, the father's eye—and others are rediscovered "by long looking." The short, end-stopped lines, offered as in the *Lost Son Sequence*, without "rational" connectives, give an impression of gradually increasing speed and power, especially as the lines begin to shorten. The "becoming" ends with a birth, with the wetness of another life, and the woman finds that she has "gone and stayed." She has burst out of darkness into

love and light ("Who took the darkness from the air?") and
found it good. And that, finally, is what she can tell her bones.
That beginnings are perpetual, that rebirth has been felt, experienced, known. The hints half-guessed, those vague intimations of
the eternal that may be half-glimpsed among the flickerings of the
temporal, have been made "clear,"

> As if released by a spirit
> Or agency outside me.
> Unprayed-for,
> And final. (CP 173)

II

My reading of the *North American Sequence* is not the first to
give attention to the patterns of thematic imagery running
throughout the six poems. Hugh Staples, in his pioneering article,
"The Rose in the Sea-Wind," writes of Roethke's imagery of
"elemental opposition: earth and water (or land and sea); fire
and darkness (or flame and shadow)." [4] Karl Malkoff accepts
Staples's emphasis upon imagery, but finds him guilty of "ignoring
complexity," of failure to recognize that "Water, for example,
appears as stagnant pond, flowing stream, and rocking, engulfing
sea, with different implications associated with each aspect. . . ." [5]
Malkoff does little with this notion, however, not bothering to
note that even in his own brief example it is motion that determines the "implications" of Roethke's imagery. As Malkoff himself acknowledges, his discussion is primarily concerned with the
content of the sequence rather than with its form, and in his
study "There is no room . . . for a detailed analysis of this
imagery. . . ." [6] My own discussion is not, perhaps, "detailed,"
but it does have the advantage of focussing upon motion and
energy, of demonstrating how Roethke's elemental images of fire,
air, earth, and water alter in meaning and value as Roethke makes
the elements speed up or slow down.

"The Longing" begins with a vision of stagnancy, a bleak place

> In a bleak time, when a week of rain is a year,
> The slag-heaps fume at the edge of raw cities:
> The gulls wheel over their singular garbage;
> The great trees no longer shimmer;
> Not even the soot dances.   (cp 187)

As always in Roethke, there is a correspondence between outer and inner weather, outer and inner landscape. In such a place, in such a time,

> the spirit fails to move forward,
> But shrinks into a half-life, less than itself,
> Falls back, a slug, a loose worm
> Ready for any crevice,
> An eyeless starer.   (cp 187)

The spirit shrinks, but it is a shrinking that promises energy, like the "shrinking" of a coiled spring. When life comes to a still-stand, it is time to "fall back" and search for a new beginning, for "any crevice" through which energy may thrust itself. There is, of course, Roethke's familiar pun on "eyeless," for when the spirit is "less than itself" the "inner I" is correspondingly "less." In section two, the narrator equates the motion of body and soul, noting that opposites demand one another, that emptiness demands fulfillment, that the thinnest moon must become less before it can be more. "Out of these nothings," he notes, "All beginnings come" (CP 188).

The "I" returns with a vengeance in the final section of the poem as Roethke turns to, as Malkoff puts it, "A Whitmanesque concentration on the first person wish. . . ." [7] *Would* is the operative verb form, a way of emphasizing the longing that has grown out of stagnation:

> I would with the fish, the blackening salmon, and the mad
>   lemmings,
> The children dancing, the flowers widening.
> I would unlearn the lingo of exasperation, all the distortions of
>   malice and hatred;
> I would believe my pain: and the eye quiet on the growing
>   rose;

> I would delight in my hands, the branch singing, altering the
>   excessive bird;
> I long for the imperishable quiet at the heart of form;
> I would be a stream, winding between great striated rocks in
>   late summer. . . . (CP 188).

Roethke's old man yearns to be moving, to be one with the migrating salmon and lemmings, with the dancing children and
widening flowers. It is interesting that the only use of the verb
to long in the poem called "The Longing" is linked with the
desire not for motion but for quiet, "the imperishable quiet at the
heart of form." However, the longing for quiet is, in turn, juxta-
posed with the wish to be "a stream," a winding form, contained
between rocks and yet flowing with energy. In the "redolent disorder of this mortal life," quiet grows out of motion just as
shadow changes suddenly into flame. The narrator realizes that he
has made a beginning out of the spiritual nothingness in which
he began, and his figure for that beginning is the escape from the
whale's mouth, an escape from darkness into darkness, from the
mouth of the whale to the mouth of the night. The dark land in
which he finds his "I" is very different from the landscape of
slag-heap, garbage, and petroleum with which the poem opens.
He has gone from stench to stench, from the "kingdom of stinks
and sighs" to the "country of few lakes," where,

> In the summer heat, I can smell the dead buffalo,
> The stench of their damp fur drying in the sun,
> The buffalo chips drying. (CP 189)

But the stink of civilization and its pollutants is very different in
Roethke's value system from the organic stink of decaying materials returning to the earth in order to begin new life. The raw
cities smell of death, but the buffalo chips have the scent of the
root cellar, that fetid womb in which even the dirt keeps breathing a small breath.

The concluding segment of the poem is alive with beginnings,
but beginnings which are possible only because the old man has

had the courage to move backward in time, in space, in degree of civilization:

> Old men should be explorers?
> I'll be an Indian.
> Ogalala?
> Iroquois. (CP 189)

The Indian remains for Roethke the symbolic figure of the wise primitive, the man who is—as Roethke himself wished to be— one with Nature. The closing lines shorten into silence, ending with the magic gutturals and labials of tribal names. Perhaps, as the echo would suggest, Roethke is glancing at Eliot and the abstract language of *The Four Quartets*. It is as if Roethke is setting out, explorer-fashion, to "unlearn the lingo of exasperation" and to discover a new language, one more elemental and less distorted by malice and hatred than is that "civilized" lingo so fraught with high-level abstraction and with euphemism. The remainder of the sequence, then, is Roethke's exploration, his search for a language full of that "imperishable quiet at the heart of form."

"Meditation at Oyster River" begins with impressions of stillness and silence, gathering darkness and incoming tide. The silence that spreads out from the word *Iroquois* at the end of "The Longing" becomes a "heard silence" as the tide-ripples move in "almost without sound" and the gulls grow silent until there is "No sound from the bay" (CP 190). It is a silence defined by absences, for Roethke reminds us of what is not there, of the gull's "cat-mewing" and "child-whimpering." And, as is so often the case in Roethke's poetry, silence and motionlessness are joined, for there is "No violence" from the bay, and the wind is so light that it turns "not a leaf, not a ripple" (CP 190). The voice of the old man echoes the "tongues of water" that come creeping in so quietly over the stones. The passage seems to be an attempt to make a quiet that speaks, an eloquent silence. The quiet tongues of the waves speak a language of diminutions, as light, sound, and motion gradually lessen toward the nothing from which all beginnings come. Finally there is only the crackling of a fire, the slight movement of a fish raven on its dead-tree perch, the reflected last light glinting faintly from black wings.

But when all has faded to the very edge of non-being, still "The self persists like a dying star . . ." (CP 190). The simile is apt, for such a star gives off energy in the form of light which goes on travelling through space long after the star has ceased to exist. The thought of death gives rise to the desire to be "with" water and "the shy beasts":

> the deer at the salt-lick,
> The doe with its sloped shoulders loping across the highway,
> The young snake, poised in green leaves, waiting for its fly,
> The hummingbird, whirring from quince-blossom to morning-
> glory. (CP 190)

The animals offer alternating images of potential and kinetic energy, for deer and snake and bird go on with the motion that is life, though the face of death rises again and again. Just so, the water coming forward "without cessation" is altered by sand-bars, kelp, and driftwood and persists in its motion despite all.

At the quiet edge, "The flesh takes on the pure poise of the spirit," and desire—the desire to be "with" the shy beasts and the water—turns to memory. The memories, appropriately enough, are memories of water, "Of the first trembling of a Michigan brook in April" and of "the Tittebawasee, in the time between winter and spring, / When the ice melts along the edges in early afternoon" (CP 191). In each case, the imagery of water is associated with beginnings, first with the tiny power of a cascade "Small enough to be taken in, embraced, by two arms" and then with the sluggish forward movement "As the piled ice breaks away from the battered spiles, / And the whole river begins to move forward, its bridges shaking" (CP 191). The poem has shifted from images of diminishing motion to these figures in which water is beginning to flow, figures which promise an ever-increasing energy as stream and river pick up speed.

In the final section, the narrator is still and moving, still sit-

ting on his rock, but able to watch "the spirit" at play, running in
and out of the small waves with "the intrepid shorebirds." He is
in that "watery drowse," that "half-sleep," which in Roethke's
poetry so often precedes the violent urge and wrestle leading to
resurrection:

> Now, in this waning of light,
> I rock with the motion of morning;
> In the cradle of all that is,
> I'm lulled into half-sleep
> By the lapping of water,
> Cries of the sandpiper.   (CP 191)

The sea is, of course, the cradle of all that is, and the gentle rocking of its saline lappings stirs preconscious memories of life in the
womb and of the birthday that begins with water. The rhythm
of life, that alternation of opposites wherein winter is forever
devising summer in its breast, goes on. As full darkness comes
down, the sea and the old man rock "with the motion of morning," the motion of new beginnings. "In the first of the moon,"
the narrator concludes, "All's a scattering, / A shining" (CP 192).
Thus the poem, which began with the "deepening light" of the
evening tide, closes with the great "All" shining with moonlight.
It is, to be sure, a scattered light, one that must be gathered and
focussed, but this light from "the first of the moon" is somehow
just right for beginning the "long journey out of the self."

That journey is a highly dynamic one—a journey without
maps, or rather, a journey for which one must make his map as
he goes along. "Going is knowing," as Roethke puts it. I think
Hugh Staples fails to realize Roethke's dynamism, and so goes
wrong in his article on the *North American Sequence*. Though
often very perceptive in his reading, Staples is given to treating
Roethke as if he were a much more didactic and static poet than
is in fact the case. For example, according to Staples, the "Meditation at Oyster River"

> explores one way out of the dilemma presented by the over-
> ture. By heroic measures a man must reject the past and its

implications, escape from the pressures of reality, and return to a temporary, though ultimately unsatisfactory condition of childlike innocence.[8]

Whenever a critic begins to talk about Roethke's work as if it were a fixed "map" leading to the Heavenly City—by the next paragraph Staples is likening the *North American Sequence* to *Pilgrim's Progress*—he inevitably begins at the same time to distort the nature of the poetry. It is not simply that Staples is wrong here—though Roethke's memories of the Michigan rivers of his past are not rejected, and Roethke would hardly use the word *reality* so carelessly as does his reader—but it is more the use of the word *must*, as if the sole purpose of the poem were to tell one how to be saved. It is true enough that, on one level, Roethke's work is, in Staples's phrase, "a quest for salvation," but it is a quest that demands a continuously altering pace and direction, for the terrain through which one journeys is changed in every instant. Roethke offers no maps; he does offer an instinctive hunger for change, growth, and development. There is no way in which a man "must" behave. There is only the going, by which we learn at last where we have to go.

The "Journey to the Interior," for example, is part of the "long journey out of the self," so that, in Roethke, the way in is the way out, the way out the way in, just as "to go forward as a spiritual man it is necessary first to go back" (SP 39). There are many detours, many blind alleys, which are found to lead nowhere only after one has risked everything by travelling down them. The first two sections of the poem offer contrasting journeys; section one, a metaphorical drive, and section two, a drive remembered. The metaphorical trip ends badly:

> the path narrowing,
> Winding upward toward the stream with its sharp stones,
> The upland of alder and birchtrees,
> Through the swamp alive with quicksand,
> The way blocked at last by a fallen fir-tree,
> The thickets darkening,
> The ravines ugly.   (CP 193)

To go forward as a spiritual man, the driver is going to have to back out, a most difficult job on such a path and with darkness coming on. The route is characterized by its increasing difficulty, for the path grows steeper as it narrows so that the car must go slower and slower until it finally stops. Thus, path, speed, and daylight all narrow toward another of those nothings from which, one hopes, all beginnings must come.

Yet the difference between the two journeys—the one ending in terror and the other in epiphany—is not entirely a matter of choosing the right road. Both routes are dangerous, but the attitude of the driver toward the danger is different in section two. The driver in section one is cautious, afraid of speed, distrusting the road. "Better to hug close," he tells himself, "wary of the rubble and falling stones" (CP 193). But the second driver, a portrait of the narrator as a young man, delights in speed and in the hazards of the road:

> I remember how it was to drive in gravel,
> Watching for dangerous down-hill places, where the wheels
>   whined beyond eighty—
> When you hit the deep pit at the bottom of the swale,
> The trick was to throw the car sideways and charge over the
>   hill, full of the throttle.
> Grinding up and over the narrow road, spitting and roaring.
> A chance? Perhaps. But the road was part of me, and its
>   ditches,
> And the dust lay thick on my eyelids,—Who ever wore
>   goggles?   (CP 193)

The speed is violent, and the driver thrusts himself into an incalculable situation as he roars over the hilltop, his daring asserted by his contempt for the sort of man who might be caught wearing goggles. The journey begins in the simple past tense, but as the pace quickens, it shifts to a flurry of participles as the drive takes on the velocity of a catalog passage:

> Always a sharp turn to the left past a barn close to the
>   roadside,

To a scurry of small dogs and a shriek of children,
The highway ribboning out in a straight thrust to the North,
To the sand dunes and fish flies, hanging, thicker than moths,
Dying brightly under the street lights sunk in coarse concrete,
The towns with their high pitted road-crowns and deep gutters,
Their wooden stores of silvery pine and weather-beaten red
    courthouses,
An old bridge below with a buckled iron railing, broken by
    some idiot plunger;
Underneath, the sluggish water running between weeds,
    broken wheels, tires, stones. . . .   (CP 193-4)

Roethke pulls out all stops to attain energy here—the short phrases, the "ing" verb forms, the alliteration, the flurry of half-sketched images. And suddenly we are in the present tense. As the driver passes the cemetery, dead snakes, dying bushes, he plunges into the realization that "I am not moving but they are . . ." (CP 194). Like his counterpart in section one, this driver has come to a stand-still. The difference is that he has arrived at stillness by attaining enormous speed, while the first driver comes to stillness by cautiously going slower and slower until at last he is unable to move forward at all. It is as if the second driver reaches a velocity so great that he hurtles across the gap of $\frac{1}{30}$ of a second which forever separates man from experiencing the instantaneous present, as if he finally arrives at a speed equal to the flowing of life itself, and thus seems not to be moving at all. At such a speed, he plunges into the eternal present—signified by the shift in tense—and the image of the sea returns, superimposed upon the grassy plain:

I rise and fall in the slow sea of a grassy plain,
The wind veering the car slightly to the right,
Whipping the line of white laundry, bending the cottonwoods
    apart,
The scraggly wind-break of a dusty ranch-house.
I rise and fall, and time folds
Into a long moment;
And I hear the lichen speak,
And the ivy advance with its white lizard feet—

On the shimmering road,
On the dusty detour.   (CP 194).

When "time folds / Into a long moment," opposites are reconciled. Sea and plain, rising and falling, become one. The dust
shimmers, perhaps with the light within light. The very plants, the
lichen and ivy are experienced more sharply, and they take on
more abundant life. Thus, the still point is reached by motion,
just as the poem must move if it is to reach the stillness and so
endure with such endurance as art has. In Roethke, as in Eliot,
time is conquered through time, through the recapturing in
memory of those moments in which time and the timeless have
had their intersection. For Roethke, of course, such moments
are always characterized by an uncommon awareness of their
dynamism, of the vitality of the greenhouse fraus, for example, or
the velocity of a careening automobile. Thus, as the driver he has
been speeds into the eternal present, Roethke's narrator becomes
one with his youthful self and finds in that reunion his own
vision of the rising and falling waters:

> I see the flower of all water, above and below me, the never
>   receding,
> Moving, unmoving in a parched land, white in the moonlight:
> The soul at a still-stand,
> At ease after rocking the flesh to sleep,
> Petals and reflections of petals mixed on the surface of a
>   glassy pool,
> And the waves flattening out when the fishermen drag their
>   nets over the stones.   (CP 194)

The journey to the interior of the continent has led to the sea;
the journey into the self has led out of the self. As the narrator
gazes into the pool he suddenly "sees," flower and water join
metaphorically, as if for a moment the lotus blossom rises in the
glassy pool. Staring at his image, the narrator finds that the water
around his reflection seems to be above him as well as below him;
there is a kind of hypnotic confusion as self and reflection of self
seem equally real and he is no longer sure "which I is I." This

image of self reflecting self in an envisioned pool is another of Roethke's attempts to capture that "friend that runs before me on the windy headlands, / Neither voice nor vision" (CP 198).

Hugh Staples, having decided that *North American Sequence* is as static a work as *Pilgrim's Progress*, makes "Journey to the Interior" correspond to Bunyan's "Slough of Despond," and thus is forced into a truly perverse reading of this passage. "This ominous illusion of eternity," Staples insists, "bears no relation to normal experience, and the poet himself acknowledges this wish in the following poem as 'foolishness with God.' " [9] Malkoff is not much better: "This eternity is annihilation of the individual. . . . And instead of transcending the self, escaping its limitations, he is in danger of losing it completely." [10] Both of these misreadings, it seems to me, are rooted in a refusal to take Roethke at his word when he says that "to go forward as a spiritual man it is necessary first to go back," or when he insists that in the history of the psyche there is "a perpetual slipping-back, then a going forward . . ." (SP 39). Roethke's sequences do not, as they are too often thought to do, move in a fixed pattern toward some ultimate salvation or "final epiphany." For Roethke, such experiences are never "final"; they are merely events that repeat themselves again and again as a man moves, in a phrase Roethke borrowed from Yeats, "from exhaustion to exhaustion." The "flower of all water" rising in "Journey to the Interior" and the rose in the sea-wind swaying in "The Rose" are both figures representing the harmonious reconciliation of opposites, the "imperishable quiet at the heart of form." There is no need to invalidate the moment of spiritual awakening in "Journey" simply because other such moments occur later in the sequence. All such experiences play their parts in the continuous movement of the spirit, and each of them must give way to make room for the next.

Thus, in the third section of "Journey to the Interior," earth, air, fire, and water merge into a single experience which turns, at last, to singing:

> In the moment of time when the small drop forms, but does
> not fall,

I have known the heart of the sun,—
In the dark and light of a dry place,
In a flicker of fire brisked by a dusty wind.
I have heard, in a drip of leaves,
A slight song,
After the midnight cries. (CP 194)

In the instant of gathering energy, that moment when stillness
seems more dynamic than motion, the narrator has "known" the
heart of the sun, which is also, in Roethke's punning poetic
strategy, the sacred heart of the Son of God. Fire and dust and
wind and the water-drip from leaves come suddenly in place, and
the narrator hears "A slight song" which foreshadows the singing
heard in the last stanza:

As a blind man, lifting a curtain, knows it is morning,
I know this change:
On one side of silence there is no smile;
But when I breathe with the birds,
The spirit of wrath becomes the spirit of blessing,
And the dead begin from their dark to sing in my sleep.
(CP 195)

To "breathe with the birds" is a figure for the making of speech
and of song, a figure carried over from the *Meditations of an Old
Woman*. Wrath turns to blessing—that is, the processes of time
and change, ordinarily felt to be hostile, are experienced as benev-
olent, as a source of beauty—when the aging man begins to make
poetry in order to compensate for the tatters in his mortal dress.
For Roethke, who believed that the poets dead stood ready to as-
sist the poets living, the image of the dead singing in the sleep of
the living is no mere metaphor. The poetic voice, like that voice
of Keats's nightingale, is immortal; the giving and giving back of
cadences goes on, generation after generation.

"The Long Waters" begins the process of spiritual renewal
once again, wearily establishing a campsite at the sea's edge and
admitting fear of "the worm's advance and retreat . . . the butter-
fly's havoc, . . . / The dubious sea-change, the heaving sands, and

. . . tenacled sea-cousins" (CP 196). For Roethke, as for Stevens, death is the mother of beauty, and the fear of the worm intensifies the narrator's delight in the world around him:

> But what of her?—
> Who magnifies the morning with her eyes,
> That star winking beyond itself,
> The cricket-voice deep in the midnight field,
> The blue jay rasping from the stunted pine.
> How slowly pleasure dies!—
> The dry bloom splitting in the wrinkled vale,
> The first snow of the year in the dark fir.
> Feeling, I still delight in my last fall.   (CP 196–97)

Section three of the poem begins as straight description of the "rich desolation" of the place where salt and fresh water meet, but it is description that turns to metaphor as the powers of memory and of imagination work their transformations, once again joining water and flowers. "These waves, in the sun," says the old man, "remind me of flowers . . ." (CP 197). The resultant journey to the past serves as preparation for the mystical fire which culminates in yet another epiphany at the poem's end:

> I see in the advancing and retreating waters
> The shape that came from my sleep, weeping:
> The eternal one, the child, the swaying vine branch,
> The numinous ring around the opening flower,
> The friend that runs before me on the windy headlands,
> Neither voice nor vision.   (CP 198)

The ever-changing sea-shape takes the appropriate form for each stage in the process of spiritual evolution; here the eternal child is, of course, the archetypal figure which signifies an opening into a larger spiritual or psychic life. The old man loses and finds himself, is gathered together and embraces all there is. Another balance, precarious and fleeting, is achieved only to vanish in the white space between poems.

"The Far Field" opens as if the vision of the eternal child had never been, opens with yet another of Roethke's narrowing journeys on which the road disappears, speed diminishes to nothing, and, finally, all the lights go dark. The means of escape is, by now, familiar—a retreat into the past, into the world of the greenhouse. There, the narrator tells us, "Among the tin cans, rusted pipes, broken machinery,—/ One learned of the eternal . . ." (CP 199). Knowledge of the eternal begins with awareness of the unchanging process of change itself. Cans and pipes rust; machines break down; flowers blossom, wither, land on the flower-dump. And that which is only living can only die—the rat and the tom-cat, the birds and young rabbits caught in the mower. Yet, the knowledge of death is but partial knowledge:

> For to come upon warblers in early May
> Was to forget time and death:
> How they filled the oriole's elm, a twittering restless cloud, all
> one morning,
> And I watched and watched till my eyes blurred from the
> bird shapes,—
> Cape May, Blackburnian, Cerulean,—
> Moving, elusive as fish, fearless,
> Hanging, bunched like young fruit, bending the end branches.
> . . . (CP 199)

The energy and motion of the birds—as well as their music—is the creative aspect of the same eternal process which has as its other aspect rust, break-down, decay, and death. The poet, for his part, demonstrates the thrust of change and development by turning to metaphor and so changing the birds to fish or fruit shapes with a twist of the active mind. Life and death are experienced as one, as the flowers growing through the entrails of a dead cat or as the rotting tree from which the flicker drums in the chickenyard.

The past contains other ways of grasping the eternal and of forgetting time and death. The narrator remembers how, as a skinny-kneed boy, he would think of the motion that is life as it transforms itself endlessly in the evolutionary process, or how he would imagine into belief the myriad transformations of incarnation after incarnation. To think of one's self as the upshot of millions of years of death, to feel one's self stuccoed all over with birds and quadrupeds, is to view time and death at some distance. From such a perspective, one's personal death shrinks in significance and one's life is but one manifestation of a single energy which writhes through many forms as it moves through time and space.

As in "Journey to the Interior," the remembrance of things past turns into an image of rapid speed building and building until a stillness is achieved:

> I feel a weightless change, a moving forward
> As of water quickening before a narrowing channel
> When banks converge, and the wide river whitens;
> Or when two rivers combine, the blue glacial torrent
> And the yellowish-green from the mountainy upland,—
> At first a swift rippling between rocks,
> Then a long running over flat stones
> Before descending to the alluvial plain,
> To the clay banks, and the wild grapes hanging from the
>   elmtrees. (CP 200)

Image leads to image, the rush of water taking the old man "to a still, but not a deep center, / A point outside the glittering current . . ." (CP 201). That point is, I think, the same *point d'appui* which Thoreau discovers in that chapter of *Walden* which explains "Where I Lived, and What I Lived For." There, Thoreau spins an image which helps us understand Roethke's still center, from which he stares "at the bottom of a river, / At the irregular stones, irridescent sandgrains . . ." (CP 201). "Time," writes Thoreau, "is but the stream I go a-fishing in. I drink at it; but while I drink I see the sandy bottom and detect how shallow it is. Its thin current slides away, but eternity remains. I would drink deeper; fish in the sky, whose bottom is pebbly with stars." Roethke's North American expedition, like Thoreau's, moves outward from the "sensual emptiness" of the city to that wilderness of the spirit from which one may survey the boundaries between time and eternity. And, again like Thoreau, who experienced his symbolic winter death and spring rebirth at Walden Pond,

Roethke's old man finds himself renewed by contemplation of
that energy which at once alters him and turns the seasons:

> I am renewed by death, thought of my death,
> The dry scent of a dying garden in September,
> The wind fanning the ash of a low fire.
> What I love is near at hand,
> Always, in earth and air. (CP 201)

The fourth and final section then moves into celebration, in
this case a blank verse hymn to continuous change, to the "immensity" contained within one man. The section begins with
an image of a protean figure, "An old man with his feet before
the fire, / In robes of green, in garments of adieu" (CP 201). The
garb is symbolic, for the green of the robes suggests perpetual renewal, while the "garments of adieu" hint at a ceaseless falling
away. So the lost self changes, a sea-shape, found and lost again
and again through myriad transformations of self toward "the end
of things, the final man" (CP 201). It would be a mistake, though
a natural one, to think of Roethke's "final man" as a static figure,
an image at last fixed and immutable. Instead, Roethke's "final
man" is cousin to Wallace Stevens's highly dynamic "philosophers' man," the hero of "Asides on the Oboe." For Stevens,

> In the end, however naked, tall, there is still
> The impossible possible philosophers' man,
> The man who has had the time to think enough,
> The central man, the human globe, responsive
> As a mirror with a voice, the man of glass,
> Who in a million diamonds sums us up.[11]

Just as Stevens's man of multi-faceted diamonds exists as a wilderness of reflections and reflections of reflections, so Roethke's "final
man" squirms with the selves he has been, with the selves he
might have been, and with those he might yet be. He is, in other
words, the impossible possible sum of human experience and
potential human experience, a finite figure vibrating with infinite
revelations. Having "had the time to think enough," the final

man alone perceives the immense energy and thrust of life as it is compressed within the clumsy instant between past and future. For such a figure, any given memory—and memory is nothing until in a single man contained—will serve to demonstrate the dynamic quality of the perpetual dance of events. The remembered moment reaches back into the past and forward into the future, altering both past and future in meaning and value, giving off energies which fructify in other moments, other lives. "The pure serene of memory in one man," then, becomes a dynamic serenity, a motion without rest, "A ripple widening from a single stone / Winding around the waters of the world" (CP 201).

"The Rose" opens with Roethke's familiar diminution of sound, sight, and motion toward that stillness in which contemplation without distraction is possible. At the edge of nothing, that moment of afterlight and near silence, the eternal child is again free from the aging flesh:

> I sway outside myself
> Into the darkening currents,
> Into the small spillage of driftwood,
> The waters swirling past the tiny headlands.   (CP 202)

That sense of movement is transformed into a metaphorical journey by ship in the first stanza of section two. The image recalls others, the old woman's bus ride, for example, or the narrator's frantic drive by car across the "slow sea of a grassy plain." Our continuous human motion is suddenly set off against the figure of the rose, a contrast that is introduced by the word *But*. "But this rose, this rose in the sea-wind, / Stays, / Stays in its true place . . ." (CP 203). However, the figure of the rose becomes a kind of mirror-image of those figurative Roethkean journeys which speed to an impression of stillness, for the "staying-power" of the rose blossoms into motion and energy, into a "Flowering," "Widening" and "struggling"

> Beyond the clover, the ragged hay,
> Beyond the sea pine, the oak, the wind-tipped madrona,
> Moving with the waves, the undulating driftwood,

Where the slow creek winds down to the black sand of the
shore
With its thick grassy scum and crabs scuttling back into their
glistening craters.   (CP 203)

The experience of energetic movement in a plant "Rooted in
stone," like the experience of stillness in the most violent motion,
seems to free the mind to journey backward in time to the
greenhouse world of order and beauty:

> I think of roses, roses,
> White and red, in the wide six-hundred-foot greenhouses,
> And my father standing astride the cement benches,
> Lifting me high over the four-foot stems, the Mrs. Russells,
> and his own elaborate hybrids,
> And how those flowerheads seemed to flow toward me, to
> beckon me, only a child, out of myself.   (CP 203)

The memory of beckoning roses is the single stone from which
energy radiates in all directions, making meanings which, decades
later, break like waves over the lovely rose in the sea-wind. And
the child who, in that early encounter with the beautiful, is
beckoned out of himself, appears as an image again and again,
racing ahead of the aging man along the windy headlands. Thus,
the figure of perpetual renewal has its roots in the past, in "The
pure serene of memory in one man."

Section three becomes a meditation upon "sound and silence"
in which the imagination conjures up sounds which become
louder and louder, culminating in the very American noise pollu-
tion of shrieking nails, roaring bulldozers, hissing sandblasters, and
"the deep chorus of horns coming up from the streets in early
morning." Just as speed builds to a stillness, noise also builds to a
stillness, and the narrator returns "to the twittering of swallows
above water" and to "that sound, that single sound, / When the
mind remembers all . . . / A sound so thin it could not woo a
bird" (CP 204). The poem has moved from silence to silence, but
with a difference. The evening quiet of the darkening current with
the morning birds gone has become an early morning quiet, a quiet

on the edge of ripeness. The narrator thinks, for example, of "light making its own silence," but the time is early summer and the place is the edge of a ripening meadow. Or he imagines that "lonely time before the breaking of morning," a time of gathering energy in which raindrops hang "Shifting in the wakening sunlight / Like the eye of a new-caught fish." The rhythms of diminishing are transformed to the rhythms of wakening and of becoming.

In the final section, the passage, poem, and sequence culminate in the image of the rose, a vision which, as Karl Malkoff has noted, is the "embodiment of unity of being for Dante and Yeats." [12] Roethke's man, who stands outside himself, "Beyond becoming and perishing, / A something wholly other," takes on the paradoxical moving stillness of the rose itself. He, too, sways and is still, is moving and unmoving in the same instant. In the image of the rose all opposites are harmoniously reconciled. Sound and silence, motion and stillness, sea and land, wind and light, are folded in the petals of the rose, which keeps and gathers all until everything comes to one and the poet and the rose dance on:

> And I rejoiced in being what I was:
> In the lilac change, the white reptilian calm,
> In the bird beyond the bough, the single one
> With all the air to greet him as he flies,
> The dolphin rising from the darkening waves;
>
> And in this rose, this rose in the sea-wind,
> Rooted in stone, keeping the whole of light,
> Gathering to itself sound and silence—
> Mine and the sea-wind's.   (CP 205)

THE FORMAL FATHER

Devising Intensity

"Form," wrote Roethke, making notes for his 1963 address at Northwestern University, "is a father: with all the ambiguities of father being operative" (28, 26). More than a decade earlier, looking back still further to his years of apprenticeship, he jotted in one of his notebooks that "I began, like the child, with some things, the little narrow forms. I thought in these I might learn to write verse and perhaps poetry would happen" (37 #110). Perhaps it is fair to say that for Roethke-the-apprentice, form was less father than mother, a comforting womb-like space capable of bearing imaginative life which he could not otherwise have conceived. The forms of the early poems were, after all, predominantly feminine forms, the forms employed by Roethke's poetic mothers—Emily Dickinson, Elinor Wylie, Louise Bogan, Leonie Adams. Thus, in his essay called "How to Write Like Somebody Else," Roethke acknowledges his debt to Elinor Wylie for the shape of "This Light," and he then goes on to describe his "spiritual romance" with Leonie Adams, a romance culminating in "The Buds Now Stretch." Roethke writes,

> I hate to abandon that poem: I feel it's something Miss
> Adams and I have created: a literary lovechild. Put it this

way: I loved her so much, her poetry, that I just *had* to
become, for a brief moment, a part of her world. For it *is*
her world, and I had filled myself with it, and I *had* to create
something that would honor her in her own terms. That, I
think, expresses as best I can what really goes on with the
hero- or heroine-worshipping young. I didn't cabbage those
effects in cold blood; that poem is a true release in its way.
I was too clumsy and stupid to articulate my own emotions:
she helped me to say something about the external world,
helped me convince myself that maybe, if I kept at it,
eventually I might write a poem of my own, with the accent
on my own speech. (SP 66)

Form as mother. Life-giving, supportive. A shape to be loved,
honored "in her own way," always there to help the clumsy and
stupid child, to help him to say and to say until, if he keeps at it,
his own speech is possible. Mamma is teaching you to talk. But
form as father, form as Roethke comes to use it in *Words for the
Wind* or in *The Far Field*, creates another relationship entirely,
one with all ambiguities operative and one which often results in
poetry of very great intensity. These later formal pieces are the
poems of a mature poet who has already created a speech all his
own, who has written some of the most innovative poems in the
language, and who is confident that "if a writer has something to
say, it will come through. The very fact that he has the support of
a tradition, or an older writer, will enable him to be more himself—or more than himself" (SP 69). The use of a form becomes
an act of love and an act of hate, a gesture of taking and of giving back with a little something added, with a greater intensity,
with more snap. It is the arrogance that leads one to think, "I
can take this god damned high style of W.B.Y. . . . and use it
for other ends, use it as well or better" (*Letters* 231). It is a defiant act and a courageous one, a way of showing that "One dares
to stand up to a great style, to compete with papa" (SP 70). No
longer a clumsy child, this is Roethke the fierce tennis player,
challenging the toughest players he can find and determined to
whip them, if not by innate ability, then by sheer intensity. He
no longer conceals his use of the technical devices of others; in-

deed, he insists that his reader be aware of them, that the reader be the judge of whether or not he has given back more than he has taken, whether or not he has managed to make his poems vibrate with the furious rhythms of his own psychic energies while working within the framework of a stanzaic form and metrical pattern that once belonged to Papa.

The technical devices by which Roethke imparts such intense vibrations to that "Ordnung" established by Papa-form are many, and he has, fortunately, indicated in his prose writings what some of them are. Of the published prose pieces, "Some Remarks on Rhythm" is doubtless the most helpful. In that essay, Roethke suggests that "memorable" speech—which is, for him, one with "intense" speech—is often "strongly stressed, irregular, even 'sprung,' if you will" (SP 74). Or that "light 'i' and short 'i' and feminine endings can make for speed, rhythmical quickness, and velocity . . ." (SP 73). He also demonstrates how direct address or the hortatory or the startling, the strange, and the absurd may be aids in the making of "memorable or passionate speech" (SP 74). Or how the creation of a dramatic tension or of a rhythmic tension playing against an established pattern may be employed to achieve that same goal. More useful, I think, than anything in the published prose, is a list included in Roethke's teaching notes, a list headed "DEVICES FOR HEIGHTENING INTENSITY." The devices are:

1. Use of symbolism.
   Intense feeling is important, but it is not enough.
2. Use of simplicity: bald statement.
   Monosyllables: movement and rush.
3. Repetition.
4. Use of constant antithesis, word against word, phrase against phrase.
5. Paradox: sense transfer.
6. Deliberate use of ambiguity (pun). (65, 2)

Roethke does not go on to explain *how* these techniques work to intensify his verse. Perhaps explanation is unnecessary. Nonetheless, I should like to hazard a few observations. Most obviously, the devices of paradox, ambiguity, and symbolism all have the effect of making words and phrases move, like Roethke's woman lovely in her bones, more ways than one. By the multiplicity of their meanings, pun, paradox, and symbol draw us into the dynamic complexity that lies beneath the static surface of language. And, at the same time, such devices remind us that the life for which the language stands, the motion that the poem represents, is equally dynamic, equally complex. Repetition, as Roethke uses it, is on the one hand a way of creating shifting patterns of symbol and pun, and on the other hand a technique with which to demonstrate that the more things remain the same, the more they change. The use of constant antithesis is, as one would expect, a way of demonstrating in language that creative tension of opposites by which the world moves. Simplified diction, the use of monosyllables, does indeed suggest "movement and rush," and any fledgling poet might benefit from comparing the effect of the Latinate diction of Roethke's apprenticeship with that of the rugged Anglo-Saxon of, say, "The Song" (CP 146) or "Infirmity" (244). In the teaching notes, Roethke writes,

> "Poets make pets of pretty, docile words," says Miss Wylie
> in her opening line of a sonnet. But such words make for a
> pretty docile poetry. Old words, tough words, Anglo-Saxon
> words, special words, but pretty be damned. . . . (28, 18)

In order to minimize repetition in writing about these late formal pieces, I have tried to work with the most dynamic poetry that Roethke made, those poems in which he seems to me most faithful to his own devices for heightening intensity. Every reader has, I suppose, a sense of the poet's self to which he wants the poet to be true. Roethke seems most himself, most a poet of dynamic intensity, in *The Dying Man;* in the *Love Poems,* some of them anyway, from *Words for the Wind;* and, most notably, in the collection of pieces he entitles *Sequence, Sometimes Metaphysical.*

The Dying Man

Rough drafts of *The Dying Man* reveal that Roethke played for some time with the notion of using as epigraph a line from W. B. Yeats—"Man has created death" (19, 19). The line concludes Yeats's short poem "Death," which begins

> Nor dread nor hope attend
> A dying animal;
> A man awaits his end
> Dreading and hoping all. . . .[1]

Roethke drops the epigraph, perhaps because, as he once put it, "I should like to think I have over-acknowledged, in one way and another, my debt to Yeats" (SP 70). *The Dying Man*, nonetheless, remains a poem about the creative possibilities inherent in the very shapelessness of the idea of death, those possibilities which "A man sees, as he dies . . ." (CP 153). Against the immense, immeasurable emptiness that is all we on earth know of Eternity, all hope and all dread may define themselves in song. It is as if the imagination delights in having the space of the abyss in which to make-believe a "Translunar Paradise" (the phrase is Yeats's) composed of language intense enough to comfort or to terrify.

I believe that Roethke establishes "dancing room," his space of creative possibility, by heavy repetition of certain deliberately vague, closely related words, words which ordinarily would weaken any poem in which they were concentrated. Such words as *what, figure, shape, thing,* and *nothing* dance around one another in a kind of celebration of "obscure shadow," a celebration in which the invisible and the half-visible take on substance (but not shape) and become for a moment, in Wallace Stevens's phrase, "invisibly clear." As Roethke uses them in *The Dying Man*, these words acknowledge the limitations of the human power to name and to define. Thus, the line "What's beating at the gate?" despite its question mark, is more than a question. The line also carries something of the thrust of declarative statement. The Great What, that mysterious, unnameable other beyond the wall, has arrived and is being announced. The ghostly "What" that beats never defines itself. It remains "Another shape" in a blurred casement, or simply a "figure" at one's back, one of many figures raving out of obscure shadow. It is the "Who" that has come and "can wait," the "all" that one dares question in the worst night of his will. It is "A spirit raging at the visible," a wraith from the "Forever" that is "what we know." And vision is not much clearer on the temporal side of the wall, this place where "What's seen recedes," for a seen "What" and a known "What" are equally insubstantial. Here one can define himself only as a dreaded "thing" or as a "final thing" or as a "nothing, leaning towards a thing." If figures out of the shadows rage at the visible, the poet, for his part, seems but "A madman staring at perpetual night." And that "perpetual night" is artificially represented by the language of darkness, vagueness, unconsciousness, blurring, and obscurity, a language which creates an artistic impression of the "immense immeasurable emptiness" against which the creative man must beat his wings as if in answer to the beating of the mysterious What upon the gate.

Establishing a poetic atmosphere as murky (and as ghostly) as that of the opening scene of *Hamlet*, Roethke acts at the same time as light-bringer to his own created world. The language of chaos and old night is played off against a language of "be-ing," a counterpoint intensified by pun and by repetition. In the beginning is the word, rolling part-way back the darkness moving on the face of the abyss. "I think a bird, and it begins to fly," Roethke writes. "By dying daily, I have come to be" (CP 155). Thought, but thought extending itself in the act of naming, creates imaginative life out of airy nothing. And, as poets have always known, imaginative life, if beautiful, must be true. If one may think a bird into flight, one may also think one's self through the many deaths of "becoming" until one comes at last to "be." Roethke makes this point punningly at the beginning of section two with a sentence which, wavering like an optical illusion, seems now to terrify and now to comfort. At first reading, the lines are straightforward enough: "Caught in the dying light, / I thought myself reborn" (CP 154). In "dying light," Roethke's equivalent of Yeats's "sensual music," the idea of rebirth is illusory, an unkind hoax. The narrator "thinks" he is reborn, but, caught in the processes of change and decay, he is sadly mistaken. Later, however, after the bird of section four has been "thought" into being, to think one's self reborn begins to sound like the same sort of trick, a poetic lifting of one's self by the bootstraps. In this reading, the poet, dying daily in a dynamic world, stays alive by continuous resurrection, by the imaginative act of giving birth over and over to a new self.

Such punning is part of a pattern in *The Dying Man*. Roethke concentrates his word-play so that it calls attention to the ambiguities of death. Karl Malkoff, I believe, catches the first of these puns, one so different from the others that I should have missed it. The poem begins with the words of the dying man himself:

> "My soul's hung out to dry,
> Like a fresh-salted skin;
> I doubt I'll use it again." (CP 153)

As Malkoff puts it, "The sweat of anxiety and terror becomes the active agent in this vision of life as a 'curing' process." [2] It is unusual in Roethke's poetic strategy—in anyone's poetic strategy—to pun in such a way that the reader is relied upon to supply the word with which to play. Nonetheless, the "cure," once Malkoff supplies it, forms so appropriate a paradox and is so characteristic of Roethke that I can only think that Roethke did intend the pun as a special pleasure for his own fit audience, fine though few. Thus, the process of living, that deterioration of the flesh, is established by a pun to be as one with the process by which the soul is preserved.

There are a few other puns, more conventional in presentation, but having a related thematic function. In section two, for example, "Places great with their dead, / The mire, the sodden wood" remind the dying man "to stay alive" (CP 154). The word *great* wriggles in its context. "Near the graves of the great dead," said Roethke's old woman at the end of her "Fourth Meditation," "Even the stones speak" (CP 170). Remembering those lines, one presumes that a place may be made "great" by the greatness of the dead who are buried in or near it. Moreover, "Places great with their dead" is almost certainly intended to echo the biblical phrase "great with child," a figure of speech suggesting immanent birth or, in this case, rebirth. The swelling of the ground with the dead hints, with the aid of the pun, at regeneration. I believe a similar pun occurs in section four, after Roethke insists that "By dying daily, I have come to be" (CP 155). One who has "thought" a bird into flight or "thought" himself into rebirth may well come to be by a related act of willful affirmation. Roethke not only comes to be, he comes to the *word* "be," the word which represents the affirmation of a self in language. To be or not to be is, as in *Hamlet,* the question. For Roethke, one way of "be-ing" is for the imagination to think a self (a being) and make it incarnate in memorable speech, to bring the "I" that dies daily to "be" through the speaking of the word. As in God's *Let there be Light,* "be" is the operative word, the magic syllable that gives birth. In the next stanza, then, Roethke may well intend us to hear "bees" and "be's" at the same time:

> All exultation is a dangerous thing.
> I see you, love, I see you in a dream;
> I hear a noise of bees, a trellis hum,
> And that slow humming rises into song . . . (CP 155)

The bees heard by the dying man are part of his "Exulting," a spiritual excitement bringing him nearer and nearer Eternity, a place (or a state) which is heard before it is glimpsed. The humming of bees comes as from a great distance, rises into song, and eventually is distinguishable as the song of birds. "They sing, they sing," cries the dying man, "but still in minor thirds." On this level, the "noise of bees" is simply a way of suggesting the drowsy sound of the imperfectly heard music which creeps by us from "that sweet field far ahead." On another level, I think, the noise of bees is the noise of "be's," the word by which the creative imagination creates what it may then celebrate in song. *Be* is the word with the property of imaginative making, whether it "be" the making of "That is no country for old men" upon the blankness of a page or the making of roses out of the darkness of Michigan winter. Throughout the poem, the dying man has been plagued by ghosts. Now, as they become more friendly, it is the sound of their voices, represented by the noise of be's and the song that rises from that noise, that draws him onward. An even more outrageous pun on the same word appears in the final stanza, in which we learn that "The edges of the summit still appall / When we brood on the dead or the beloved" (CP 156). When we brood, that is, not only on those whom we love but on those who loved "be," who exercised the creative power of language.

There are other puns in the same lines. The word *appall*, for example, which suggests a whitening at the edges of darkness ("Dawn's where the white is") as well as having its more apparent meaning, that of making pale by frightening or terrifying. Or the word *brood*, which means, to be sure, to dwell moodily on a subject, but which also retains something of its root sense, that of warming into life, especially with the breath. It is a brooding which may "hatch" the dead, giving them life in much the same way that a bird may be "thought" into flight. Once again, the puns make the sense of the line waver ambiguously between comfort and terror. There are still other puns in *The Dying Man* which might be mentioned, puns on *I* and *eye*, for example, or on Yeats's *A Vision* and the loquacious man who "dared to fix his vision anywhere," or on the variety of meanings in each use of the word *still*. These, however, are more obvious than the puns I have already discussed, and they have, at least in this poem, less thematic significance.

Paradox, as Roethke uses it in *The Dying Man*, is much more than mere rhetorical flourish. The entire poem is rooted in paradox, particularly in those paradoxes of Christian mysticism that Roethke comes to use more and more in the later poems as a kind of one-upmanship in the face of reason. "All possibilities," read an early draft of the poem, "Play in the presence of death" (40 #157b). The dying man, like the mystic, can see in the "play" of possibilities the reconciliation of seeming opposites, can see the darkness that is light, the motion that is stillness, the animosity that is love, the death that is life.

Some sense of the pervasiveness of paradox in *The Dying Man* may be gained simply by underscoring a few of the poem's more obvious paradoxical statements: "What's done is yet to come," or "I breathe alone until my dark is bright," or "I die into this life, alone yet not alone," or "I shall undo all dying by my death," or "By dying daily, I have come to be." Taken in isolation such lines might seem, and indeed might be, a stylistic affectation, the sort of "rhetorical flourish" I mentioned earlier. However, when each statement is seen to be but a part of a pattern of paradoxical statements and ideas, each makes its own significant contribution to the rhetorical texture of the poem. The "flourish," meaningless in casual isolation, becomes, in the context of the whole, a moving instant in a flowing larger gesture which has both direction and meaning. That gesture, it seems to me, indicates Roethke's direction that is all, a direction leading away from the linear, the logical, and the analytical and toward the immediate, the intuitive, and the mystical. Paradox is, after all, the simultaneous affirmation of truths which are logically incompatible. As such, it is an effective technique for presenting in language a world which is extremely complex and highly dynamic, a world in which opposites interact so rapidly and with such violence that they sometimes blend into a momentary relationship which we experience as a unified force, an energy.

Such paradoxical blending is the key to the structure of "The Dying Man" as well as making up a large part of its texture. It does not seem to me that the poem moves from death to life nor from dark to light nor from terror to comfort—those directions so often taken by Roethke's poetry. Rather, I think, it moves from one level of perception to another, from, if you like, the rational to the mystical, from seeing by "the dying light" of the sensual world to seeing by that "gentlest light" that descends upon the narrator as he approaches the "sweet field far ahead" with its singing birds. There, and in that light, dark and light, death and life, hatred and love, being still and still moving, are seen to be joined in harmonious and beautiful reconciliation. The opposites come suddenly in place, and in their couplings they release the energy that turns the world and that brings all dying men, at last, to be. That same energy is "The fury of the slug beneath the stone," the rage to live, to be, to be something more. In my opinion Malkoff errs in asserting that the slug is "Roethke's comfortless symbol of the eternal in the temporal." [3] I should say, rather, that the slug's fury is closely akin to the human dread of "the thing I am" which serves as motive for change, growth, and development. It is the primordial rage, the force that drives the evolutionary process.

Richard Hugo, one of Roethke's students in 1947, recalls a classroom incident which may reveal a good bit about theme and meaning in *The Dying Man*. "The second half of the Roethke final," Hugo recalls, "usually consisted of one question, a lulu like, 'What should the modern poet do about his ancestors?' 'Do you mean his blood ancestors or the poets who preceded him?' I asked. 'Just answer the question,' Roethke growled." [4] *The Dying Man* may, I think, be read as the professor's poetic answer—or one of his answers—to his own question. Roethke's growled reply to Hugo suggests, as does the poem, that one's blood ancestors and one's literary ancestors pose similar problems which must be dealt with in similar ways. Roethke thinks of himself as the son of many fathers, but foremost among them are Otto the florist and Yeats the poet. And in both of these relationships, all of the ambiguities of "father" are indeed operative. In the third section of *The Dying Man*, the fathers merge into a single shadowy figure, a figure inspiring pity, awe, not a little fear, and a vague sense of guilt:

> A ghost comes out of the unconscious mind
> To grope my sill: It moans to be reborn!
> The figure at my back is not my friend;
> The hand upon my shoulder turns to horn.
> I found my father when I did my work,
> Only to lose myself in this small dark.   (CP 154)

The sense of guilt, perhaps, is more clearly defined later, when the poet acknowledges that "When figures out of obscure shadow rave, / All sensual love's but dancing on a grave" (CP 154). One's ancestors, of course, are always at one's back, a fact that can make a man wondrous uncomfortable when he feels—as all sons occasionally feel—the weight of ghostly disapproval, feels that "The figure at my back is not my friend."

What is one to do with such enemies? Roethke answers the question in section four, the section called *The Exulting*. First, there is a sketch of the blood ancestor and then one of the literary ancestor:

> I saw my father shrinking in his skin;
> He turned his face: there was another man,
> Walking the edge, loquacious, unafraid.
> He quivered like a bird in birdless air,
> Yet dared to fix his vision anywhere.   (CP 155)

And then Roethke adds, "Fish feed on fish according to their need: / My enemies renew me, and my blood / Beats slower in my careless solitude" (CP 155). The image is of a kind of Oedipal cannibalism; the son chews up the old man, blood, bones, and stones, taking from him what really matters—his energy, his potency, the ground-beat of his psychic and biological rhythms. And from such feeding he finds himself "renewed" and, paradoxically, free of the ingested ancestors who are now flesh of his flesh, bone of his bone. He is, as he puts it, "alone yet not alone."

The eucharistic ritual seems to release the poet from fear and rancor. The terrified backward glances of *What Now?* and of *The Wall* are replaced by exultation, by singing, by an almost divine thrusting-forward. The word *love* appears again and again, the word being celebrated by the act of repetition. "[H]ow I love the moon!" cries the poet, or "I love the world; I want more than the world. . . ." Such love, of course, is markedly different from that "sensual love" which had seemed "but dancing on a grave" earlier in the poem. This is a higher love, of the order that undoes all dying by the lover's death. In movement, in tone—even in the cannibalistic imagery—*The Dying Man* is reminiscent of Roethke's piece of prose-turned-poem that he calls "A Tirade Turning." The "Tirade" begins with a furious assault on Roethke's "more tedious contemporaries," those "Roaring asses, hysterics, sweet-myself beatniks, earless wonders happy with effects a child of two could improve on . . ." (SP 151). The fun goes on for three pages of vitriolic attack on the enemy, on "the two-bit cisatlantic tough guys making like Marlon Brando on a motor-scooter, Edna St. Vincent Millay on a raft, Rupert Brooke in a balloon, Robert P. Tristram Coffin on a blueberry muffin" (SP 153). But at last the prose turns to poetry, the hatred to a more complex relationship embracing both love and hate:

> Are not you my final friends, the fair cousins that I loathe and
> love?
> That man hammering I adore, though his noise reach the very
> walls of my inner self;
> Behold, I'm a heart set free, for I have taken my hatred and
> eaten it,
> The last acrid sac of my rat-like fury;
> I have succumbed, like all fanatics, to my imagined victims;
> I embrace what I perceive!
> Brothers and sisters, dance ye,
> Dance ye all!   (SP 154)

It is rage, both here and in *The Dying Man,* that half-creates and half-justifies the intensity of language. In *The Dying Man,* however, it is a rage directed against one's mortal limits, against the ancestors who, on the one hand, establish hereditary boundaries to one's growth and who, on the other, seem always to have surpassed by far the best that one has been able to do. That fury, close cousin to "The fury of the slug beneath the stone," must be taken and swallowed, for it is the nourishment which allows development and which, once digested and assimilated, sets the heart free. Thus, the final image of the poem, an image as puzzling as it is powerful, seems to be saying that only the man who knows (and dares to face) the rage to be "something more" is really alive. He must be willing to evolve continuously, to be ever-changing, yet must keep whatever foot, fin, or wing the evolutionary process provides that might help move him onward:

> [H]e dares to live
> Who stops being a bird, yet beats his wings
> Against the immense immeasurable emptiness of things.
>   (CP 156)

The Love Poems

Asked in 1961 by Paul Engle and Joseph Langland to select his favorite poem for their *Poet's Choice*, Roethke chose a love poem, the one that had provided the title for his fifth volume. "Allow me," he wrote, "a purely personal choice: 'Words for the Wind.'"

> For those who are interested in such matters: the poem is an epithalamion to a bride seventeen years younger. W. H. Auden had given us his house, in Forio, Ischia, for several months, as a wedding present. It was my first trip to Europe. A real provincial, I was frightened by Italy, but within a few days, the sun, the Mediterranean, the serenity of the house changed everything. I was able to move outside myself—for me sometimes a violent dislocation—and express a joy in another, in others: I mean Beatrice O'Connell, and the Italian people, their world, their Mediterranean.[1]

All of this is charming enough, but notice especially that love is expressed as motion, perhaps is experienced as motion, as a moving outside of the self, as "a violent dislocation." The figure is not, I believe, carelessly chosen. For Roethke, love and motion are one, and the *Love Poems* of *Words for the Wind* may be best read as a dissertation on love which is, at the same time, a dissertation on motion. It is a dissertation which takes on an uneasy unity from its diversity, for it is an attempt to capture the multiplicity of motion, to suggest the myriad flowing shapes that love may take.

The action of the sequence is essentially the struggle of the poet-protagonist to know—to know a woman, to know the grammar of least motion, to know the motion of the deepest stone, to know Eternity, to know the Love that is all. Knowing, however, is not easy when what must be known is "A shape of change, encircled by its fire" (CP 119). Beatrice O'Connell may be the cause and end of movement in "Words for the Wind," but she is a quite different Beatrice in, say, "The Dream," and quite others still—if, indeed, she appears at all—in "I Knew a Woman" or in "The Sensualists." The sequence might be taken as a tribute to the infinite variety of Roethke's lovely wife, but I suspect it is more likely a tribute to the variousness of love itself, to womankind's ability to be at one moment the evanescent "shape of change" of "The Dream" and at another moment the "lovely tits" of "The Sensualists." And, of course, in at least one of the poems, "Plaint," it is no woman who is loved, but God. And death. Roethke, I think, is most moved to love by motion itself; by the motion of his wife, of any lovely woman, but by other motions as well—the leaping of stones, the walking of wind, the rising of the moon, the migration of birds and fish, the swinging around of "The sharp stars"—is moved to love even by the motion of that garden which metamorphizes into "a river flowing south." He is in love, too, with the answering motions of his own body and spirit, the rising and falling of his flesh, the "violent dislocations" of his ego, with the all but kinesthetic sense of moving toward spiritual oneness with another, with others, with the very stones.

It is this sense of motion answering motion in dance-like give and take that forms the intuitive basis for Roethke's mysticism, for his most happy marriages of loving and knowing. As early as 1942, discussing the "Ballad of the Clairvoyant Widow," Roethke had been willing to assert belief in "a deep and abiding energy in all living things which can aid our human strength and contribute to our destiny. I don't think," he had continued then, "this is just mystical bunk . . ." (Letters 97). But a decade and a half later, writing in Words for the Wind, he is far better able to translate that belief into poetry. The "deep and abiding energy" is still present, not only in "living things," but in the "motion of the deepest stone" as well, in the whirl of which all things are made.

> I find my loving heart,
> Illumination brought to such a pitch
> I see the rubblestones begin to stretch
> As if reality had split apart
> And the whole motion of the soul lay bare:
> I find that love and I am everywhere. (CP 135)

It is the physicist's world that Roethke sees in his moment of "illumination," a world in which "all's in motion," which is to say, a world in which motion is all. It is the physicist's world, that is, except for one thing: for Roethke, the motion seen in the heart of the rubblestones is spiritual in nature, is "the whole motion of the soul." To that motion of the soul he gives the name "Love." Love is, quite literally, what makes the world go round, is, in fact, the going round itself. And if all is motion, if all things pulsate to the rhythm that is "the whole motion of the soul," then it makes sense to say, as Roethke does, "Each one's himself, yet each one's everyone," or even "I taste my sister when I kiss my wife" (CP 132). All are brothers and are sisters as well, being of one insubstantial substance with the energy which pulses everywhere and is life. The dance of energy is the same for atoms and amoebae, for sunflowers and for rodents, for human beings, for the galaxy, for the universe itself. All things respond to all things; all energy fields exert an attraction on all other fields. And "All things," says the poet, "bring me to love" (CP 125).

The *Love Poems* begin with the poet's dream of a woman, a kind of precognition in which

> I met her as a blossom on a stem
> Before she ever breathed, and in that dream
> The mind remembers from a deeper sleep:
> Eye learned from eye, cold lip from sensual lip. (CP 119)

The loved woman gradually becomes more substantial as the sequence builds to such poems as "I Knew a Woman," "She," "The Other," "The Sententious Man," and "The Sensualists," and then fades again in "The Surly One," "Plaint," and "Memory." The sequence might be said to move from a prefiguring dream of an ideal love, a dream in which, as if in empathetic celebration, "The deer came down, out of the dappled wood" (CP 120), to a different dream, this one a memory, in which the loved one turns to go and in which

> A doe drinks by a stream,
> A doe and its fawn.
> When I follow after them,
> The grass changes to stone.   (CP 141)

Thus, the sequence begins a little before the beginning and ends somewhere beyond the end. The motion that moves the poet, that "shape of change, encircled by its fire," is experienced before the loved woman, the "creaturely creature," is encountered in the flesh, perhaps before she is even born. And the woman remains as dream-memory after she has gone, her image faded but not disappeared. Like any experience, the love experience is not contained between hat and boots, even when the hat and boots are those of a lovely woman. It has roots in what has been and is pulled by what will be; and it may be "known" (the point of the sequence, remember, is to know) only in the full contextualist sweep of its energy, its backward reach and forward thrust in time and space.

The motion of time, like the motion of space, leads Roethke to a sense of the Oneness of all things. If "each one's everyone" because in space "all's in motion," it is equally true that in the sweep of time, "Whatever was, still is," that flower and seed *are* the same. All events are joined in the dynamic movement of time just as all things are as one thing in the energetic whirl of space. This, says Roethke is "a song tied to a tree" (CP 125), for the tree is his most frequent symbol of organic change, growth, and development. The "she" of the sequence moves in every way, swaying in space, frolicking "like a beast," and at the same time is an "event," a creature containing all that the evolutionary process can contain and reaching out to be more still:

The breath of a long root,
The shy perimeter
Of the unfolding rose,
The green, the altered leaf,
The oyster's weeping foot,
And the incipient star—
Are part of what she is.
She wakes the ends of life.   (CP 125)

Like the dying man who kept his wings yet stopped being a bird, Roethke's lady retains the oyster's foot, the root's breath, yet contains as well the potential energy of "the incipient star." The woman herself, evolving from root toward the pure burning of the star, is as much in process as is the love-event of which she is a part. And the background against which she has her being and against which love grows and develops is in process as well, a stage setting of receding fields, floating stars, rippling water, pulsing noons, migrating birds and fish, stretching stones, journeying vines, and gardens which are rivers "flowing south," gardens in which all flowers are "flow-ers."

The use of such imagery is, to be sure, an important technique in representing the dynamism of Roethke's world at loveplay; however, there are other, more subtle, of his "devices for heightening intensity" at work in the sequence as well. Some of them are felt in the rhythms of the love poems, and Roethke was highly conscious of their effect. For example, in the comment following "Words for the Wind" in *Poet's Choice*, Roethke writes,

> The piece is written in a line-length that interested me from the beginning ("Open House," "The Adamant," and the like). But here the beat is a good deal swifter, the rhythms more complex. I would like to think, of course, that something other than the usual has been effected in an old form.[2]

It is interesting, since Roethke invites the comparison, to try to see why the three-beat line of "Words for the Wind" seems to have so much more velocity than have lines of the same length in

Open House. Obviously the rhythms of "Words for the Wind" are less uniform than are those of any single poem from the first volume. That is, the basic iambic pattern stretches alarmingly at times, only to snap back into shape in the next section, sometimes even the next line, of the poem. In other words, like his woman lovely in her bones, Roethke plays it quick and plays it light and loose. Let the first stanza, typically atypical, serve as illustration:

> Love, love, a lily's my care,
> She's sweeter than a tree.
> Loving, I use the air
> Most lovingly: I breathe;
> Mad in the wind I wear
> Myself as I should be,
> All's even with the odd,
> My brother the vine is glad.   (CP 123)

One change, immediately apparent after one rereads the three-beat *Open House* poems, is that Roethke has, in "Words for the Wind," managed to make the line unit and the unit of thought less predictably identical to one another. Lines three and four and lines five and six, for example, are strongly enjambed, and line four completes one thought unit and contains another. Thus all thought is not, as in the early Roethke, divisible into three- or six-beat aphorisms.

Nor are the lines, especially the beginnings of lines, so drearily iambic. The first foot of every line of "Open House" is perfectly regular, whereas this first stanza of "Words for the Wind" opens with a spondee, has two lines beginning with trochees, and has another line—"All's even with the odd"—which might be read as beginning with a spondee. Because all lines in "Words for the Wind" *end* regularly, that is, with an accented syllable, the effect of beginning many lines with a trochee or spondee is to nail line to line by accents, to create a kind of spondaic effect *between* the lines of the poem which preserves the thrust of the rhythm. We "land running," so to speak. Moreover, the process of "turning the line over," shifting it back to iambs after its beginnings in trochee or spondee, requires that unaccented syllables must fall together somewhere, either in the link between trochaic and iambic feet or in a pyrrhic foot. The effect is to speed the line or, as Roethke puts it, to make "the beat a good deal swifter." The accents are concentrated at the beginnings and ends of lines, and the rush of the middle syllables is responsible for our sense of unusually rapid pace.

Some of the difference between the velocity of the three beat line in "Words for the Wind" and the velocity of that used in *Open House* might well be attributed to Roethke's application of the second of his "DEVICES FOR HEIGHTENING INTENSITY," the "Use of simplicity: bald statement. *Monosyllables: movement and rush.*" Roethke mentions "Open House" and "The Adamant" as examples of early poems in the same line length as "Words for the Wind," but his two examples are probably the best of their kind. Such poems as "Orders for the Day" or "Genesis" or "Reply to Censure" or "Lull" are perhaps more typical of Roethke's early three-beat line. They are built of words like *Intricate phobias, malignant, collective, pedantry, inveterate, fortitude, elemental, quiescent, circumvent,* and *virulent.* Words for the wind, on the other hand, are short words, most often the names of elemental things: *sun, earth, stones, stream, plain, field, sea, wind.* There are occasional polysyllabic adjectives—*tremulous, incipient, hilarious* —but very few for a poem of 125 lines. On the whole, a comparison of the diction of the *Open House* poems with that of "Words for the Wind" proves Roethke correct in his theory that "intensity" (which he equates, at least in part, with velocity) is heightened by the use of the monosyllable, by adherence to "simplicity" as motto. And what is true of "Words for the Wind" is true, generally, for the *Love Poems* sequence of which it is a part. In fact, the progressive intensification of Roethke's verse as he grows to poetic maturity is directly linked to, among other things, his dual tendencies toward increasing complexity in rhythm and increasing simplicity in diction.

Throughout the sequence, Roethke makes frequent use of others of his "DEVICES FOR HEIGHTENING INTENSITY," most notably the devices of repetition and ambiguity; and these techniques, together with those already mentioned, serve to give the sixteen love poems a stylistic unity that reinforces that more obvious unity growing out of their common patterns of image and theme. The dynamism at work in both style and content is experienced in "The Dream," the very first poem in Roethke's arrangement. Essentially, "The Dream" is a celebration of the power of feminine motion, a celebration during which the male narrator is stirred from being purely the celebrant-observer until he becomes at last a participant, an acting partner. In the early going, the woman sets the pace. She ripples toward the narrator, loves the wind, loves him, gradually slows to a steadiness in the wind; he, on the other hand, is primarily a watcher and a helpless one at that. He cannot even choose *not* to see her, for when he turns his face away, her image remains with him. For two stanzas, save for a tentative touching of her shifting shadow, our hero remains motionless, while the woman, a kind of goddess of flux, "A shape of change, encircled by its fire," presides over a universe of dancing bushes and stones, rippling water, flowing air, and singing birds. In the third stanza, the woman slows to sigh, and "in that long interval" she loans him "one virtue" by which he lives. The juxtaposition of lines would suggest that the loaned virtue has to do with the "grammar of least motion," motion, I take it, that is efficient and graceful. At any rate, the loan churns earth, air, fire, and water into foam, and the narrator begins a slow dance which gradually quickens to a climax in which he, who has been come *toward* from the beginning, finally is able to come *to* love, to come *into* his own:

> She turned the field into a glittering sea;
> I played in flame and water like a boy
> And I swayed out beyond the white seafoam;
> Like a wet log, I sang within a flame.
> In that last while, eternity's confine,
> I came to love, I came into my own.   (CP 120)

The last line is a fair example both of Roethke's use of repetition and of his use of ambiguity. As I have suggested before,

Roethke is the master of the sharply limited, elemental vocabulary, and that quality of limitation makes for a marked repetition of the names of the most common of things—fire, water, wind, earth, stones, birds, lights, and so on. But in these *Love Poems* he begins to intensify still further the quality of repetition that has marked his verse since the *Lost Son* pieces. More and more often the same word will appear twice—even three times—in a single line, and the effect is one of enormous compression, of powerful, almost magical forces gathering themselves in the echoing sounds of the repeated word. By my count, there are eight such lines in the thirty-two lines of "The Dream," one line out of every four that is intensified by internal repetition. Most of them are tortuous, phrase playing against phrase, the repeated words shifting back añd forth in meaning or value or both with each sounding and re-sounding. "Eye learned from eye," Roethke writes, "cold lip from sensual lip." Or "The water rippled, and she rippled on." Or "Love is not love until love's vulnerable." Or, as a more common use of repetition, but one clearly linked to intensification, "The bushes and the stones danced on and on." In almost every case, the repeated words are related to the twin themes of love and motion, and in several instances their shifting meanings underscore Roethke's characteristic ambiguities. The last line of the poem links the narrator's coming to and coming into with the earlier coming toward of his dream vision. It calls attention to his new-found active role, reminds us that his dance-like swaying "out beyond the white seafoam" has, paradoxically, been the way *in,* a moving out that has led him "into [his] own." Coburn Freer argues rather unconvincingly that the final line is an allusion to the parable of the Prodigal Son, that "in spite of making the poet vulnerable, love provides a means of self-inheritance." [3] But leaving the Prodigal Son aside, Freer is right enough here. Surely one of the things the line says is that by losing himself the narrator has found himself. The way out of the self, strangely enough, turns out to be the way to self-inheritance. But this is true on more levels than the spiritual. "To come" is a common enough idiom for sexual climax, and Roethke is too good a poet not to be aware of the ambiguity. In this sense, to "come into" one's own love is indeed, to use Roethke's phrase, "a violent dislocation," but it is a dislocation that is an expression of joy and one that is very much a part of claiming one's inheritance as a man. Freer, still pushing the Prodigal Son theme, goes on to remark, apparently in all innocence, that "In the very first poem of the sequence, [Roethke] said that he 'came into his own': clearly this was premature. . . ." [4] Roethke would have enjoyed that, I think, especially since sexual climax attained while dreaming of a woman "Before she ever breathed" is, as Freer says, "clearly . . . premature."

Critics have tended to pass over "All the Earth, All the Air" with a sentence or two, but I find the poem remarkable as an attempt to harness the tensions at work during a moment of what Faulkner might have called "terrific arrest." The poem seems to me to present an instant in which potential energy is about to become kinetic, "the moment of time when the small drop forms, but does not fall," as Roethke puts it in "Journey to the Interior." Specifically, the poem is "about" a man impelled by desire, by his joy in a woman's beauty, to "fall" in love; however, as with the formed drop of "Journey to the Interior," impulse and inertia combine momentarily in a precarious balance and he does not fall. It is as if he is caught like an urn figure in the act of stepping over the threshold of his own ego, as if the poem stops him, foot in air, about to leave himself and thus experience that "violent dislocation" in which he will "see and suffer [himself] / In another being at last" (CP 126).

The opening stanza of "All the Earth, All the Air" encapsulates neatly the warring impulses that animate the poem as a whole. The passage is marked by repetition used with a venegeance, repetition, in fact, bordering on redundancy:

> I stand with the standing stones.
> The stones stay where they are.
> The twiny winders wind;
> The little fishes move.
> A ripple wakes the pond.   (CP 121)

That stones should be "standing" comes as small surprise, and that such stones "stay where they are" is still less a surprise. And we should rather expect that "twiny winders"—whatever they are —should "wind." As the cab driver in *The Catcher in the Rye* says, though of fish, not of twiny winders, "It's their *nature*, for Chrissake." The nature of Roethke's narrator, however, is less certain. That word *stand* in the first line is wonderfully ambiguous, and one of its connotations is that of making a conscious choice, as in "I'll take my stand" or "I stand on my Constitutional rights." It implies a taking of sides, in this case a siding with the stones *because*, like nothing else in the pond, "The stones stay where they are." Read in this way, the first two lines have a logical connection and the effect of the repetition is something more of the emphatic and something less of the redundant. More important, the lines establish a character for the speaker. He is a man trying to locate himself, a difficult business in a world of shifting landmarks. After all, when "A ripple wakes the pond," even the standing stones must dance a little to the weighty music of moving water.

In the final stanza the narrator is still holding on, his desperation emphasized once again by repetition:

> In a lurking-place I lurk,
> One with the sullen dark.
> What's hell but a cold heart?
> But who, faced with her face,
> Would not rejoice?   (CP 122)

He knows where he is at last and has given a name to his lurking-place. He is in hell, but lurking in the sullen dark of a lurking-place is set off rhetorically against the joy of being "faced with her face." Such facing is a chance which does redeem all sorrows and which holds out the promise of resurrection to come. If hell is the suffering of being unable to love, "The truly beautiful" have still the power to harrow the damned out of the cold darkness of their own hearts and into largeness of life. The redeeming power—that which leads to laughter, joy, warmth, and finally to love—is always experienced as motion. "When she shakes out her hair," the narrator becomes "A man rich as a cat." Or, he says,

> When, easy as a beast,
> She steps along the street,
> I start to leave myself. (CP 121)

To start to leave one's self in such pursuit is a first step toward coming into one's own, a paradox that is by now familiar enough. And, as is so often Roethke's way, the energy of the climactic moment is represented linguistically by the intensifying device of ambiguity. "I start to leave myself" can be read in three ways: most obviously, as "I myself start to leave," suggesting pursuit; most significantly, as another of Roethke's images for love as a moving outside of the self; and, most forgivably, given the provocation, as yet another euphemism for sexual climax. Both the gathered energy of the image of the hero's coiling for action and the compressed intensity of language are released into the lovely movement of the ten poems that follow. After them, as if the energy has gradually dissipated itself, the remainder of the sequence diminishes toward stillness.

"Words for the Wind" and "I Knew a Woman," the two poems which follow immediately after "All the Earth, All the Air," are the high points of the sequence and are, for that matter, among the best pieces that Roethke ever wrote. In them he pulls out all his tricks for intensifying poetry, especially the devices of paradox, pun, repetition, and antithesis. Paradox, for instance, is vital to both poems, for it is the stuff of which the narrating character is woven. No longer lurking in the hell of a cold heart, the poet takes on in "Words for the Wind" and in "I Knew a Woman" the role of the martyr-clown, the wise (which is to say "knowing") fool. He is, he acknowledges, "no longer young," a "fond and foolish man" who must make do with "old bones" and with eyes that "dazzle" at the flowing shape of the woman he loves. She is incredible, almost awesome—swaying, playing, waking, breaking, frolicking, wandering, and, of course, moving continuously and in more ways than one. (The word *motion* or various forms of the verb *to move* appear nine times in the two poems, always in close connection with the woman.) And to all this, the poor narrator must respond as best he can, dancing round and round like a tame and toothless bear in a comic, scruffy, yet strangely dignified romp. His is a condition of blessed suffering, of blissful martyrdom, in which he bears the difficult burden of joy. The way of the lover leads through humiliation to humility and, like the way of the religious mystic, beyond humility to enlightenment. We see this process suggested in the final stanza of "Words for the Wind":

> She breaks my breath in half;
> She frolics like a beast;
> And I dance round and round,
> A fond and foolish man,
> And see and suffer myself
> In another being at last. (CP 126)

Or again in "I Knew a Woman," when, after nibbling meekly from his lady's hand and "Coming behind her for her pretty sake," the lover concludes,

> I'm martyr to a motion not my own;
> What's freedom for? To know eternity.
> I swear she cast a shadow white as stone.
> But who would count eternity in days?
> These old bones live to learn her wanton ways:
> (I measure time by how a body sways). (CP 127)

To "know" another, to know others, engenders a painful self-knowledge out of self-sacrifice; and such knowing, at least in "I Knew a Woman," sets a man free "To know eternity." Thus, if the fool persists in his foolishness, he becomes wise.

Pun is the proper language of paradox in Roethke, and these poems are no exceptions. The closing lines, quoted above, from "Words for the Wind" dance round and round, changing meanings rather than partners. To "see one's self" in another (and thus gain self-knowledge) is a common experience. But perhaps "another being" is merely a way of speaking of a different state of consciousness, a movement away from "Being myself" to being a different, "an other" being. And the sexual pun ought to be obvious enough. If we suffer fools, gladly or otherwise, must we also "suffer ourselves" when our folly is reflected in "another being"? Or, in "I Knew a Woman," what does the poet mean when he writes, "She was the sickle; I, poor I, the rake, / Coming behind her for her pretty sake"? (CP 127). Coburn Freer remarks that "the poem's witty sexual puns . . . are obvious enough and hardly require elucidation," [5] but I wonder if he is fully cognizant of all the shapes that Roethke's bright containers can contain. That word "behind" is tricky. For example, in addition to completing the mowing metaphor (itself a sexual pun), the rake's coming behind his lady may suggest simple appreciation of the southern charm of a north-bound woman. Further still, our rake may be testifying to a bit of sexual chivalry, a timing of his climax "behind" hers so that the woman lovely in her bones may have her due satisfaction. Such a reading provides another level of meaning for the line "I'm martyr to a motion not my own." And again, though perhaps a bit far-fetched, to "come behind" the lady suggests sexual positioning, an interpretation which might lend a bawdy appropriateness to those "English poets who grew up on Greek" and who are, Roethke insists, the proper chorus to sing her "choice virtues." Thus, ambiguity begets ambiguity; a pun in one line creates, in a dynamic and organic way, alternate readings in another, in others. "All's even with the odd," a line from "Words for the Wind," allows at least two readings of every word but *the*, and as *All* or *even* or *odd* shifts in value, it alters each of the others in turn and alters, too, the sense of "I'm odd, and full of love," a line coming eight stanzas later. In "I Knew a Woman," those English poets who grew up on Greek lead us to remember that "Turn, and Counter-turn, and Stand," in addition to their sexual suggestiveness, are the English equivalent of the Greek *strophe, antistrophe,* and *epode.* Apparently the woman, by her movement, becomes a kind of Muse whose turn and re-turn serve as inspiration for the poet's turns of language. "Counter-turn," after all, is also a term for the rhetorical device of repeating words in an inverse order, as in "(She moved in circles, and those circles moved)." Among the things she teaches, then, is creative writing, and this poem, with its turning and counter-turning of word against word, phrase against phrase, is both a celebration of her body's motion and a demonstration of what a poet can learn about poetics through the study of "how a body sways."

Both poems are marked by an almost tortuous density of repetition. "Words for the Wind" contains eleven lines in which some one word appears twice (though it does not always appear in exactly the same form), and my count does not include such near-misses as "Loving, I use the air / Most lovingly" (CP 123). "I Knew a Women" pushes repetition even harder, having eight of these echoing lines among its total of twenty-eight. And to intensify his effect, Roethke tends to throw such lines at us in clusters:

> When small birds sighed, she would sigh back at them;
> Ah, when she moved, she moved more ways than one:
> The shapes a bright container can contain!   (CP 127)

There is playfulness here as well as movement and intensity. In fact, in all of these devices Roethke's language is language taking pleasure in itself, delighting in its own moving shapes. Despite the inescapable overtones of comic martyrdom or of humiliating suffering, these are essentially happy poems. For the wise fool, both moved and moving, there is joy in "knowing," with, as Roethke would say, all the ambiguities of the word operative.

The next three poems, "The Voice," "She," and "The Other," develop further the idea of the woman as Beatrice-figure, the source of poetic rhythms as well as inspiration. In "The Voice" and "She" it is her "true voice," her "lovely song," that awakens the answering voice of the poet. "Desire exults the ear," he says, and at last

> Bird, girl, and ghostly tree,
> The earth, the solid air—
> Their slow song sang in me.   (CP 128)

Or, in "She," the lady's "low soft language" turns into a duet in which "We sing together; we sing mouth to mouth" (CP 129). Desire, it turns out, exults not only the listening, passive ear, but the poetic ear as well, the "ear" engaged in the act of song-making. In "The Other" the poet's tongue, his creative organ, is aroused by his lady's motion rather than by her voice. "She moves and I adore: / Motion can do no more" (CP 130). These lines, of course, are ambiguous. They seem to mean both that no motion is capable of doing more than does her motion and that motion has no higher purpose than to be the cause of adoration. In any case, the poem itself is clearly the act of adoration; it is another of Roethke's musical gestures in which the motion of language self-consciously responds to the motion of a body. Malkoff misreads, I believe, in assuming that it is the poet who "watches his beloved with the 'absent gaze' of a child who 'stares past a fire.'" [6] Surely, in the context of the poem, one who has been lolling "all Tongue" and adoring the motion of the beloved is unlikely to be adoring with "absent gaze." It is she who is young and careless, he who is neither, and therein lies much of the sadness in the music of the poem. The aging lover whose "old bones" once lived "to learn her wanton ways" now has his wish, but knowing "her careless ways" proves a mixed blessing. "Aging," he says, "I sometimes weep, / Yet still laugh in my sleep" (CP 130).

"Love's progress" has been costly in terms of energy. None of the three poems has the vitality of "Words for the Wind" or "I Knew a Woman." The rhythms have simplified and have slowed to the pace of that "slow song" absorbed by the poet in "The Voice." Roethke's devices for intensifying language are used most sparingly, and the absence of those devices is felt. The pervasive sense that one has of these poems is that they tell of a diminished impulse, of a noon pulsing away, of motion stayed as well as pulled, of laughter and tears that counteract one another.

The strategy of "The Sententious Man" seems to me highly complex. Ordinarily, we think of "sententiousness" as an appropriate characteristic of the aging clown who, Polonius-like, is "At times, indeed, almost ridiculous— / Almost, at times, the Fool."

And here, some might feel, the narrative persona wears a mask which is an uncomfortably close likeness to the face beneath; Roethke himself is often the sententious man, a poet much given to the aphoristic couplet, the rhymed maxim, the memorable apothegmatic line. Perhaps, then, the title with its inescapable connotations of pithy pomposity is ironic, part of Roethke's comic view of himself as lover and poet. However, Roethke's fool is never so foolish as he claims to be. He is, after all, one who has been "schooled in pain" and who has graduated with honors. The *sententiae* that he utters are not of the stuff fools think about, and they are marked by humility rather than pomposity. It may be that Roethke is up to an old trick here. In his essay called "Verse in Rehearsal," he recalls some suggestions made during his apprenticeship by "one of the best technicians among modern poets," Rolfe Humphries. Humphries had looked at an early draft of "Genesis" and objected to "its conventional rhymes: desire-fire; shock-rock; mirth-birth; sky-die" (SP 33). He went on to suggest that "What I think could be done with this kind of poem is deliberately advertise the conventional by calling it 'Poem with Old Rhymes' or something like that, and then work in the idea by way of counterpoint to the simplicity, and have it come out in the end, the emotion breaking the pattern . . ." (SP 33). Glancing at the work sheets of "The Sententious Man," Roethke could hardly have missed the epigrammatic quality of most of what he had written. No unit of thought takes up more than two lines, each stanza concludes with a closed couplet, and all lines are strongly end-stopped, often by periods. The effect, as Roethke knew as well as anyone, might well suggest scissors and paste, a verse-form modelled on the almanac. In Malkoff's words, "the reader is frequently called upon to decide whether a particular line is governed by its relation to the poem as a unit or by its effectiveness as an epigram." [7] But the mature poet has technical resources at his command that were not available to the apprentice who wrote, say, "The Conqueror." For one thing, he adopts the strategy that Humphries had suggested years before. He gives his poem a title which advertises the conventional patterns of his utterances, then works the dynamic content of the poem against those patterns so that emotion moves in counterpoint to the "sententious" form. The energy of thought is seen in arrest, "As if a lion stooped to kiss a rose, / Astonished into passionate repose" (CP 131).

Richard Hugo remembers occasions in the classroom when Roethke expressed admiration for Yeats's skill at handling enjambment; Hugo also remembers that at those times Roethke remarked that he himself found it difficult to write run-ons.[8] In "How to Write Like Somebody Else" Roethke writes of his practice of end-stopping lines with a kind of testy defensiveness. Insisting that his debt to Yeats has been over-acknowledged, Roethke concludes this way:

> One simple device provides, I believe, an important technical difference: in the pentameter, I end-stop almost every line— a thing more usual when the resources of the language were more limited. This is not necessarily a virtue—indeed, from many points of view, a limitation. But it is part of an effort, however clumsy, to bring the language back to bare, hard, even terrible statement.   (SP 70)

If Hugo's memory is correct, Roethke could not always avoid taking some of those points of view from which his aphoristic line looked like a limitation. But Hugo also says, and here he is surely correct, that Roethke covers this flaw by using "subtle and expert tonal and harmonic carry-overs from one line to the next so that the end-stops, which would be excessive for most poets, call a minimum of attention to themselves in Roethke."[9] Here of course, by titling his poem "The Sententious Man" Roethke himself calls maximum attention to the rough-hewn shape of his statements. Nonetheless, the "carry-overs," as Hugo calls them, are there—harmonic, tonal, associational, energetic.

The direction in which the lines "carry" is clear enough. Word links with word. The inert "loveless stone" of the first stanza passes through ice and fire and fire and ice to reappear in "the motion of the deepest stone" of stanza six. The impulse, line after line, is toward greater speed and intensity until motion purifies

the "True lechers" of stanza one and turns them into the strength-
ening bridegroom and his bride of the closing lines:

> I'm tired of brooding on my neighbor's soul;
> My friends become more Christian, year by year.
> Small waters run toward a miry hole—
> That's not a thing I'm saying with a sneer—
>
> For water moves until it's purified,
> And the weak bridegroom strengthens in his bride.   (cp 132)

To "become more," however timidly, is never to be sneered at.
Though Roethke's "deepest stone" swarms with revelations not to
be found by Rotarians in their Sunday pews, their attempt to
move toward Love is, like his own, an effort that strengthens and
purifies.

Appropriately, "The Pure Fury" and "The Renewal," though
love poems, are primarily poems of spiritual becoming, of movement toward "purification." "The Pure Fury" begins in reminis-
cence, an account of an archetypal "fearful night" through which
the poet "read nothing . . . / For every meaning had grown
meaningless" (CP 133). The encounter with nothing, the "death"
of meaning, is the descent into hell that leads to cosmic resurrection:

> Morning, I saw the world with second sight,
> As if all things had died, and rose again.
> I touched the stones, and they had my own skin.   (cp 133)

After the dark night, in other words, comes union with the very
stones, a motion answering the motion at the deep heart of things.
But tense is important in Roethke. That feeling is gone and now
he loves "a woman with an empty face." She is a fascinating figure,
a kind of Goldie Hawn as La Belle Dame Sans Merci. The woman
is not, I think, the same one who appears earlier in the sequence,
or, if she is the same, she is now viewed through eyes that have
been much disillusioned. She remains a force—still beautiful, still
enticing—but she is also vacuity personified, the apotheosis of
mindlessness:

> I love a woman with an empty face.
> Parmenides put Nothingness in place;
> She tries to think, and it flies loose again.
> How slow the changes of a golden mean:
> Great Boehme rooted all in Yes and No;
> At times my darling squeaks in pure Plato.   (CP 133)

Malkoff offers a passage from Paul Tillich as source for this stanza, and I find his evidence most convincing. According to Tillich, "Plato used the concept of nonbeing because without it the contrast of existence with the pure essences is beyond understanding." [10] Apparently Roethke's darling squeaks a language that is as purely nonbeing as one is likely to find on the shadowy wall of Plato's cave.

Small wonder that the next stanza begins, "How terrible the need for solitude." The poet affirms his own rage to live, to be something more. In this case he wishes to become once again the "thing he almost was" in that first stanza when the stones took on his skin and when the trees came closer "with a denser shade." His woman is so much the spirit of mindlessness, of nonbeing, that a dream of her *is* a dream of death, a dreamed experience like that of the long night during which all things died and rose again. In fact, she has taken the poet's breath away, and, with his breath, she has possession of both his life-giving and creative force. She is the abyss near which he lives, the incarnation of the meaninglessness and nothingness that he once read through his fearful night. And the poet hopes to stay "Until my eyes look at a brighter sun / As the thick shade of the long night comes on" (CP 134). Like death itself, a woman so vacuous has a certain creative potential; she, too, is a nothingness that may precede resurrection. The poem takes its energy from its central paradox. Nonbeing, meaninglessness, is a denial of life, but there is hope for the rising of a "brighter sun" out of so much darkness. It may be that in a dark time, the I will again begin to see.

As its title suggests, "The Renewal" is also concerned with an "Illumination" growing out of a darkness, this time a darkness that "hangs upon the waters of the soul" (CP 35). Here, however, the woman has all but vanished from the poem and it is the energy of the poetic imagination that celebrates itself by creating "glories," specifically glories of motion. Roethke begins like a stage magician, a scruffy sleight-of-hand man amusing an audience (one that includes his own less magically gifted self) by asking what trick it would like to see performed, what glories it would like to see him produce out of thinnest air. The answer, itself in the form of a question, sets the poet the task of bringing "Motions of the soul" within the reach of his imaginings. His specialty, it seems, is converting desires into experiences or, as he puts it, "I teach my sighs to lengthen into songs" (CP 135). The song-poem must be "experienced," we should remember, and not be merely a "talking about" sort of thing.

The desire must be turned to song; the interrogative must become an exclamation. In the process the poet-magician goes a dark way, down into one of those watery drowses that so often in Roethke precedes the urge and wrestle of resurrection:

> Dark hangs upon the waters of the soul;
> My flesh is breathing slower than a wall.
> Love alters all. Unblood my instinct, love.
> These waters drowse me into sleep so kind
> I walk as if my face would kiss the wind.   (CP 135)

Renewal is marked by growing rhetorical intensity, by a preponderance of monosyllables, by repetition and counter-turning: "I know I love, yet know not where I am" (CP 135). The "I" turns and turns again in the line, and there is a frantic quality to the action:

> I saw the dark, the shifting midnight air.
> Will the self, lost, be found again? In form?
> I walk the night to keep my five wits warm.   (CP 135)

And out of these desperate questings and questionings emerge the exclamations that become the poet's answering illumination—an illumination to be found "in form," in the taut rhythms and rhymes of the final stanza. There Roethke finds in "the deepest stone" the motion that pulses at the loving heart of the world; it is "As if reality had split apart / And the whole motion of the soul lay bare" (CP 135). The language flashes from the straightforward to the metaphorical and back again at a pace rapid enough to blur distinctions. At the peak of illumination the poet *sees* "the rubble-stones begin to stretch," but the splitting apart of reality and the laying bare of the soul's motion occurs in the realm of "As if." Then, in the twinkling of a colon, we are back in the world of statement, half-literal, half-metaphorical, entirely mystical: "I find that love, and I am everywhere" (CP 135). The love found, the sense of being "everywhere," is a new reality, a "glory" neither literal nor imagined, but partaking of both the literal and the imagined and transcending both. Thus Roethke creates the verbal effect of a motion so rapid that the soul is simultaneously in the dimension of the "real" and the imagined. And for the magician, speaking and listening, half-perceiving and half-creating, to experience such a motion comes very close indeed to being "everywhere."

The rest of the sequence carries on the protagonist's struggle to know, though what remains to be known is a weary and sometimes fearful knowledge. Like Frost's oven bird, the poet must learn how to speak of a diminished thing. The rhythmic energy of the sequence, somewhat renewed in "The Sententious Man," "The Pure Fury," and "The Renewal," begins to slacken again, though "The Sensualists" possesses a certain seedy vitality. A common poem in common meter about what Mother would have termed "common" people, it does nonetheless explore another aspect of love's motion. "There is no place to turn," the woman laments, "You have me pinned so close," and in the final stanza she adds, "I hate this sensual pen" (CP 136). (Roethke is punning again, this time on *pen* as the poet's tool.) Even the man, by this time an uneasy rider, "rides" in a kind of pen of which the unpadded walls are "those lovely tits." This motion, violent enough that "The bed itself begins to quake," does not lead to an epiphany of stillness as does, say, the mad and holy car ride of *North American Sequence*, but rather to a limpness, to fatigued and painful impotence. There is, of course, one other motion in the poem, the tiptoeing away down the hall of that ghostly figure who, "Affrighted from her wits" had been standing beside the quaking bed. The woman may be The Mother—any mother—who comes to cast a spectral shadow over the adult sensuality of those who were, as we all were, once children and innocent. "All sensual love's but dancing on a grave," as Roethke put it in "The Dying Man." Or, if the child may be said to be father to the man, the ghostly visitor may be the virgin that is mother to the sensuous woman. In a related sense, she may be the dream woman from the first poem of the sequence. The passing of that dreamy shadow leaves the poet in a nightmarish reality complete with burning forehead and parching tongue. In any case, her departure—taking her breath *with* her and *from* the lovers—signifies, for good or ill, the passing of an innocence and a purity from the relationship of the two who now must find their way in a fallen world, the world of men. That Malkoff, who is so often very good in his readings, should see in the spectral woman "the familiar ghost in the wall (symbol of father and sexual guilt)," [11] and thus turn "A woman . . . pure as a bride" into Otto Roethke is a warning against the dangers of rigidifying Roethkean symbols. In reading a dynamic poet, context is all.

"Love's Progress" and "The Surly One" are poems taken over by *fear*, the word that dominates the final stanza of each. The takeover is most apparent in "Love's Progress," which begins with daring, with "The possibles we dare" (CP 137), and ends with fear for one's own joy, fear of one's own self. The theme of knowing emerges again, this time connected to a very different kind of pun from that of "I Knew a Woman," for here the overtones are more tragic than comic. "A woman's naked in water," chants the poet, "And I know where she is." That "know where" is linked to the "nowhere" of stanza four: "Father, I'm far from home, / And I have gone nowhere." It is as if Roethke is saying "I know where I am when I'm lost." "Where?" we ask. And the answer is "Nowhere." He is, after all, with the woman ("I have considered and found / A mouth I cannot leave"), and knows where *she* is, but he can locate the place only as "far from home . . . no-

where." The final stanza of the poem is an imaginative creation of
that "nowhere" that the poet has come to "know" by going there:

> The close dark hugs me hard,
> And all the birds are stone.
> I fear for my own joy;
> I fear myself in the field,
> For I would drown in fire.   (CP 138)

The dark builds its own kind of "pen," and the birds, usually
associated with the powers of song-making and graceful movement, have been turned stone-still. The ambiguity of "I fear for my
own joy" captures nicely the protagonist's pain. On the one hand,
his joy is so consuming that, like the log singing in its flame, he
must fear that it will destroy him utterly. On the other hand, he
must fear the loss of joy, for its existence seems most precarious.
One fears for one's own joy, in this sense, as one is said to fear
for one's own health.

In "The Surly One" love has, indeed, ended in heart-break, and
the poet has become a terrifying figure mean enough to get away
with telling his neighbors "when to laugh." He keeps a dog less
ferocious than he is. Not even the howling ghosts he has feared
for so long are as terrifying to him as he is to himself. Like Young
Goodman Brown, brandishing his staff in his forest rage, the most
terrible thing in a woodland of horrors, the narrator need fear no
shade more than he fears his own:

> Ghost cries out to ghost—
> But who's afraid of that?
> I fear those shadows most
> That start from my own feet.   (CP 138)

In "Plaint" rage gives way to a quieter despair, a sameness
"Day after somber day" that is Roethke's special idea of hell. "In
hell," he says, as though defining the concept, "there is no
change." (CP 139). A resurrection of spirit is required, but the
poet lacks the knowledge "that / Could bring [him] to [his] God"
(CP 139). Faced with the dead end of dust, failing light, late

November, he remembers that the way forward is sometimes the way back, the way up sometimes the way down:

> I lived with deep roots once:
> Have I forgotten their ways—
> The gradual embrace
> Of lichen around stones?   (cp 139)

Notice the sad play over the words *deep roots*, the delicacy of the question that answers itself, the sense of the forgotten turning to remembrance, the weary rhythms of a speaker half in love with the death that is only a deeper sleep. Perhaps, the narrator suggests, in that deep sleep grows the root of a tree of knowledge that leads a man, not from but toward his God.

"The Swan" is really two poems, an interesting study in Roethke's ability to modulate the intensity of his verse. Section one is a last fling at the old rage. It celebrates the "coursing blood," the impassioned life "certain as a bull" (CP 140). All the intensifying devices return; repetition and antithesis, paradox, ambiguity, the clacking play within a single line of hard consonant against consonant—even some internal rhyme to give the ear the effect of a shorter, more compact line than is actually seen on the page.

> We think too long in terms of what to be;
> I live, alive and certain as a bull;
> A casual man, I keep my casual word,
> Yet whistle back at every whistling bird.
> A man alive, from all light I must fall.
> I am my father's son, I am John Donne
> Whenever I see her with nothing on.   (cp 140)

The repetition and "counter-turning" of words is obvious enough, as are the ambiguity of "keep," the paradox of the poet's being at once his father's son and John Donne, the internal rhymes of the fifth and sixth lines, and the half-comic rhyme that closes the stanza. This is Roethke manifesting abundancy—even redundancy —of life, repeating the word itself as if the sound had magic properties, singing at last the phallic oneness of all vital men when confronted by the eternal woman "with nothing on."

But the poet sings in praise of another kind of "nothing" in part two of the poem. Liquids and sibilants take over, and the devices for intensification vanish as the poet retreats into the silence that waits at the poem's end. The desire for lively life gives way to the longing for lovely death—for that "nothing of which all is made." The rhythms slow, the rhymes become more and more faint, until at last we come to the word *god*, and the rest is the quiet blankness of wordless space.

The sequence, which began with a dream, ends with one, this time a dream of death in which "The outside dies within" and "The wind dies on the hill" (CP 141). Loving and knowing blend, for the loved one "knows all I am" and "Love's all. Love's all I know" (CP 141). This is an ambiguous kind of knowing, though the ambiguities reinforce one another. Whether the poet has learned that love is all—the lesson to be found in the dance at the heart of the deepest stone—or whether he is merely saying that he has specialized too narrowly, that he knows nothing but love and will thus be left adrift should love fail him, one is, finally, what one knows. Love is all he knows and all he is.

In the closing lines he starts to follow the doe and fawn who reappear like shadows from an earlier dream, but the way turns hard; the organic, yielding grass changes to stone. The effect is that of a closing door; the intrusion of reality, of the present upon remembered bliss. We are back with the standing stones of "All the Earth, All the Air" and far from the loving stones which wore the poet's own skin in "The Pure Fury" or those which revealed "the whole motion of the soul" in "The Renewal."

I am not certain, but in these *Love Poems* I sometimes think that Roethke is deliberately manipulating his poetic techniques in such a way that the reader is supposed to feel the varied rhythms of love, the peaks and valleys of excitement. In other words, though fully in command of a host of tricks for generating intensity, he pulls punches on occasion, allows a slackening of dramatic, rhythmic, and linguistic tensions in those poems which demonstrate the failing passion of the relationship. In any case, I think him a better poet over the long haul of *Sequence, Sometimes Metaphysical*. There, though the pursuit of God, like the pursuit of a woman, has its dark times, Roethke insists that, like joy, despair has its own terrible intensity. And such intensity requires every trick at his disposal if it is to be adequately created in language.

Sequence,
Sometimes Metaphysical

Roethke once described *Sequence, Sometimes Metaphysical* as "a hunt, a drive toward God; an effort to break through the barrier of rational experience." [1] For Roethke the motion of such a hunt or drive was both exhilarating and terrifying. If on the one hand he felt drawn by the love of God and by a desire to come at last face to face with transcendent reality, on the other hand he feared the encounter might utterly destroy him. After all, if one *should* at last break through the barriers of the rational, what lay on the other side? Roethke knew only too well the terrors of the dim regions beyond those barriers. He had himself tottered on the windy edge of the rational more than once, and, though he liked to poke fun at the dreariness of reason's "hutch," he knew first hand that the leap into the abyss was no jump for the timid. Moreover, should the journey reach an end, even a perfect end, should one lose himself in finding God, what then? There are terrors in perfection, terrors even in too great joy. We cling to our sense of self, for it is all that we have ever known, all that we have ever certainly possessed.

As might be expected, then, from its beginning in a dark time to its ending in a joyous dance, Roethke's *Sequence* is a journey which both comforts and terrifies. Is it not a smooth progression from the dark to celestial light. Sometimes, the poet knew, it is necessary to go back in order to move ahead. And so the spirit's progress is represented as uncertain, halting, frequently falling back into despair. The sequence moves fitfully, its protagonist torn between the desire which reaches out and the fear which clings to what one has and is. Thus, the *Sequence* is "Metaphysical," I take it, because the "metaphysical manner" is well suited to the reconciliation of diverse images and attitudes, to creating precarious unities from the scattered materials of life and to the presentation of paradox. And it is "Sometimes" metaphysical because the spiritual journey has moments calling for pure lyricism, moments when opposites come suddenly in place and when all paradoxes vanish into irrelevance. For such moments another "manner" is required and is supplied.

Perhaps no poem of Theodore Roethke's has received more sensitive and intelligent critical commentary than has "In a Dark Time." [2] Nevertheless, the poem illustrates so well Roethke's genius for making his medium one with his message that I hope I may be excused a few observations of my own. To my knowledge, some of the most pervasive characteristics of the poem have never received comment. The use of various forms of paradox, the use of puns, especially repeated puns, and the careful balancing of question and exclamation are, perhaps, too obvious to seem worthy of comment. They are, however, devices which reinforce and strengthen the poem, devices which help to make the experience of reading the poem mirror the experience which is the occasion for and the subject of the poem. Most commentators, Roethke among them, agree that the poem is "about" a kind of mystical revelation. Roethke himself says it is "about" an attempt "to break from the bondage of the self, from the barriers of the 'real' world, to come as close to God as possible." [3]

In his attempt to render that experience poetically, Roethke has used (depending on what one counts) about a dozen paradoxical statements in a twenty-four line poem. Beginning with the first line, in which we are told that "In a dark time, the eye begins to see," and continuing through the last, in which "one" mysteriously becomes "One," paradox is the basic substance of the poem. The poet-narrator meets his shadow "in a deepening shade," precisely the place in which, reason tells us, a sharply outlined individual shadow *cannot* be discerned. The narrator is "a lord of nature," yet this lordly creature weeps, a most un-lordly sort of behavior, to a natural object, a tree. The narrator knows purity, but it is a sinful purity, a "purity of pure despair." In the world of the poem, midnight comes "in broad day." A man goes far to find his identity, yet the identity is found only in a "Death of the self." "Natural shapes" are on fire with "unnatural light." The final stanza is a bramble patch of paradox and mystery. The poet insists that his is a dark light, that as a fallen man he climbs, that the mind must somehow enter itself. Roethke's comments on the latter image are of interest: "this suggests (visually at least) an androgynous act, a hole disappearing into itself, 'crawling into your hole and pulling your hole after you,' the folk saying has it." [4] All of this is wonderfully mysterious; one *may*, as Roethke suggests, be able to visualize what happens when "The mind enters itself, and God the mind, / And one is One, free in the tearing wind," but whatever happens, it is not an experience to be explained in purely rational terms. Like pulling a hole in after one's self, Roethke's escape to freedom in the final stanza is a good trick, and one never performed under the roof of reason's "dreary shed."

The confounding of reason with paradox is, of course, precisely what Roethke intends. Having accepted the conditions laid down by the first line, the reader enters a world in which the only certainty is the mysterious complexity of things, a world in which nothing is its solid self. To call into question the conventional values and expectations of the world is the commonplace use that poets make of paradox; few, however, have used the device more effectively than does Roethke in "In a Dark Time." If the reader can get into the poem at all, he does so because Roethkean paradox shoves him, in effect, through "the barrier of rational experience." He must give up his hold on "the 'real' world," as Roethke called it, and begin to see in the darkness that is light. To accept the poem, to find that its paradoxes "make sense," is to go at least part-way down the narrator's winding path, a path which may, after all, turn out to be a cave.

Roethke's puns strengthen "In a Dark Time" both structurally and thematically. As an example, it seems certain that Roethke is playing with the words *eye* and *I*. For one thing, the poem begins with an "eye" as subject and quickly moves to a repeated first person pronoun. In line one "the eye begins to see," but in line two "*I* meet my shadow in the deepening shade." Such a linkage is valid thematically, for it asserts subtly the relationship between identity and vision. In the world of the poem, a man is what he begins to see. The quality of vision is what determines "Which I is *I*?" Structurally, the "eye" of stanza one becomes the "I" that is searching for identity. Perhaps we are supposed to remember Emerson's "I" becoming a "transparent eyeball," as we encounter Roethke's Emersonian reference to "A steady stream of correspondences."

The "eye" pun is related to another bit of word play. The self dies in a "long, tearless night," and in the last line of the poem one is "free in the tearing wind." "Tearless" may, of course, be taken to mean either *without rip* or *without teardrops*. I suspect that both are intended. The long night is oppressive, without seam or breathing space. At the same time, neither the indifferent darkness nor the narrator sheds tears over the "Death of the self," for such death is "good death," is part of the process by which one comes to be "free." The "Lord of nature" has stopped weeping. The "tearing wind," according to John Crowe Ransom, is part of "a storm from heaven," is "a tearing but cleansing wind to sweep all the foolishness of the mind away." [5] I agree, but Roethke also wants us to hear the word as "tear-ing." "I feel," he writes, "there is a hope in the ambiguity of 'tearing'—that the ambient air itself, that powers man once deemed merely 'natural,' or is unaware of, are capable of pity; that some other form or aspect of God will endure with man again, will save him from himself." [6]

There are other puns. "Shadow" is played off against "shade," and surely the adjective "fallen" bears both physical and spiritual meanings in the phrase "A fallen man." When Roethke cries "The edge is what I have," he is turning the idiom "to have the edge" to good use. Roethke's edge, his creative advantage, is the perilous edge on which he walks, the edge between life and death, between the death of the self and the birth of the self.

As is the case with his use of paradox, Roethke's puns suggest something of the enormous complexities of life. And, perhaps more important, some of his puns are so interdependent that they form an organic poetic structure that imitates the organic nature of Roethke's view of the world. We hear the dual possibilities in "tearing," for example, largely because "Tearless" and "the eye" and the "weeping lord" have come before. As we have so often seen before, then, a given word in the poem, a serious pun, may change in meaning and value because of the weight of others coming before and after, just as the experience of the instant alters in meaning and value in the context of other experiences, other instants.

The spirit journeys toward God through alternate moments of revelation and uncertainty. In Roethke's poem, these moments are represented by exclamations and questions. There are three of each. The exclamations all seem to be cries of wonder at the terrifying beauty of the visions that have been earned and dared. "The day's on fire!" the poet exclaims. And, again, in the next stanza,

> A steady storm of correspondences!
> A night flowing with birds, a ragged moon,
> And in broad day the midnight come again!

The first of the three questions is primarily rhetorical, "What's madness but nobility of soul / At odds with circumstance?" but the others show the anguish of the human voyager struggling to be reborn and yet wishing not to die. I believe that we are meant to pair the questions, that the matter of whether the place among the rocks is a cave or a path is directly related to the question of "Which I is I?" If the place among the rocks (toward which the poem moves) is a cave, then the journey comes to a dead end, to a kind of tomb. There is no escape, no freedom. The walls of the cave and the closed window against which the heat-maddened fly buzzes are, in value and function, one and the same. On the other hand, if the opening among the rocks is a path, it is a way through and he who seeks and finds such an opening is the successful adventurer, the spiritual path-finder. The two questions form one: am I a trapped and helpless thing like the fly, or am I capable as a man, however fallen, of climbing out to freedom, however "tearing"? What *is* man? Which I *is* I?

Generally, the poem moves from the "In" of "In a dark time" to the "out" of the fallen man who climbs "out of [his] fear." Or, perhaps, from that initial "In" to the last line's "free *in* the tearing wind," a much different sort of confinement. It begins in division and ends in a precarious unity. It begins with human tears and ends with tears of grace and pity shed by "the ambient air itself." It begins in the darkness of spiritual ignorance and ends in the dark light of the knowledge of God.

It is darkness that connects "In a Dark Time" with "In Evening Air." The darkness found in evening air, however, is very different from the darkness which comes in broad day and in which we "begin to see." There is nothing of the supernatural about the growing darkness of evening, and the air is alive, as Wallace Stevens once put it, "with wormy metaphors." The spiritual problem of the poet-protagonist is that of how to live in the "real" world after the sense of oneness with God has passed. It is a form of the problem facing Keats when he discovers that "the fancy cannot cheat so well / As she is fam'd to do," and that he must always come back to "The weariness, the fever and the fret." In evening air, Roethke experiences withdrawal pangs and finds the mystical moment only in memory:

> Once I transcended time:
> A bud broke to a rose
> And I rose from a last diminishing.   (CP 240)

The poet's identification with the bud's breaking to become the rose is underscored by the "rose" pun, but the tense is past and the moment occurred "Once" only.

As comfort against the terrors of growing darkness, Roethke

makes a poem about the powers of "making" as a means of keeping, holding, possessing. "A dark theme keeps me here," he begins, and I take the word *keeps* to have *preserves* as its primary meaning in this context. He then asks, "Who would be half possessed / By his own nakedness?" More cry than question, those lines reach back over twenty years to the title poem of Roethke's first volume, *Open House*. Spiritual nakedness was, for Roethke, one of the prerequisites for the writing of honest poetry:

> I'm naked to the bone,
> With nakedness my shield.
> Myself is what I wear:
> I keep the spirit spare.   (CP 3)

The need, then, is to be *wholly* possessed by his own nakedness before one can *make* a broken music, a music with, perhaps, some power to preserve life. "I'll make a broken music," Roethke says, "or I'll die." Human making and divine making are joined in the next stanza as Roethke prays, "Make me, O Lord, a last, a simple thing / Time cannot overwhelm." Note that both human and Godly making are invoked as a means of keeping or holding life against the flowing waters of Time.

Stanza three develops further these themes of destroying and preserving. Looking down "the far light," the poet "*beholds*" "the dark side of a tree," a living, growing organism with which he may identify to some extent. The word *behold* punningly combines the powers of looking and holding. To behold is to "hold" with the eye, perhaps with the heart. But the powers are limited, and "when I look again, / It's lost upon the night." The poet "holds" the darkness that remains, embraces "Night . . . a dear proximity." By seizing or arresting the darkness, embracing it as "dear," one gains some power over it. In the final stanza the poet finds himself in a feeble circle of light cast by "a low fire." The darkness comes down around him. Even in this state, he may be more than a helpless observer. Punning richly, he says, "I bid stillness be still." The line offers multiple meanings, but all of them assert a human power, the power to command stillness. The human being may choose to maintain (keep) silence, or he may break it. He may remain motionless, or he may move. Roethke intends the line to be highly ambiguous, but I suspect that he wants us to realize that to "still" stillness—whether to stop it or to silence it—is to act, to say human things in a human voice, perhaps to make a poem. After all, one cannot command stillness (silence) without breaking it. At the very least, the line is a hymn to man's control, however inadequate, over the silence of the coming dark.

In the last lines, "I see in evening air, / How slowly dark comes down on what we do," the key words seem to me to be "slowly" and "do." Clearly, the poet is expressing wonder at the *slowness* with which dark comes down, rather than awe (or fear) at the simple fact of its coming down at all. Doing and making are, in this poem at least, ways of keeping and holding. The dark may come down swiftly on what we *are*, but what we *do*, the poem that we make, becomes the foster child of *slow* time and partakes of eternity. "In Evening Air" *makes* its point by *making* of Roethke's voice "a simple thing / Time cannot overwhelm." The poem is at once prayer and the answer to prayer.

Such solace does not appear in "The Sequel," a poem which plumbs the depths of doubt and despair. The poet begins by questioning his experiences with the air, both the ambient, "tear-ing" wind of "In a Dark Time" and the evening air in which dark comes slowly down "on what we do." The poet has come to know the difficulty of knowing. "Was I too glib about eternal things?" he asks. "Whom do we love? I thought I knew the truth; / Of grief I died, but no one knew my death" (CP 241). Not only has he come to doubt the "truth" that he once "glibly" knew, he has discovered that his "death" has passed unnoticed by the universe, and, if unnoticed, that even that experience suddenly seems unreal.

The two stanzas that follow explain what the narrator has lost, why he "died of grief." They form a retrospective account of a moment of vision, a moment of intimacy with wind and air. The shift to past tense is vital and has not always been sufficiently

taken into account by Roethke's readers.[7] As in "In Evening Air,"
the narrator looks back to a time when time was transcended.
Here the experience is represented as a dance in the wind, a dance
in which the poet's partner is, as Mills puts it, "his guide, his
Beatrice" and also "the *anima* or soul which is a female principle
in the male." [8] The power of the poet's calling is evoked, for the
creature is "A shape called up out of my natural mind." The poet's
vocation is, in turn, to call, to use the powers of his voice to
create. And, having created or called up, he finds himself capable
of entering his own creation, his own fiction. All of nature, nestling and partridge and bird and moon, join with him and his
Beatrice in the dance of the imagination. Like Adam, the poet
takes part in creation by naming, by *calling* the nestling his. And
like Adam, his term in Eden is short-lived. With the coming of
"outrageous dawn," the narrator's love leaves him.

> She left my body, lighter than a seed;
> I gave her body full and grave farewell. . . .
> A light leaf on a tree, she swayed away
> To the dark beginnings of another day.   (CP 241)

The leaving leaf is to the tree, Roethke suggests, as the guide-
anima figure-Muse is to the poet, to the self. The identification
of the protagonist of the *Sequence* with the tree that appears and
reappears throughout is quite clear in this passage.

The final stanza returns to present tense, drops the narrative
form of the second and third stanzas. Once again, the dance having ended, we are left with questions. "Was nature kind? The
heart's core tractable?" The nature of nature is at question; was
it benign? Was it, as it seemed, related by sympathy to man? And
did the heart learn, was it altered by the experience? There are no
answers, but the next line reminds us that mutability is part of
the nature of nature, that even the elements are subject to
entropy, to wavering and failing. "Leaves, leaves, lean forth and
tell me what I am," the poet begs. The leaves are, of course,
linked by imagery with the dancing shape from the "natural

mind," but they are also reminders of mortality and of the organic nature of life. Like the apple of Stevens's monocled uncle, a leaf

> serves as well as any skull
> To be the book in which to read a round,
> And is as excellent, in that it is composed
> Of what, like skulls, comes rotting back to ground.[9]

At the same time, the leaf is, as Thoreau knew, the pattern from which one may trace "all the operations of Nature. The Maker of this earth but patented a leaf." Roethke's tree, as if in reply, turns into flames, presumably the slow fire of decaying, changing leaves, which is at once a manifestation of the life process and the outward sign of death. The narrator, on the other hand, finds himself in a colorless cell, a prison in which the beauty of decay is absent. His denial of desire manifests itself in the fear of motion. He confines himself to intermittent pacing, a motion kept safely within "dead-white walls."

The message spelt from Roethke's leaves leads to "The Motion," one of the best poems of the *Sequence*. The poem offers about as many "motions" as has the soul itself. Its verbs squirm with life. We *stretch, embrace, grieve into, beget, meet, rise up, take up, stride, fare-forth, alter, reach, act, share, live,* and, of course, *move.* This energetic motion is a reaffirmation of the life-giving power of desire, both sexual and spiritual. The Love of God (which begets in us our love of God) and our love of the act of love are the forces by which we "move" and thereby "live." "By lust alone," says the poet, "we keep the mind alive." In "The Motion," even the relationship between the mind and the physical world seems the occasion for a sexual pun: "To meet the world, I rise up in my mind." Presumably, the offspring of this flowing intercourse between the imagination and the things of the earth is poetry, is "The Motion."

The central paradox of this poem, as in so many of Roethke's poems, is that all this motion, all this urge and wrestle, becomes a source of stability and comfort. Stretchings of the spirit and lustings of the mind lead to "the certainty of love." The voice of the poem insists that "By striding I remain." Amid the altering of all things, and despite love's continuous faring-forth, we reach "this final certitude, / This reach beyond this death . . ." (CP 243). Like a bicyclist, Roethke finds stability in motion. The constancy of change is the only constancy we shall know, and in our ceaseless putting down and taking up, our lusting and grieving, we find that motion, the love of motion and the motion of love, endures as our "final certitude." This paradox is captured in the magnificent closing line, "O, motion O, our chance is still to be!" Our chance to *be* "still" (motionless, at rest) lies in our ability to synchronize our motion with "the motion" that is life. If we accept change and growth and process, if we accept each moving instant's offer of "still" (yet) another chance "to be," if we wed our motion to the flow of time, we lose our dread of speed, conquer our motion sickness, and have the sensation of stillness while very much in flux. By striding, as Roethke puts it, we remain. To stand against the motion of life, to deny desire, is death.

"Infirmity," the next poem in the *Sequence*, accepts the judgment of "The Motion," for "there is no choice." To deny desire is to deny love; to deny decay is to deny growth. And, deny as he will, man finds the process goes on. He still must feel the "failure" of autumn. However, acceptance of motion as the way of things is not entirely comforting. The strength of "Infirmity" is its ability to present the quiet courage of acceptance and affirmation. The narrator sees only too clearly that "the way up is the way down," that spiritual purity is purchased at the cost of the decay of the flesh. "Eternity's not easily come by," he notes sadly, but he will endure what must be endured (and will manage to sing as he does so).

"Infirmity" is a religious poem, beginning in love of the self and ending in the love of Christ. The tone of the opening stanza is gently self-mocking. It is only human to love one's self, to play Narcissus and bow down before our own grave mirrored images. And it is human to fear the loss of that self, the loss of identity. The poet's cry is everyman's cry, "Oh, to be something else, yet still to be!" (CP 244). The universal dream is to have a fresh start, to reach a higher state, without letting go of what one has and is. And it is a foolish dream, however beautiful it may be.

As Whitman once suggested, we take identity from our bodies, and the hero of "Infirmity" is finding that there is little left of his body that he cares to call his own. His own bodily fluids are drained from one end and artificial ones are pumped in at the other: "Today they drained the fluid from a knee / And pumped a shoulder full of cortisone" (CP 244). Yet, as the flesh "breaks down," a "pure extreme of light / Breaks" on the aging man. The soul "delights," answering its own kind of light to light. Once again, as in "In Evening Air," "breaking" is associated with a spiritual "break through," with a moment of vision. Roethke's hero, hardly one of "the meek," finds that he has been granted a kind of grace and comfort. The seeker of the eternal finds that the eternal has sought and found him, that he has inherited love, not wrath.

The prison of self-love is "broken." "Dead" to himself and to all he holds "most dear," the narrator samples Eternity, finds himself "beyond the reach of wind and fire." His brief vision of Eternity is metaphorically expressed in the fourth stanza.

> Deep in the greens of summer sing the lives
> I've come to love. A vireo whets its bill.
> The great day balances upon the leaves . . .   (CP 244)

The moment of epiphany does not last, but neither is it totally lost. The bird's song echoes in the "inner ear," and the permanence and the "balance" found in that song are reflected by the "stillness" of the next three lines:

> My ears still hear the bird when all is still;
> My soul is still my soul, and still the Son,
> And knowing this, I am not yet undone.   (CP 244)

Roethke fought hard against editorial deletion of any of those "still's." [10] Their cumulative effect is to call attention to what the narrator has found to be "still" amid the motion of life. The things which partake of the stillness of Eternity are Christ, the mortal-immortal Son of God; the soul, which is mysteriously one with Christ, and thus immortal; and the bird's song, wordless, but with a message of grace and love. These are the certainties which sustain the voyager in the midst of flux. With *knowledge*, unqualified knowledge, of these "still" things, the narrator is able to go on, to set out to "come by" the Eternity he has glimpsed, however difficult the way. "At the end," he sets out to teach himself to see (and hear) behind his physical decay the "unwinding" and the purification of the spirit. It is not a lesson to be comprehended by the usual senses in the usual ways; the eyes must hear, the ears must see, "How body from spirit slowly does unwind / Until we are pure spirit at the end."

"The Decision" completes the change from denial and fear to commitment and courage. Much of the first stanza is in the past tense, a description of a phoebe's song which haunted the narrator when he "was young." The song of the phoebe is a "slow retreating" from song, a reluctant song reminding him of "The sleepy sound of leaves in a light wind." Our hero finds himself poised between phoebe and vireo, between the drowsy lotus-land of childhood and the Eternity which must be bought at the cost of all that one has and is. The "Decision" is made in the white space between the stanzas. As the second stanza begins, the narrator exclaims that "Rising or falling's all one discipline," Roethke's own version of "The way up is the way down." *Discipline*, of course, is a word that moves more ways than one. Primarily it is used here as a synonym for "course of study," or "lesson," but it also has the force of "punishment." Our traveller finds himself in the position of an experimental rat who is shocked if he acts and shocked if he does not. "Discipline" is unavoidable. The paradox of that first line is followed by another paradox in the second: "The line of my horizon's growing thin!" (CP 245). Here is growth, but growth toward thinness, the growth of one no longer young. The life process begins to impose limitations, and one's journeying is seen more and more clearly to have but one end.

Still turned toward the past, still listening to the "retreating" song, the narrator calls on the darkness at his back for guidance. "Which is the way?" he cries. The answer is loud silence. And, having been instructed in the way, he turns, putting forever "behind him" the idea of "running from God," of escaping change and process by preserving one's self in some museum case of the memory. The way through the dark will not be easy, but he has the power to endure as he struggles forward like one who "turns to face on-coming snow."

In any birth—spiritual or physical—the "turning" is decisive and painful. Though one crisis is past, much remains to be suffered before one emerges, victorious or otherwise. And so "The Marrow" begins in pain. All's cheerless, dark and deadly. The wind brings no new message of hope or faith, and the mist swarms with intimations of mortality. "What's the worst portion in this mortal life?" asks the poet, and for once he seems to answer himself with certainty. The worst of *this* life is one thing he knows, but it is not the knowledge that he desires with such passion. It is not the knowledge for which he bleeds his bones.

The second stanza sets forth the dangers and rewards of contemplation, of "Brooding on God." On the one hand, one risks losing his soul, risks death itself; on the other, contemplation may make one wholly evolved, may give one a sense of his worth and identity as a man. One thing is sure. Having seen the "white face" that shines brighter than "the sun" (surely "the Son" is brought to mind by the pun), the "desire" to see it again, to see it more clearly, to touch, to possess if possible, becomes a burning, an intolerable rage for more. The agony of separation is the subject of stanza three. In the absence of vision, the poet cries for an answer: "Godhead above my God, are you there still?" As usual, Roethke's "still" carries at once the force of "yet," of "still," and of "silent." But the conversation is one-sided, and Roethke can only hope to be heard, not answered. His shout is both lament and prayer. "Lord, hear me out, and hear me out this day: / From me to Thee's a long and terrible way" (CP 246).

The final stanza is a kind of summing up, a weighing of what he has been against what he must become. The lines "I was flung back from suffering and love / When light divided on a storm-tossed tree" are difficult, though I agree to some extent with Karl Malkoff that the poet "envisions himself as a tree struck by lightning, by all the love and suffering involved in human existence." [11] The tree is surely the tree that is wept to in "In a Dark Time," that is beheld and lost in "In Evening Air," and that turns to purest flame in "The Sequel." Though it is usually identified with the poet (as a symbol of organic growth), here it becomes also *the* Tree of suffering and love, the cross. When light "divides" on the tree, it creates the "dark side" of the tree, the side which is dimly seen "in a dark time" or "in evening air." The tree as instrument of torment and death is dark and terrible, but as Christian symbol of resurrection and self-sacrificing love, it is also a source of hope and comfort. The dual nature of the tree reflects the dual nature of God—God the terrible judge and God the sweet redeemer. Roethke feels this duality in the anticipated terrors of sickness and death and in the promised joys of a larger life after death. It is important to notice the verb forms here. The narrator *was* "flung back," but now, at this point in the *Sequence*, he "would be near" once again.

The terrible death-in-life that seemed reflected in every line of the first stanza seems to have passed. Our hero has apparently undergone a spiritual transformation of some sort in the course of "The Marrow." I believe a clue to what has happened is found in the repetition of the word *will* in the first and final stanzas. Surely Roethke intends that we connect the slain will of the last stanza with the "will to die" which his drinking is said to breed in stanza one. If we make that connection, we see that the narrator's spiritual life depends upon his ability to slay the will to slay himself. The "will to die" is, of course, the great enemy of the growth process. It is the force of inertia, the pull of the known and the familiar and the past. *Will*, as it is used here, is the opposite of *desire*, the force which drives one to brood on God that one may at last become a man. The human "will to

die" must be surrendered to the will of God, which is that great
energy which moves everything toward the ripeness that is all.

The poet has learned that to come to "know" (as the poem
moves toward that word), he must pay the price of marrow, must
"bleed his bones." But he has learned, too, that "Men must endure / Their going hence even as their coming hither," that the
process of growth and decay has its own rhythm, to which men
must learn to dance.

Something of that rhythm moves "I Waited," a poem beginning in windless dust and ending in gusty gladness. Wind here,
as elsewhere in the *Sequence,* suggests the breath of the Creator,
the spirit which animates our clay and moves the world. In his
"Dark Time" Roethke was momentarily "free in the tearing
wind," but since then he has had second thoughts about being an
"intimate of air." He finds that the wind comes close, "like a shy
animal," but that he is no longer one with it, that it has nothing
new to say. And so he waits for "the wind to move the dust," but
no wind comes.

The poem makes use of the metaphor of the journey to describe spiritual changes. The poet begins without "inspiration,"
his dust unmoved by wind. He is terribly conscious of the weight
of his body, the "airlessness" of his heavy bulk, which thwarts his
determination to rise. "It was as if I tried to walk in hay, / Deep
in the mow, and each step deeper down," he says. Nevertheless,
he is granted a momentary vision, an instant in which

> I saw all things through water, magnified,
> And shimmering. The sun burned through a haze,
> And I became all that I looked upon.
> I dazzled in the dazzle of a stone.   (CP 247)

The "dazzle," the sense of oneness with all things, the brightness
of the sun that is also The Son—these are the characteristics of
Roethke's moments of mystical awareness. But, as always, such
moments do not last. "And then a jackass brayed. A lizard leaped
my foot. / Slowly I came back to the dusty road." And, again,

the absence of vision that has been makes the journey more difficult than ever.

> And when I walked, my feet seemed deep in sand.
> I moved like some heat-weary animal.
> I went, not looking back. I was afraid.   (CP 247)

The way is a steep path between stony walls (the place among
the rocks turns out not to be a cave, after all), and the poet finds
himself on a plateau overlooking the sea. "And all the winds
came toward me. I was glad."

Like the final stanza of "The Marrow," "I Waited" looks both
backward and forward. On the one hand, it summarizes the spiritual journey that has taken place thus far in the *Sequence;* on the
other, it does move from the agony of "The Marrow" to the word
glad, a word which serves as a kind of password into the final
four works of *Sequence, Sometimes Metaphysical.*

"The Tree, the Bird" is a poem which moves from motion to
stillness and returns to motion again. The narrator begins by
walking through enchanted fields, fields which rise up to meet
him, fields filled with snails which nod to him, light which
meets him, and clouds which call to him. Clearly this is one
aspect of Roethke's mysticism, that sense of loving kinship with
all things, with the earth itself.[12] "Yet when I sighed," he says, "I
stood outside my life," and that sensation is less euphoric. He
finds himself "Part of a tree still dark, still, deathly still . . ."
(CP 248). Such unnatural "stillness" must have special meaning
to a poet, must represent a special terror. Absolute stasis, the total
absence of motion, must be terrifying to a man who views life as
a perpetual journey. Yet even the becalmed tree bears a singing
bird, a bird whose song is painful to Roethke and which he
answers with "The lonely buzz behind my midnight eyes," with
a cry that is a "still cry." And then the tense shifts and the day
comes, and with it motion and joy. As always, "the present falls
away," for life is motion and the now is forever vanishing just
ahead of our efforts to capture it. The bird takes wing, a figure of
aspiration, grace, and beauty. And, like the bird, Roethke beats

wings against the sky to try to go beyond into the Eternal. Surely "stretch" is a pun in the next to last line. The "stretch" of joy is both a unit of measurement (as a "stretch" of road) and a tugging or wrenching (as one "stretches" a sweater to alter its shape). Joy is stretching him, making him larger, making him rise up, and at the same time the rest of the journey (and of the *Sequence*) is a "stretch" of joyful sailing. Still, a stretch, even a stretch of joy, is to be "endured" if one is anxious to arrive at his destination. The scenery may be lovely, but after much travelling one would be home. And being stretched *by* joy, however uplifting, causes growing pains. Thus, paradoxically, joy is to be "endured," "The dire dimension of a final thing."

"The Restored" is different in tone and form from the poems that have come before. Roethke turns to the short line and to anapests with the effect of a general lightening of the tonal darkness through which he has passed. The rhymes are essentially those of light verse, too comic in their linkings to have worked in, say, "The Marrow" or "In a Dark Time." The rhymes of "bowl" and "soul," for example, or of "thought" and "shot" protect us and the narrator from the dangers of taking ourselves and the poem too seriously. Indeed, the idea of so colloquial a soul, one that cries "I'm like to die" and who sounds like an old tennis player with a wing "gone dead," is primarily an idea that leads us to laughter, not tears. The message of the poem is, clearly, that the poet's soul is maimed when he is too rational, too thoughtful, and is restored when he relies on intuition and emotion, on raging and wailing. Fair enough. But the message read in the poem's medium suggests that among those things "restored" have been the poet's love of dance and motion, his ability to smile, his ability to experience gladness and joy. The poem delights in its own unusual rhymes and dancing meter, and delight seems bright and warm indeed after the "midnight" that has been. The voice of the poet is, for the first time in the *Sequence, Sometimes Metaphysical*, the voice of a "happy man," the sort of man to whom "The Right Thing" happens.

In writing of the defects of Roethke's poetry, Karl Malkoff accused the poet of relying too greatly on the aphorism, on the single line which "often threatens to become an oversimplification which evades rather than confronts reality." As an example of one such failed aphorism, Malkoff cites "The right thing happens to the happy man," a line which, he suggests, is either platitudinous or comes dangerously close to being so.[13] Malkoff's judgment seems accurate when "The Right Thing" is read outside of its context in the *Sequence, Sometimes Metaphysical*. The refrain line at issue does indeed appear to be oversimplified, naive, an evasion of reality. However, "The right thing happens to the happy man" read in the context of the poems that have gone before takes on something of the ring of an earned truth.

It is not, after all, as if the "happy thing" happens to the man who is "right." That *would* be light opera, the Disney version of things as they aren't. It is the "right" thing that happens, the "right" thing in the sense of its being the proper or fitting thing taking place at its proper or fitting time. In context, the line (and the poem) becomes the culmination of the movement of the entire sequence toward perfect acquiescence to the motion of life, to the will of God. Ripeness is all, and "happy" is the man who can endure that truth. Such a man is a kind of religious stoic, is definitely not an optimist or a booster. And his acquiescence has been hard-won. It has been conceived in an agony of bone marrow; it has contended with the fear of life and with the love of death and it has survived both.

The happy man is the man who surrenders his will to the supreme will, the force which drives the universe through its continuous changes. He has learned to be still and still moving, to lie motionless on the current and so move with the flow of things, even as the slow night comes down. On the other hand, those who surround him are "Time-harried prisoners of *Shall* and *Will*," men who think to impose "willfully" their rigid patterns upon an ever-flowing reality. They would "probe" the mysteriousness of the motion of things in order to predict and control the future, to organize their own destinies. One of the ways in which one can exert control over his destiny is, of course, through "self-destruction," the arrogant act of the will which Roethke overcame in "The Marrow." The human will, faced with affliction, becomes the will to die. The "happy man," however, can wait, can bear affliction until it cries out. Because he has made his peace with mutability, he is able to form prayers praising change and the mystery which is the source of all change. "The Right Thing" is itself such a prayer, and thus Roethke and his "happy man" are discovered to be in the same attitudes, performing the same actions. The only piece in the *Sequence* not written in the first person, "The Right Thing" nevertheless joins poet and protagonist as the poem develops.

The villanelle, with its tight interlocking rhymes and strict formal pattern, would seem to be an inappropriate form in which to celebrate change. However, in Roethke's hands the villanelle becomes a highly dynamic medium, one wholly capable of conveying its dynamic message. In Roethke's poem, there is a moment in which form wavers, almost disappears, and then reemerges, much altered in shape, meaning, and value. The most obvious "wavering" is Roethke's departure from the pattern of the villanelle in stanzas three and four. The refrain lines should alternate as the final lines of stanzas two, three, four, and five; yet in "The Right Thing" Roethke repeats "The right thing happens to the happy man" as the final lines of consecutive stanzas. Moreover, in its paradigmatic form, the first refrain line ought to read "Let others probe the mystery if they can," but Roethke strays further from that form each time he uses the line. When we last see it, the line reads "Till mystery is no more: No more he can," and the original form is barely visible, is, indeed, glimpsed at the point of disappearance. Even the rhymes of the poem move from the perfect to the imperfect and then return in the final stanza to form exact rhymes with stanza one.

"The bird flies out, the bird flies back again," writes Roethke. "The hill becomes the valley and is still" (CP 250). The poem mirrors that action most effectively. The lines do go out and return, and, like the bird, altered by virtue of having flown, the lines are altered each time they appear by what has come before, by inevitable shifts in context. "Let others probe the mystery if they can" becomes "Till mystery is no more: No more he can," and, like the hill, *"is still."* The roots of the final form of the line still exist; in the ending is (still) the beginning. The villanelle itself becomes a non-villanelle as the form breaks down; yet "The Right Thing" has "the soul" of a villanelle, remains a villanelle in every important sense. The poem is a world in process about a world in process, a hymn to change that is an ever-changing hymn.

As was the case in "The Restored," Roethke suggests that the power of human thought is pretty puny stuff. The mystery of continuous change cannot be probed or delved by reason, but it *can* be experienced, praised, and even represented artistically. The (happy) man who accepts change as the way of things finds that "mystery is no more." He is the man content to "learn by going where [he] has to go," the man who, having put aside seeking after his destiny, rests assured that his destiny is seeking after him. Standing outside of the whirl of the small becoming great, the great becoming small, the happy man surrenders his will, confident that whatever happens to him, it will be "the right thing," the "happening" that moves in accordance with the Will that is the source and end of movement.

"Once More, the Round" is an ending that does not end. The dance goes on and on, like a musical round, like a spiralling gyre, like the evolutionary process. The hero of *Sequence*, once one who ran from God, now finds that his "true self runs toward a Hill," a hill that is, perhaps, both the elevation leading upward to God and the grave. The way up and the way down become, truly, one and the same. The eye, which in a dark time began to see, now "sees" that the Unknown can, indeed, be known (if one will only stop trying to know it) and that the mysterious Hill is "More! O More! visible" (CP 251). We come back to the beginning, come "round" to the eye, but it is an altered eye, an altered self that has survived "Infirmity" and "The Motion" to "adore" the dance of life.

The life Roethke loves is a process, a cosmic dance with Bird, Leaf, Fish, and Snail in which the Eye half-perceives and half-creates all of the dancers. The abiding Leaf, ever-decaying, never to be decayed, and the questing Snail, ever evolving, never to be evolved, are Roethke's partners. They suggest the rhythm (and the limits) of the dance. Nothing is ever lost; nothing ever fully arrives. And it is Love and the love of Love which moves them all.

Blake is evoked, both by name and by imitation, as the representative poet-mystic, the visionary who saw the sun to be a choir of angels chanting "holy, holy, holy." The eye of such a poet has the "altering power" in abundance, making Blake one of the mystical brotherhood of singers who, perhaps, are as one singer in the cosmic vision.

We come, at the end which is not an end, to One, which is where we began in "In a Dark Time." There *one* became *One*. Now "everything comes to One." The sense of Oneness has enlarged to include all of creation, all of the dancers. Some of the loneliness of the "dark time" has been dispelled, and the motion here is that of the dance, not of "the tearing wind." The third "dance on," like Gertrude Stein's third rose, suggests infinite repetition. The dance goes on, still and still moving, into the silence beyond the poem.

Like the aging instant which forever vanishes just ahead of us, each poem in *Sequence, Sometimes Metaphysical* has independent worth and identity, yet each is enlarged in meaning and value by its relationship to other of the poems and to the whole. And, like that vanishing instant, each poem in the *Sequence* destroys itself to make way for the next poem. Ever decaying, never to be decayed; ever evolving, never to be evolved, the poems of *Sequence, Sometimes Metaphysical* prove that each ending is a new beginning, and that endings and beginnings alike are "perpetual." The sequence of twelve poems may not wholly master the complexities of a world in process, but, taken together, the poems represent a remarkable attempt to wed the motion of the creative mind to the motion that is life itself.

Afterword

As I write these words I am ending four years of life, scholar-fashion, with Theodore Roethke. That is not over-long, I realize, for a literary study. Nor is it so long as many of his colleagues, his friends, and some of his students spent with him, and they in fashion much more direct and intense. But my four years have been intense enough, marked by strange dreams, strong emotions, and unusually close relationships with a few of those fortunate ones who sat in Roethke's classroom at the University of Washington. Leafing through the notebooks, reading poems in their germinal states, looking at the letters and the teaching notes, I have known quite unscholarly extremes of compassion and awe. At times I have felt something of the hatred that Roethke so often felt for himself. And I have known something like love for him, too, as if in all that reading of Roethke's private and public writing I have now and then touched, or nearly touched, the man.

Therefore I do not wish to use these "after words" to try to decide whether Roethke was "a truly great poet" or just "a major one" or—worse still—merely "an important poet." [1] That is, in the short run, a foolish game, played with undefined and perhaps undefinable terms. The long run will define the terms as well as they can be defined; perhaps at last the "long run" is itself the only term that matters. My study, I hope, indicates that Roethke wrote his poems carefully, that he was a craftsman, a word-smith of many well-chosen strategies. As such, I suppose it unintentionally becomes a small piece of favorable evidence, a bit of testimony from a friendly witness, in a trial that ought to go on for quite a while. In the meantime, there was this man, and he wrote poems.

About the poems I have said most of what I have to say. Their genius, I maintain, lies in the meaning communicated beyond the denotation of their words. When Roethke is at his best, "meaning" is a complex of forces, a musical expression growing out of the pre-conscious resonances of the language, out of the play of sound against sound, out of the energy of primitive rhythms, out of the extension of sense through ambiguity, out of the explosion of sense through paradox, out of the telescoping and juxtapositioning of images, out of an intensification through repetition and variation. For Roethke, "meaning" is always a medium in motion, a vibration beginning in the poet's psyche, passing into language through the flesh and bone of his voice box, passing then into the bone and flesh of the listener's ear and from there into the nerve endings, the fingertips, the blood, and the pulse. In Roethke's classroom, meaning *is* motion; and the lesson is to be felt as experience, not cribbed in cold blood from the poet's lecture notes.

I have not intended to explicate poems but, as I said in my "Introduction," to present a way of looking at them, one that concentrates closely upon what Roethke tried to do and very often did do in his art and craft. The genius of the poetry is not, I realize, confined to the sequences, much less to the sequences I have examined in this book, though Roethke does exploit the sequence as an important device for representing the protean nature of experience, for representing the de-creation of form as a necessary prelude to the creation of new and further form. It is my hope that the boundaries of this study have some elastic in them, that what I have said of Roethkean vision and technique may be stretched without undue strain to cover poems I have not discussed. For example, almost all that I have said of Roethke's maneuvering of the villanelle form in "The Right Thing" can be as well applied to "The Waking." If I may be forgiven for quoting myself, each of the poems "is a world in process about a world in process." In each "there is a moment in which form wavers, almost disappears and then re-emerges, much altered in shape, meaning, and value." Such shape-shifting is highly appropriate to "The Waking," a poem celebrating the "always" that falls away whenever we near it and one which finds its only steadiness in the "shaking" by which the world advances. Similarly, much of my discussion of the devices used in the *Greenhouse Sequence*, especially that of the techniques at work in "Frau Bauman, Frau Schmidt, and Frau Schwartze," can be transplanted into the bleached valleys of the "Elegy for Jane." Like the three ladies, Jane has the power to transfer her energy creatively to the life around her, and it is that power which commends her to the memory and to the apotheosizing force of the imagination. Like the fraus, too, Jane is "not here," and yet the rush of images, the alliteration and manipulation of vowel and consonant, and the intensification and proliferation of verbs re-creates the bird-like quickness of her bodily rhythms so effectively that she seems to move again and breathe again and *be* again. She is gone yet "still hovering," just as the poet, neither father nor lover, is simultaneously both and more. As is usual in Roethke, "reality" is caught from the corner of the eye, an insubstantial flickering between affirmation and denial.

If these and like transplantations prove fruitful, as I hope they will, I am content. I would like to think that my work has its conclusion somewhere beyond its last word. That would be a fitting open-ending for a study of Roethke.

About the man who wrote the poems I have little to add. Near the beginning of my study, the editor of a small magazine of verse told me I would need "an electric cage" to hold Roethke, and I think the editor was right. *The Glass House* will not hold him, though it will continue to be a useful book. Others, especially those who lived and worked closely with Roethke for years, have caught more of the quick of him. Robert Heilman [2] and Arnold Stein,[3] for example, intelligent men both, wise enough to see the face beneath Roethke's many masks and to understand the "running costs" he met day after day in being the kind of poet he was, have written sketches which allow us to feel some of the energy with which he was both blessed and cursed. And there is David Wagoner's *Straw for the Fire*, his attempt to arrange the poet's notebooks to combine "prose and poetry and shifts of mood in a way that Roethke's own conversation did, complete with associational leaps." [4] It will remain, I suspect, the next best thing to a seat in Roethke's classroom.

What I have to say about the man Roethke is not new, but it is good news nonetheless to those dark closets where our fears hide. Thoreau's experiment has been tried again, and its conclusion upheld: "if one advances confidently in the direction of his dream, and endeavors to live the life he has imagined, he will meet with a success unexpected in common hours." And Whitman's experiment, too, his poetic incarnation of an eternally healthful self. Galway Kinnell quotes a description of Whitman by "someone who knew him both before and after the publication of *Leaves of Grass*": " '*He was quite gray at thirty. He had a look of age in his youth, as he now has a look of youth in his age.*' " Kinnell concludes, "If Whitman's poetry in some sense consists of wishes, it is useful for our faith in his enterprise to know that they came true in his own flesh." [5]

It is impossible to say just when Roethke's enterprise began. But it is clearly announced in that sophomoric manifesto from his undergraduate days: "I have faith in myself. I'm either going to be a good writer or a poor fool" (SP 6). The going was never easy. As others have noted, poetry came hard for him. He was never the child prodigy, the *Wunderkind*. The agonies of the beginning notebooks, the slow progress of the apprentice work, the stiffness of *Open House* show that. He learned that he had to *be* more in order to *do* more, that the stuff from which his poetry had to be carved was pure psychic energy, the extremes of suf-

fering and of joy. "A poem that is the shape of the psyche itself;
in times of great stress, that's what I tried to write" (SF 178).
Finally such poems are there, a success unexpected in common
hours. "Frau Bauman, Frau Schmidt, and Frau Schwartze," "The
Lost Son," "Words for the Wind," "I Knew a Woman," "The
Dying Man," "The Far Field," "The Rose," "In a Dark Time,"
"The Waking." Dynamic fixtures, irreducible facts beyond the
need for prizes or awards.

"A man goes far," he wrote, "to find out what he is" (CP
239). Now for him the going and the finding are one; the motion
of the world, of the man, of his art—everything comes to One,
and dances on.

A SELECTED BIBLIOGRAPHY

Berryman, John. "From the Middle and Senior Generations." *American Scholar*, 28 (Summer 1959), 384–390.

Blessing, Richard. "The Shaking that Steadies: Theodore Roethke's 'The Waking.'" *Ball State University Forum*, 12 (Autumn 1971), 17–19.

———. "Theodore Roethke: A Celebration." *Tulane Studies in English*, 20 (1972), 169–180.

———. "Theodore Roethke's Sometimes Metaphysical Motion." *Texas Studies in Literature and Language*, 14 (Winter 1973), 731–749.

Boyd, J. D. "Texture and Form in Theodore Roethke's Greenhouse Poems." *Modern Language Quarterly*, 32 (December 1971), 409–424.

Burke, Kenneth. "The Vegetal Radicalism of Theodore Roethke." *Sewanee Review*, 58 (Winter 1950), 68–108.

Ciardi, John. *Mid-Century American Poets*. New York: Twayne, 1950.

Ciardi, John, Stanley Kunitz, and Allan Seager. "An Evening with Ted Roethke." *Michigan Quarterly Review*, 2 (October 1967), 227–242.

Deutsch, Babette. "The Poet and His Critics: A Symposium." *New World Writing*, 19 (1961), ed. Anthony Ostroff.

Dickey, James. "The Greatest American Poet." *Atlantic*, 222 (November 1968), 53–58.

———. "Theodore Roethke." *Poetry*, 105 (November 1964), 119–122.

Donoghue, Denis. "Roethke's Broken Music," in *Theodore Roethke: Essays on the Poetry*, ed. Arnold Stein. Seattle and London: University of Washington Press, 1965.

Eberhart, Richard. "On Theodore Roethke's Poetry." *Southern Review*, n.s. 1 (July 1965), 612–620.

Everette, Oliver. "Theodore Roethke: The Poet as a Teacher." *West Coast Review*, 3 (Spring 1968), 5–11.

Freer, Coburn. "Theodore Roethke's Love Poetry." *Northwest Review*, 11 (Summer 1971), 42–66.

Galvin, Brendan. "Kenneth Burke and Theodore Roethke's 'Lost Son' Poems." *Northwest Review*, 11 (Summer 1971), 67–96.

Gustafson, Richard. "In Roethkeland." *Midwest Quarterly*, 7 (Autumn 1965), 167–174.

Hayden, Mary H. "Open House: Poetry of the Constricted Self." *Northwest Review*, 11 (Summer 1971), 116–138.

Heilman, Robert B. "Theodore Roethke: Personal Notes." *Shenandoah*, 16 (Autumn 1964), 55–64.

Heyen, William. *Profile of Theodore Roethke*. Columbus, Ohio: Charles E. Merrill Co., 1971.

———. "Theodore Roethke's Minimals." *Minnesota Review*, 8 (1968), 359–375.

Hobbs, John. "The Poet as His Own Interpreter: Roethke on 'In a Dark Time.' " *College English*, 33 (October 1971). 55–66.

Hoffman, Frederick J. "Theodore Roethke: The Poetic Shape of Death," in *Theodore Roethke: Essays on the Poetry*, ed. Arnold Stein. Seattle and London: University of Washington Press, 1965.

Holmes, John. "Poems and Things." *Boston Evening Transcript*, March 24, 1941, p. 9.

———. "Theodore Roethke." *American Poetry Journal*, 17 (November 1934), 2.

Kramer, Hilton. "The Poetry of Theodore Roethke." *Western Review*, 18 (Winter 1954), 131–146.

Kunitz, Stanley. "News of the Root." *Poetry*, 73 (January 1949), 222–225.

———. "Roethke: Poet of Transformations." *New Republic*, 152 (January 23, 1965), 23–29.

———. "The Poet and His Critics: A Symposium." *New World Writing*, 19 (1961), ed. Anthony Ostroff.

LaBelle, Jenijoy. "Theodore Roethke and Tradition: 'The Pure Serene of Memory in One Man.' " *Northwest Review*, 11 (Summer 1971), 1–18.

Lee, Charlotte. "The Line as a Rhythmic Unit in the Poetry of Theodore Roethke." *Speech Monographs*, 30 (March 1963), 15–22.

Lucas, John. "The Poetry of Theodore Roethke." *The Oxford Review*, 7 (1968), 39–64.

McLeod, James R. *Theodore Roethke: A Bibliography*. Kent, Ohio: Kent State University Press, 1973.

McLatchy, J. D. "Sweating Light from a Stone, Identifying Theodore Roethke." *Modern Poetry Studies*, 3 (1972), 1–24.

McMichael, James. "The Poetry of Theodore Roethke." *The Southern Review*, n.s. 5 (Winter 1969), 4–25.

———. "Roethke's North America." *Northwest Review*, 11 (Summer 1971), 149–159.

Malkoff, Karl. *Theodore Roethke: An Introduction to the Poetry*. New York and London: Columbia University Press, 1966.

Martz, Louis L. "A Greenhouse Eden," in *Theodore Roethke: Essays on the Poetry*, ed. Arnold Stein. Seattle and London: University of Washington Press, 1965.

Martz, William J. *The Achievement of Theodore Roethke*. Glenview, Illinois: Scott, Foresman and Company, 1966.

Mazzaro, Jerome. "Theodore Roethke and the Failures of Language." *Modern Poetry Studies*, 1 (July 1970), 73–96.

Meredith, William. "A Steady Storm of Correspondences: Theodore Roethke's Long Journey Out of the Self," in *Theodore Roethke: Essays on the Poetry*, ed. Arnold Stein. Seattle and London: University of Washington Press, 1965.

Mills, Ralph J., Jr. "In the Way of Becoming: Roethke's Last Poems," in *Theodore Roethke: Essays on the Poetry*, ed. Arnold Stein. Seattle and London: University of Washington Press, 1965.

———. *Theodore Roethke*. Minneapolis: University of Minnesota Press, 1963.

———. "Toward a Condition of Joy: Patterns in the Poetry of Theodore Roethke." *Northwestern University Tri-Quarterly Review*, 1 (Fall 1958), 25–29.

Ostroff, Anthony, ed. "The Poet and His Critics: A Symposium." *New World Writing*, 19 (1961), 189–219.

Pearce, Roy Harvey. "Theodore Roethke: The Power of Sympathy," in *Theodore Roethke: Essays on the Poetry*, ed. Arnold Stein. Seattle and London: University of Washington Press, 1965.

Ransom, John Crowe. "On Theodore Roethke's 'In a Dark Time.' " *New World Writing*, ed. Anthony Ostroff, 19 (1961).

Roethke, Theodore. *The Collected Poems of Theodore Roethke*. Garden City, New York: Doubleday and Company, Inc., 1968.

———. *On the Poet and His Craft: Selected Prose of Theodore Roethke*. Ed. Ralph J. Mills, Jr. Seattle and London: University of Washington Press, 1965.

———. *Selected Letters of Theodore Roethke*. Ed. Ralph J. Mills, Jr. Seattle and London: University of Washington Press, 1968.

———. *Straw for the Fire: From the Notebooks of Theodore Roethke*, 1943–63. Selected and arranged by David Wagoner. Garden City, New York: Doubleday and Company, Inc., 1972.

Schwartz, Delmore. "The Cunning and the Craft of the Unconscious and Preconscious." *Poetry*, 94 (June 1959), 203–205.

Scott, Nathan A. "The Example of Rothke," in *The Wild Cry of Longing*. New Haven: Yale University Press, 1971, pp. 76–118.

Seager, Allan. *The Glass House: The Life of Theodore Roethke*. New York: McGraw-Hill Book Company, 1968.

Seymour-Smith, Martin. "Where Is Mr. Roethke?" *Black Mountain Review*, 1 (Spring 1954), 40–47.

Slaughter, William R. "Roethke's Song." *Minnesota Review*, 8 (1968), 342–344.

Snodgrass, W. D. " 'That Anguish of Concreteness'—Theodore Roethke's Career," in *Theodore Roethke: Essays on the Poetry*, ed. Arnold Stein. Seattle and London: University of Washington Press, 1965.

Spender, Stephen. "The Objective Ego," in *Theodore Roethke: Essays on the Poetry*, ed. Arnold Stein. Seattle and London: University of Washington Press, 1965.

Staples, Hugh B. "Rose in the Sea-Wind: A Reading of Theodore Roethke's 'North American Sequence.' " *American Literature*, 36 (May 1964), 189–203.

Stein, Arnold. "Roethke's Memory: Actions, Visions, and Revisions." *Northwest Review*, 11 (Summer 1971), 19–31.

———. Ed. *Theodore Roethke: Essays on the Poetry*. Seattle and London: University of Washington Press, 1965.

Truesdale, C. W. "Theodore Roethke and the Landscape of American Poetry." *Minnesota Review*, 8 (1968), 345–358.

Wain, John. "The Monocle of My Sea-Faced Uncle," in *Theodore Roethke: Essays on the Poetry*, ed. Arnold Stein. Seattle and London: University of Washington Press, 1965.

NOTES

Introduction

1. Oliver Everette, "Theodore Roethke: The Poet as Teacher," *West Coast Review*, 3, No. 1 (1968), 6.
2. Everette, pp. 6–7.

The Student Literary Criticism

1. D. H. Lawrence, *The Complete Poems of D. H. Lawrence*, ed. Vivian de Sola Pinto and Warren Roberts (New York: Viking Press, 1971), p. 182.
2. Lawrence, p. 183.
3. Lawrence, p. 182.

Uncollected Poems

1. The passage is in a letter to me, dated February 28, 1972. I am grateful to Richard Hugo for a good deal of help with Roethke.
2. *American Poetry Journal*, 17 (November 1934), 3–6.
3. *Commonweal*, 14, No. 23 (October 7, 1931), 544.
4. *Poetry: A Magazine of Verse*, 40 (April–September, 1932), 316.
5. *Poetry: A Magazine of Verse*, 40 (April–September, 1932), 316–317.
6. *American Poetry Journal*, 17 (November 1934), 3–6.
7. *The Atlantic Monthly*, 159, No. 1 (January 1937), 47.
8. *Poetry: A Magazine of Verse*, 53 (December 1938), 141.

Open House

1. Karl Malkoff, *Theodore Roethke: An Introduction to the Poetry* (New York: Columbia University Press, 1966), p. 22.
2. Malkoff, p. 20.
3. Jenijoy LaBelle, "Theodore Roethke and Tradition: 'The Pure Serene of Memory' in One Man," *Northwest Review*, 11, No. 3 (Summer 1971), 3–4.
4. John Holmes, *Boston Evening Transcript*, 24 March 1941, p. 9.
5. Malkoff, p. 23.
6. Malkoff, p. 33.
7. See LaBelle, 3–4.
8. I have taken the comment from "The Achievement of Theodore Roethke," an unpublished address to the English Graduate Organization in autumn 1972.

The Notebooks: 1938–1948

1. Stanley Kunitz, "News of the Root," *Poetry*, 73 (January 1949), 225.
2. Karl Malkoff, *Theodore Roethke: An Introduction to the Poetry* (New York: Columbia University Press, 1966), p. 45.
3. Allan Seager, *The Glass House: The Life of Theodore Roethke* (New York: McGraw-Hill Book Co., 1968), p. 153.
4. Arnold Stein, "Introduction," *Theodore Roethke: Essays on the Poetry*, ed. Arnold Stein (Seattle: University of Washington Press, 1965), p. xiii.
5. *The Glass House*, p. 147.
6. *The Glass House*, p. 144.
7. *The Glass House*, p. 90.
8. *The Glass House*, p. 101.
9. *The Glass House*, p. 101.
10. Stein, p. xiv.
11. *The Glass House*, p. 161.

THE EDGE OF MANY THINGS
The *Greenhouse Sequence*

1. Louis L. Martz, "A Greenhouse Eden," in *Theodore Roethke: Essays on the Poetry*, ed. Arnold Stein (Seattle: University of Washington Press, 1965), p. 27.
2. John Wain, "The Monocle of My Sea-Faced Uncle," in *Theo-*

dore Roethke: Essays on the Poetry, ed. Arnold Stein (Seattle: University of Washington Press, 1965), p. 61.

3. Kenneth Burke, "The Vegetal Radicalism of Theodore Roethke," *Sewanee Review,* 58 (Winter 1950), 68.

4. Burke, 69.

5. Karl Malkoff, *Theodore Roethke: An Introduction to the Poetry* (New York: Columbia University Press, 1966), p. 48.

6. From "The Achievement of Theodore Roethke," an unpublished address to the English Graduate Organization in autumn 1972.

7. "The Achievement of Theodore Roethke."

8. Malkoff, pp. 50–55.

9. Malkoff, p. 53.

10. Martz, "A Greenhouse Eden," p. 29.

The Opening Knock and the Lost Son

1. Stephen Spender, "*Words for the Wind,*" *New Republic,* 141 (August 10, 1959), 22.

2. Stanley Kunitz, "Roethke: Poet of Transformations," *New Republic,* 152 (January 23, 1965), 24.

3. From "The Achievement of Theodore Roethke," the unpublished address to the English Graduate Organization of the University of Washington, autumn 1972.

4. Kunitz, "Roethke: Poet of Transformations," 25.

5. Kunitz, "Roethke: Poet of Transformations," 25.

6. T. S. Eliot, "Ulysses, Order, and Myth," *The Dial,* 75, No. 5 (November 1923), 483.

7. Evelyn Underhill, *Mysticism: A Study in the Nature and Development of Man's Spiritual Consciousness* (New York: World Publishing Co., 1965), p. 31.

8. William Heyen, "Theodore Roethke's Minimals," *Minnesota Review,* 8, No. 4 (1968), 368, 370.

9. "The Achievement of Theodore Roethke."

10. Kenneth Burke, "The Vegetal Radicalism of Theodore Roethke," *Sewanee Review,* 58 (Winter 1950), 96–98.

11. Malkoff, p. 79.

The Old Woman's Meditations and the *North American Sequence*

1. Arnold Stein, "Roethke's Memory: Actions, Visions, and Revisions," *Northwest Review,* 11, No. 3 (Summer 1971), 24–25.

2. Allan Seager, *The Glass House: The Life of Theodore Roethke* (New York: McGraw-Hill Book Co., 1968), p. 140.

3. *The Glass House*, p. 141.

4. Hugh Staples, "The Rose in the Sea-Wind: A Reading of Theodore Roethke's 'North American Sequence,'" *American Literature*, 36, No. 2 (May 1964), 195.

5. Karl Malkoff, *Theodore Roethke: An Introduction to the Poetry* (New York: Columbia University Press, 1966), p. 178.

6. Malkoff, p. 189.

7. Malkoff, p. 177.

8. Staples, 198.

9. Staples, 199.

10. Malkoff, p. 181.

11. Wallace Stevens, *The Collected Poems of Wallace Stevens* (New York: Alfred A. Knopf, 1957), p. 250.

12. Malkoff, p. 188.

THE FORMAL FATHER

The Dying Man

1. William Butler Yeats, *The Collected Poems of William Butler Yeats* (New York: Macmillan & Co., 1956), p. 230.

2. Karl Malkoff, *Theodore Roethke: An Introduction to the Poetry* (New York: Columbia University Press, 1966), p. 152.

3. Malkoff, p. 157.

4. Richard Hugo, "Stray Thoughts on Roethke and Teaching." Hugo was kind enough to let me see an essay, still in rough form, which he is preparing for publication.

The Love Poems

1. Theodore Roethke, "Words for the Wind," in *Poet's Choice*, ed. Paul Engle and Joseph Langland (New York: Dell Publishing Co., 1962), p. 99.

2. Engle and Langland, p. 100.

3. Coburn Freer, "Theodore Roethke's Love Poetry," *Northwest Review*, 11, No. 3 (Summer 1971), 51.

4. Freer, 56.

5. Freer, 52.

6. Karl Malkoff, *Theodore Roethke: An Introduction to the Poetry* (New York: Columbia University Press, 1966), p. 127.

7. Malkoff, p. 223.

8. Richard Hugo in a letter to me, October 18, 1972.

9. Hugo's letter, October 18, 1972.

10. Paul Tillich, *The Courage to Be* (New Haven: Yale University Press, 1959), p. 32. Malkoff develops the idea fully in *Theodore Roethke*, pp. 131–134.

11. Malkoff, p. 126.

Sequence, Sometimes Metaphysical

1. Theodore Roethke, "On 'In a Dark Time,'" in *The Contemporary Poet as Artist and Critic: Eight Symposia*, ed. Anthony Ostroff (Boston: Little Brown, 1965), p. 49.

2. Particularly the symposium edited by Anthony Ostroff which included essays by John Crowe Ranson, Babette Deutsch, Stanley Kunitz, and Roethke himself. Originally published as "The Poet and His Critics: A Symposium," in *New World Writing*, 19 (1961), 189–219, the four studies were reprinted as one of the eight symposia cited above.

3. Roethke, "On 'In a Dark Time,'" p. 49.

4. Roethke, "On 'In a Dark Time,'" p. 52.

5. John Crowe Ransom, "On Theodore Roethke's 'In a Dark Time,'" in *The Contemporary Poet as Artist and Critic: Eight Symposia*, ed. Anthony Ostroff (Boston: Little Brown, 1965), p. 35.

6. Roethke, "On 'In a Dark Time,'" p. 53.

7. See, for example, Karl Malkoff's *Theodore Roethke: An Introduction to the Poetry* (New York: Columbia University Press, 1966), p. 212 or Ralph J. Mills, Jr.'s essay called "In the Way of Becoming: Roethke's Last Poems" in *Theodore Roethke: Essays on the Poetry*, ed. Arnold Stein (Seattle, University of Washington Press, 1965), p. 131.

8. Ralph J. Mills, Jr., "In the Way of Becoming," p. 131.

9. Wallace Stevens, *The Collected Poems of Wallace Stevens* (New York: Alfred A. Knopf, 1957), p. 14.

10. Finding that editors had changed the line to "My ear can hear the bird," Roethke scrawled the following across the galley proofs: "I know that makes four still's in two lines, but it's a nice effect & more accurate. Leave this in, and I won't complain about those damned semi-colons which have been substituted for colons, thereby distorting the meaning." Box 20, folder 50 of the University of Washington's Roethke Collection.

11. Malkoff, p. 216.

12. Malkoff describes the passage as the experience of "an 'I-Thou' relationship with every existing thing." *Theodore Roethke*, p. 217.

13. Malkoff, pp. 223–224.

Afterword

1. Karl Malkoff, *Theodore Roethke: An Introduction to the Poetry* (New York: Columbia University Press, 1966), pp. 224–225.

2. Robert B. Heilman, "Theodore Roethke: Personal Notes," *Shenandoah*, 16 (Autumn 1964), 55–64.

3. Arnold Stein, "Introduction," in *Theodore Roethke: Essays on the Poetry* (Seattle: University of Washington Press, 1965), pp. ix–xx.

4. David Wagoner, "Introduction," in *Straw for the Fire: From the Notebooks of Theodore Roethke, 1943–63* (Garden City: Doubleday & Company, 1972), p. 13.

5. Galway Kinnell, "Whitman's Indicative Words," *The American Poetry Review*, 2, No. 2 (March/April 1973), 10.

INDEX